# Azure Data and AI Architect Handbook

Adopt a structured approach to designing data and AI solutions at scale on Microsoft Azure

**Olivier Mertens**

**Breght Van Baelen**

BIRMINGHAM—MUMBAI

# Azure Data and AI Architect Handbook

**Group Product Manager**: Ali Abidi

**Publishing Product Manager**: Anant Jain

**Content Development Editor**: Priyanka Soam

**Technical Editor**: Devanshi Ayare

**Copy Editor**: Safis Editing

**Project Coordinator**: Farheen Fathima

**Proofreader**: Safis Editing

**Indexer**: Sejal Dsilva

**Production Designer**: Prashant Ghare

**Marketing Coordinator**: Vinishka Kalra

First published: August 2023

Production reference: 1310723

Published by Packt Publishing Ltd.

Grosvenor House

11 St Paul's Square

Birmingham

B3 1RB

ISBN 978-1-80323-486-1

www.packtpub.com

*This book is a tribute to the memory of my grandfather, Andre, a pioneer in the field of technology, and his wife, Lilliane. Further gratitude to my parents, Brigitte and Marc, my brother, Nicolas, my girlfriend, Jen, and everyone who stood by my side unconditionally.*

*- Olivier Mertens*

*To my parents, Marc and Carmen, and grandparents, Guillaume and Monique, for their loving support and dedication. To my brother, Dries, who has been my career-long soundboard and fellow data-enthusiast. To my girlfriend, Jing, for giving me the perseverance along this journey.*

*- Breght Van Baelen*

# Contributors

## About the authors

**Olivier Mertens** is a cloud solution architect for Azure data and AI at Microsoft, based in Dublin, Ireland. In this role, he assisted organizations in designing their enterprise-scale data platforms and analytical workloads. Next to his role as an architect, Olivier was selected as an advanced cloud expert for AI. In this role as a domain expert, he has led the technical expertise of his field in the corporate markets of Europe, the Middle East, and Africa at Microsoft. Before his time at Microsoft, he worked as a data consultant at Microsoft Partners in Belgium.

Olivier is a lecturer at PXL Digital Business School, a keynote speaker for AI, and holds a master's degree in information management, a postgraduate degree as an AI business architect, and a bachelor's degree in business management.

**Breght Van Baelen** is a Microsoft employee based in Dublin, Ireland, and works as a cloud solution architect for the data and AI pillar in Azure. He provides guidance to organizations building large-scale analytical platforms and data solutions. In addition, Breght was chosen as an advanced cloud expert for Power BI and is responsible for providing technical expertise in Europe, the Middle East, and Africa. Before his time at Microsoft, he worked as a data consultant at Microsoft Gold Partners in Belgium.

Breght led a team of eight data and AI consultants as a data science lead. Breght holds a master's degree in computer science from KU Leuven, specializing in AI. He also holds a bachelor's degree in computer science from the University of Hasselt.

# Acknowledgement

This goes out to our highly skilled colleagues whose contributions have had a direct impact on the development of this book: Justin Venter, Diogo Vaz Guedes, Frederic Van Kelecom, Luke Moloney, David Browne and to our managers, Karim Shawki and Gary Keegan, for the continued support.

# About the reviewers

**Aleksei Zhukov** is a fully certified Microsoft data engineer and architect. He has 10+ years of practical experience in different roles closely related to data – mobile network design engineer, data analyst, BI and DWH developer, architect and team lead, DWH product owner, and ETL developer. Different business domains are also covered for professional years (mostly, telecommunication and consulting). He is well known in the Power BI world as one of the top official community contributors.

**Aaron Saikovski** has over 30 years of commercial information technology expertise, spanning a broad range of technologies and industries. His skill set is centered around software and platform engineering, specifically in the Microsoft Azure platform. He works primarily in the platform, DevOps, and site reliability engineering space. Aaron has a software development background in GoLang, Python, PowerShell, and Bash scripting. He specializes in **Infrastructure as Code (IaC)** technologies such as Terraform, Bicep, and ARM templates.

**Remon van Harmelen** started his career as a software developer. Later, he became intrigued by Azure and made a career change to become an Azure consultant. He worked for several consulting parties and as part of multiple multinational projects, ranging from lift-and-shift migration to creating data analytical platforms. Now working for Microsoft as a cloud solution architect, he spends his days supporting customers on their Azure journeys.

# Table of Contents

# Part 2: Data Engineering on Azure

## 3

## 4

# 5

# Part 3: Data Warehousing and Analytics

# 6

# Part 4: Data Security, Governance, and Compliance

## 10

## 11

# Preface

With data quickly becoming an essential asset of any business, the need for cloud data and AI architects has never been higher. *The Azure Data and AI Architect Handbook* will assist any data professional or academic who is looking to advance their skill set in cloud data platform design. This book will help you understand all the individual components of an end-to-end data architecture and how to piece them together into a scalable and robust solution.

The book introduces core data architecture design concepts and Azure data and AI services. Cloud landing zones and best practices are explained to build up an enterprise-scale data platform from scratch. Next, you will get a deep dive into various data domains, such as data engineering, business intelligence, data science, and data governance. You'll learn about various methods for ingesting data into the cloud, designing the right data warehousing solution, managing large-scale data transformations, extracting valuable insights, and how to leverage cloud computing and (generative) AI to drive advanced analytical workloads. Finally, you will discover how to add data governance, compliance, and security to a solution.

By the end of this book, you will have gained the necessary expertise to become a well-rounded Azure data and AI architect.

## Who is this book for?

This book is for anyone looking to elevate their skill set to the level of an architect. Data engineers, data scientists, business intelligence developers, and database administrators will learn how to design end-to-end data solutions and get a bird's-eye view of the entire data platform. Although not required, basic knowledge of databases and data engineering workloads is recommended.

## What this book covers

*Chapter 1, Introduction to Data Architectures*, introduces methods of getting business value from data to solidify any long-term data strategy. You will then get an introduction to our architecture reference diagram to give a first glance at what a bare-bones data architecture may look like. You will then learn what challenges businesses can face when retaining an on-premise-only data strategy.

*Chapter 2, Preparing for Cloud Adoption*, explains the economic and technical benefits of using the Azure cloud and gives an introduction to Microsoft's Well-Architected Framework (WAF), which is used by all data and AI architects at Microsoft to guarantee high quality in the design of any data platform. Finally, you will learn how to set up a data and AI landing zone to start your journey to the Azure cloud.

*Chapter 3, Ingesting Data into the Cloud,* discusses the different ways of ingesting data in Azure and various reference architectures (e.g., Lambda, Kappa, and so on) to best match any requirements. You will learn how to land any streaming or batch data in scalable Azure data lakes according to best practices.

*Chapter 4, Transforming Data on Azure,* covers data pipelines – the key components to move data between on-premises and Azure and between various Azure components. Pipelines can move data based on a specific event, on a schedule, or in near real time, also called a streaming pipeline. You will learn about the various techniques for automating such data pipelines utilizing orchestration of the pipelines as jobs. You will also learn how to handle both batch and streaming data when orchestrating data transformations in Azure.

*Chapter 5, Storing Data for Consumption,* looks at best practices for early data orchestration and storage design. You will also learn about the different types of data, the requirements for different data serving methods, and the Azure resources that can be used to meet the functional and technical storage requirements for a data platform.

*Chapter 6, Data Warehousing,* covers the different ways of creating data warehouses in Azure, where every warehouse comes with its own pros and cons. You will learn what metrics are taken into account when choosing the right warehousing option.

*Chapter 7, The Semantic Layer,* explains how to implement a semantic layer in a data warehouse to improve the ease of use for end/business users. The semantic layer will hide many of the underlying complexities occurring in earlier stages of the data processing, allowing a wider audience to perform queries against the data warehouse.

*Chapter 8, Visualizing Data Using Power BI,* explains the options for designing enterprise dashboards and reports to render KPIs. You will learn various ways of integrating Power BI with other components of the data platform to allow for fast and easy visualization of key data.

*Chapter 9, Advanced Analytics Using AI,* looks at how to leverage the Azure AI services to analyze or transform data or generate new data. You will learn key questions to ask yourself to set up a solid AI strategy and get an in-depth view of the Azure OpenAI service, Azure Cognitive Services, and the Azure Machine Learning workspace, along with knowledge of the entire MLOps process.

*Chapter 10, Enterprise-Level Data Governance and Compliance,* covers data governance, which has quickly become a key component of every cloud data platform at scale. You will learn about core concepts within the world of data governance and how Microsoft Purview addresses many of the needs in this area. Furthermore, you will learn about data governance frameworks to help get you started on your governance journey.

*Chapter 11, Introduction to Data Security,* looks at how Azure was designed with security in mind. You will learn about the different layers of data security, along with some core Microsoft and Azure services to make security and monitoring airtight.

## Conventions used

There are a number of text conventions used throughout this book.

`Code in text`: Indicates code words in text, database table names, folder names, filenames, file extensions, pathnames, dummy URLs, user input, and Twitter handles. Here is an example: "Dedicated SQL pools allow the usage of `INSERT` and `UPDATE  T-SQL` statements like relational databases, but also have a lot of dissimilarities."

A block of code is set as follows:

```
AttemptedLoginLogs
| where Timestamp >= ago(7d)
| sort by Timestamp, Identity desc
```

| take 100When we wish to draw your attention to a particular part of a code block, the relevant lines or items are set in bold:

```
CREATE TABLE dbo.DimCustomer
(
    CustomerKey INT IDENTITY NOT NULL,
    CustomerAlternateKey NVARCHAR(15) NULL,
    CustomerName NVARCHAR(80) NOT NULL,
    EmailAddress NVARCHAR(50) NULL,
    Phone NVARCHAR(25) NULL,
    StreetAddress NVARCHAR(100),
    City NVARCHAR(20),
    PostalCode NVARCHAR(10),
    CountryRegion NVARCHAR(20)
)
WITH
(
    DISTRIBUTION = REPLICATE,
    CLUSTERED COLUMNSTORE INDEX
);
```

**Bold**: Indicates a new term, an important word, or words that you see onscreen. For instance, words in menus or dialog boxes appear in **bold**. Here is an example: "To connect to on-premises files in a folder, use the **File system** linked service, as illustrated in *Figure 3.11*."

> **Tips or important notes**
> Appear like this.

## Get in touch

Feedback from our readers is always welcome.

**General feedback**: If you have questions about any aspect of this book, email us at customercare@packtpub.com and mention the book title in the subject of your message.

**Errata**: Although we have taken every care to ensure the accuracy of our content, mistakes do happen. If you have found a mistake in this book, we would be grateful if you would report this to us. Please visit www.packtpub.com/support/errata and fill in the form.

**Piracy**: If you come across any illegal copies of our works in any form on the internet, we would be grateful if you would provide us with the location address or website name. Please contact us at copyright@packt.com with a link to the material.

**If you are interested in becoming an author**: If there is a topic that you have expertise in and you are interested in either writing or contributing to a book, please visit authors.packtpub.com.

## Reviews

Please leave a review. Once you have read and used this book, why not leave a review on the site that you purchased it from? Potential readers can then see and use your unbiased opinion to make purchase decisions, we at Packt can understand what you think about our products, and our authors can see your feedback on their book. Thank you!

For more information about Packt, please visit packtpub.com.

## Share Your Thoughts

Once you've read *Azure Data and AI Architect Handbook*, we'd love to hear your thoughts! Scan the QR code below to go straight to the Amazon review page for this book and share your feedback.

https://packt.link/r/1-803-23486-5

Your review is important to us and the tech community and will help us make sure we're delivering excellent quality content.

# Download a free PDF copy of this book

Thanks for purchasing this book!

Do you like to read on the go but are unable to carry your print books everywhere?

Is your eBook purchase not compatible with the device of your choice?

Don't worry, now with every Packt book you get a DRM-free PDF version of that book at no cost.

Read anywhere, any place, on any device. Search, copy, and paste code from your favorite technical books directly into your application.

The perks don't stop there, you can get exclusive access to discounts, newsletters, and great free content in your inbox daily

Follow these simple steps to get the benefits:

1.  Scan the QR code or visit the link below

https://packt.link/free-ebook/9781803234861

2.  Submit your proof of purchase
3.  That's it! We'll send your free PDF and other benefits to your email directly

# Part 1:
# Introduction to Azure
# Data Architect

This part mainly focuses on business and data strategy alignment, the economic and technical benefits of using the cloud for data, and making the first preparations for moving data to the cloud.

This part has the following chapters:

- *Chapter 1, Introduction to Data Architectures*
- *Chapter 2, Preparing for Cloud Adoption*

# 1

# Introduction to Data Architectures

With data quickly becoming an essential asset of any business, the need for cloud data architects has never been higher. The key role these professionals fulfill is to provide the technical blueprints of any cloud data project and expertise on data architectures as a whole. A skilled data architect is proficient in many steps of the end-to-end data processes, such as data ingestion, data warehouses, data transformations, and visualization.

It is of utmost importance that data architects are familiar with the benefits and drawbacks of individual resources as well as platform-wide design patterns. Typically, aspiring data architects have a background as **business intelligence** (**BI**) developers, data engineers, or data scientists. They are often specialized in one or more tools but lack experience in architecting solutions according to best practices.

Compared to a developer profile, an architect is more focused on the long term and the bigger picture. The architect must keep in mind the overarching business strategy and prioritize certain aspects of the architecture accordingly. To equip you with the necessary skills to do so, you will be introduced to methods of getting business value from your data, to solidify any long-term data strategy.

This chapter will also introduce you to a wide-purpose referential data architecture. This architecture will be used as a guideline throughout this entire book and will become more and more defined as the chapters go on.

Finally, on-premises data architectures nowadays face a variety of challenges. You will explore these challenges and look at how a business can benefit from either a cloud or a hybrid cloud solution.

In this chapter, we're going to cover the following main topics:

- Understanding the value of data
- A data architecture reference diagram
- Challenges of on-premises architectures

# Understanding the value of data

Data generation is growing at an exponential rate. 90 percent of data in the world was generated in the last 2 years, and global data creation is expected to reach 181 zettabytes in 2022.

Just to put this number in perspective, 1 zettabyte is equal to 1 million petabytes. This scale requires data architects to deal with the complexity of big data, but it also introduces an opportunity. The expert data analyst, Doug Laney, defines big data with the popular *three Vs framework*: **Volume**, **Variety**, and **Velocity**. In this section, we would like to explore a fourth one called **Value**.

## Types of analytics

Data empowers businesses to look back into the past, giving insights into established and emerging patterns, and making informed decisions for the future. *Gartner* splits analytical solutions that support decision-making into four categories: **descriptive**, **diagnostic**, **predictive**, and **prescriptive** analytics. Each category is potentially more complex to analyze but can also add more value to your business.

Let's go through each of these categories next:

- **Descriptive analytics** is concerned with answering the question, "*What is happening in my business?*" It describes the past and current state of the business by creating static reports on top of data. The data used to answer this question is often modeled in a data warehouse, which models historical data in dimension and fact tables for reporting purposes.

- **Diagnostic analytics** tries to answer the question, "*Why is it happening?*" It drills down into the historical data with interactive reports and diagnoses the root cause. Interactive reports are still built on top of a data warehouse, but additional data may be added to support this type of analysis. A broader view of your data estate allows for more root causes to be found.

- **Predictive analytics** learns from historical trends and patterns to make predictions for the future. It deals with answering the question, "*What will happen in the future?*" This is where **machine learning** (**ML**) and **artificial intelligence** (**AI**) come into play, drawing data from the data warehouse or raw data sources to learn from.

- **Prescriptive analytics** answers the question, "*What should I do?*" and prescribes the next best action. When we know what will happen in the future, we can act on it. This can be done by using different ML methods such as recommendation systems or explainable AI. Recommendation systems recommend the next best product to customers based on similar products or what similar customers bought. Think, for instance, about **Netflix** recommending new series or movies you might like. Explainable AI will identify which factors were most important to output a certain prediction, which allows you to act on those factors to change the predicted outcome.

The following diagram shows the value-extracting process, going from data to analytics, decisions, and actions:

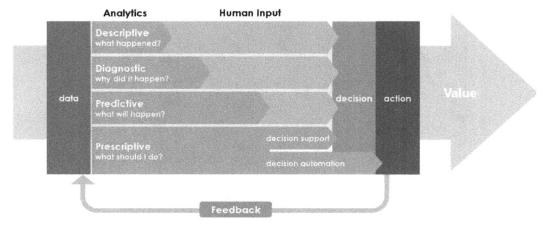

Figure 1.1 – Extracting value from data

Just as with humans, ML models need to learn from their mistakes, which can be done with the help of a **feedback loop**. A feedback loop allows a teacher to correct the outcomes of the ML model and add them as training labels for the next learning cycle. Learning cycles allow the ML model to improve over time and combat data drift. Data drift occurs when the data on which the model was trained isn't representative anymore of the data the model predicts. This will lead to inaccurate predictions.

As ML models improve over time, it is best practice to have human confirmation of predictions before automating the decision-making process. Even when an ML model has matured, we can't rely on the model being right 100 percent of the time. This is why ML models often work with confidence scores, stating how confident they are in the prediction. If the confidence score is below a certain threshold, human intervention is required.

To get continuous value out of data, it is necessary to build a data roadmap and strategy. A complexity-value matrix is a mapping tool to help prioritize which data projects need to be addressed first. This matrix will be described more in detail in the following section.

## A complexity-value matrix

A complexity-value matrix has four quadrants to plot future data projects on. These go from high- to low-value and low- to high-complexity. Projects that are considered high-value and have a low complexity are called "quick wins" or "low-hanging fruit" and should be prioritized first. These are often **Software-as-a-Service** (**SaaS**) applications or third-party APIs that can quickly be integrated into your data platform to get immediate value. Data projects with high complexity and low value should not be pursued as they have a low **Return on Investment** (**ROI**). In general, the more difficult our analytical questions become, the more complex the projects may be, but also, the more value we may get out of it.

A visualization of the four quadrants of the matrix can be seen as follows:

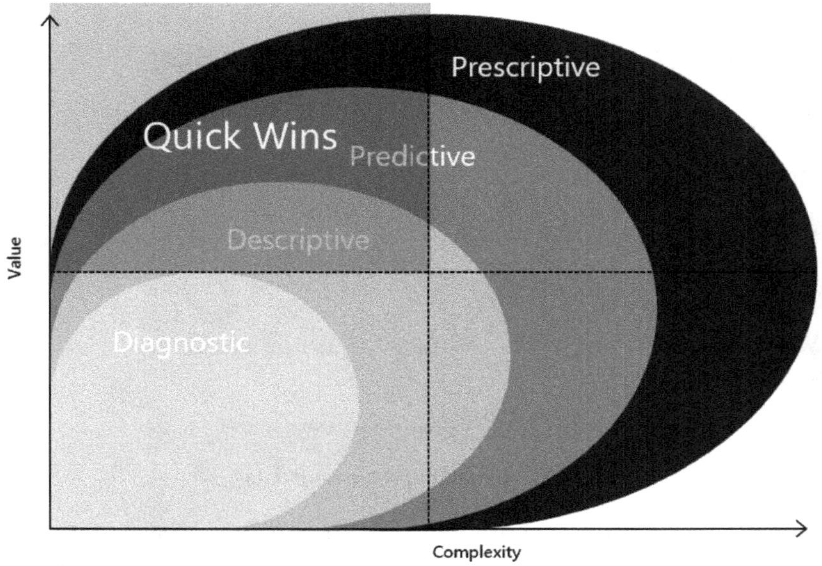

Figure 1.2 – The four quadrants of a complexity-value matrix

Often, we think of the direct value data projects bring but do also consider the indirect value. Data engineering projects often do not have a direct value as they move data from one system to another, but this may indirectly open up a world of new opportunities.

To extract value from data, a solid data architecture needs to be in place. In the following section, we'll define an abstract data architecture diagram that will be referenced throughout this book to explain data architecture principles.

## A data architecture reference diagram

The reference architecture diagram that is abstractly defined for now in *Figure 1.3* shows the typical structure of an end-to-end data platform in a (hybrid) cloud:

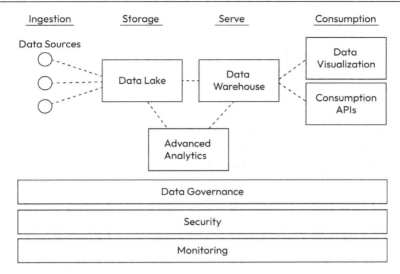

Figure 1.3 – A typical structure of an end-to-end data platform in a (hybrid) cloud

This reference diagram shows the key components of most modern cloud data platforms. There are limitless possible adaptations, such as accommodating streaming data, but the diagram in *Figure 1.3* serves as the basis for more advanced data architectures. It's like the *Pizza Margherita* of data architectures! The architecture diagram in *Figure 1.3* already shows four distinct layers in the end-to-end architecture, as follows:

- The ingestion layer
- The storage layer
- The serving layer
- The consumption layer

Next to these layers, there are a couple of other key aspects of the data platform that span across multiple layers, as follows:

- Data orchestration and processing
- Advanced analytics
- Data governance and compliance
- Security
- Monitoring

Let's cover the first layer next.

## The ingestion layer

The ingestion layer serves as the data entrance to the cloud environment. Here, data from various sources is pulled into the cloud. These sources include on-premises databases, SaaS applications, other cloud environments, **Internet of Things (IoT)** devices, and many more. Let's look at this layer in more detail:

- First, the number of data sources can vary greatly between businesses and could already bring a variety of challenges to overcome. In enterprise-scale organizations, when the amount of data sources can reach extraordinary levels, it is of exceptional importance to maintain a clear overview and management of these sources.

- Secondly, the sheer variety of sources is another common issue to deal with. Different data sources can have distinct methods of ingesting data into the cloud and, in some cases, require architectural changes to accommodate.

- Thirdly, managing authentication for data sources can be cumbersome. Authentication, which happens in a multitude of ways, is often unique to the data source. Every source requires its own tokens, keys, or other types of credentials that must be managed and seamlessly refreshed to optimize security.

From a design perspective, there are a few other aspects to keep in mind. The architect should consider the following:

- **Data speed**: Will incoming data from the source be ingested periodically (that is, batch ingestion) or continuously (that is, data streaming)?

- **Level of the structure of the data**: Will the incoming data be unstructured, semi-structured, or structured?

Regarding data speed, data will be ingested in batches in the vast majority of cases. This translates to periodical requests made to an **application programming interface** (**API**) to pull data from the data source. For the more uncommon cases of streaming data, architectural changes are required to provide an environment to store and process the continuous flow of data. In later chapters, you will discover how the platform architecture will differ to accommodate the streaming data.

Finally, the level of structure of the data will determine the amount of required data transformations, the methods of storing the data, or the destination of data movements. Unstructured data, such as images and audio files, will require different processing compared to semi-structured key-value pairs or structured tabular files.

*(Add what data ingestion services will be discussed later in the book).*

# The storage layer

The definitions of the following layers can vary. Over the course of this book, the storage layer refers to the central (often large-scale) storage of data. Data lakes are the most common method for massive storage of data, due to their capacity and relatively low cost. Alternatives are graph-based databases, relational databases, NoSQL databases, flat file-based databases, and so on. The data warehouse, which holds business-ready data and is optimized for querying and analytics, does not belong to the storage layer but will fall under the serving layer instead.

Decisions made by the architect in the storage layer can have a great effect on costs, performance, and the data platform in its entirety. Here, the architect will have to consider redundancy, access tiers, and security. In the case of a data lake, a tier system needs to be considered for raw, curated, and enriched data, as well as a robust and scalable folder structure.

*(Add what data storage services will be discussed later in the book).*

# The serving layer

In the serving layer, preprocessed and cleansed data is stored in a data warehouse, often regarded as the flagship of the data platform. This is a type of structured storage that is optimized for large-scale queries and analytics. The data warehouse forms one of the core components of BI.

The major difference between a data warehouse and the aforementioned data lake is the level of structure. A data warehouse is defined by schemas and enforces data types and structures. Conversely, a data lake can be seen as a massive dump of all kinds of data, with little to no regard for the enforcement of specific rules. The strong level of enforcement makes a data warehouse significantly more homogeneous, which results in far better performance for analytics.

The cloud data architect has various decisions to make in the serving layer. There are quite a few options for data warehousing on the Azure cloud, as follows:

1.  First, the architect should think about whether they want an **Infrastructure-as-a-Service (IaaS)**, a **Platform-as-a-Service (PaaS)**, or a SaaS solution. In short, this results in a trade-off between management responsibilities, development efforts, and flexibility. This will be discussed more in later chapters.

2.  Next, different services on Azure come with their own advantages and disadvantages. The architect could, for example, opt for a very cost-effective serverless SQL solution or leverage massive processing power in highly performant dedicated SQL pools, among numerous other options.

After deciding on the most fitting service, there are still decisions to be made within the data warehouse. The architect will have to determine structures to organize the data in the data warehouse, also known as **schemas**. Common schemas are star and snowflake schemas, which also come with their own benefits and drawbacks.

*Chapter 6, Data Warehousing*, will teach you all the necessary skills to confidently decide on the right solution. *Chapter 7, The Semantic Layer*, will introduce you to the concept of data marts, subsets of a data warehouse ready for business consumption.

## The consumption layer

The consumption layer is the final layer of an end-to-end data architecture and typically follows the serving layer by extracting data from the data warehouse. There are numerous ways of consuming the data, which has been prepared and centralized in earlier stages.

The most common manner of consumption is through data visualization. This can happen through dashboarding and building reports. The combination of a data warehouse and a visualization service is often referred to as **BI**. Many modern dashboarding tools allow for interactivity and drill-down functionality within the dashboard itself. Although technically it is not a part of the Azure stack, Power BI is the preferred service for data visualization for Azure data platforms. However, Microsoft allows other visualization services to connect conveniently as well.

Another way to consume data is by making the data available to other applications or platforms using APIs.

*Chapter 8, Visualizing Data Using Power BI*, will teach you how to extract data from the data warehouse in various ways and visualize it using interactive dashboarding. In this chapter, you will also discover methods to perform self-service BI, allowing end users to create their own ad hoc dashboards and reports to quickly perform data analysis.

## Data orchestration and processing

Contrary to the four layers mentioned previously, there are a couple of other core components of the data platform that span across the entire end-to-end process.

Data orchestration refers to moving data from one place to another, often using data pipelines. This process is often done by data engineers. When data is moved from one stage to the next, data undergoes transformations in the form of joining data, deriving new columns, computing aggregations, and so on. For example, when data is moved from a data lake to a data warehouse, it must be transformed to match the data model, which is enforced by the data warehouse. Another example is when moving data between tiers (raw, curated, and enriched tiers) in the data lake, where the data becomes more and more ready for business use whenever it moves up a tier.

Data pipelines allow data engineers to automate and scale the orchestration and processing of data. These components are critical to the performance and health of the data platform and must be monitored accordingly.

Here are two common methods of performing orchestration and processing:

- **Extract-Transform-Load** (ETL)
- **Extract-Load-Transform** (ELT)

In both cases, data is extracted from a source and loaded to a destination. The main difference between both methods is the location where the transformations take place. These will be further discussed in *Chapter 4, Transforming Data on Azure*. This chapter will also teach you how to create and monitor data pipelines according to best practices.

## Advanced analytics

For analyses that may be too complex to perform in the serving layer, an analytics suite or data science environment can be added to the architecture to perform advanced analytics and unlock ML capabilities. This component can often be added in a later stage of platform development, as it will mostly not influence the core working of the other layers. A data platform in an early phase of development can perfectly exist without this component.

One option for the advanced analytics suite is an ML workspace where data scientists can preprocess data, perform feature engineering, and train and deploy ML models. The latter may require additional components such as a container registry for storing and managing model deployments. The **Azure Machine Learning** workspace allows users to create and run ML pipelines to scale their data science processes. It also enables citizen data scientists to train models using no-code and low-code features.

Apart from an environment for data scientists and ML engineers to build and deploy custom models, the Azure cloud also provides users with a wide array of pre-trained ML models. Azure Cognitive Services encompass many models for **computer vision** (**CV**), speech recognition, text analytics, search capabilities, and so on. These models are available through ready-to-use API endpoints. They often involve niche cases but, when used correctly, bring a lot of value to the solution and are exceptionally fast to implement.

*Chapter 9, Advanced Analytics Using AI*, will go deeper into end-to-end ML workflows, such as the connection to data storages, performing preprocessing, model training, and model deployments. This chapter will also introduce the concepts of **ML operations**, often referred to as **MLOps**. This encompasses **continuous integration and continuous development** (**CI/CD**) for ML workflows.

## Data governance and compliance

The more a data platform scales, the harder it becomes to maintain a clear overview of existing data sources, data assets, transformations, data access control, and compliance. To avoid a build-up of technical backlog, it is strongly recommended to start the setup of governance and compliance processes from an early stage of development and have it scale with the platform.

To govern Azure data platforms, Microsoft developed Microsoft Purview, formerly known as Azure Purview. This tool, which is covered in *Chapter 10, Enterprise-Level Data Governance and Compliance*, allows users to gain clear insights into the governance and compliance of the platform. Therefore, it is essential to the skill set of any aspiring Azure data architect. In this chapter, you will learn how to do the following:

- Create a data map by performing scans on data assets
- Construct a data catalog to provide an overview of the metadata of data assets
- Build a business glossary to establish clear definitions of possibly ambiguous business terms
- Gain executive insights on the entire data estate

## Security

With the growing rise of harmful cyber-attacks, security is another indispensable component of a data platform. Improper security or configurations may lead to tremendous costs for the business. Investing in robust security to prevent attacks from happening will typically be vastly cheaper than dealing with the damage afterward.

Cybersecurity can be very complex and therefore should be configured and managed using the help of a cybersecurity architect. However, certain aspects of security should fall into the responsibilities of the data architect as well. The data architect should have the appropriate skill set to establish data security. Examples are working with row- or column-level security, data encryption at rest and in transit, masking sensitive data, and so on.

*Chapter 11, Introduction to Data Security*, will teach you all that is necessary to ensure data is always well protected and access is always limited to a minimum.

## Monitoring

Disruptions such as failing data pipelines, breaking transformations, and unhealthy deployments can shut down the workings of an entire data platform. To limit the downtime to an absolute minimum, these processes and deployments should be monitored continuously.

Azure provides monitoring and health reports on pipeline runs, Spark and SQL jobs, ML model deployments, data asset scans, and more. The monitoring of these resources will be further discussed in their own respective chapters.

# Challenges of on-premises architectures

Cloud computing has seen a steep rise in adoption during the last decade. Nevertheless, a significant chunk of businesses hold on to keeping their servers and data on-premises. There are certain reasons why a business may prefer on-premises over the cloud. Some businesses have the perception of increased security when keeping data on their own servers. Others, generally smaller businesses, may not feel the need to optimize their IT landscape or simply are not keen on change. Organizations in strictly regulated industries can be bound to on-premises for compliance. Whichever the reason, on-premises architectures nowadays come with certain challenges.

These challenges include, among other things, the following:

- Scalability
- Cost optimization
- Agility
- Flexibility

Let's go through these challenges in detail.

## Scalability

Organizations with a rapidly enlarging technological landscape will struggle the most to overcome the challenge of scalability. As the total business data volume keeps growing continually, an organization faces the constant need of having to find new ways to expand the on-premises server farm. It is not always as simple as just adding extra servers. After a while, extra building infrastructure is needed, new personnel must be hired, energy consumption soars, and so on.

Here, the benefit of cloud computing is the enormous pool of available servers and computing resources. For the business, this means it can provision any additional capacity without having to worry about the intricate organization and planning of its own servers.

## Cost optimization

Businesses that completely rely on on-premises servers are never fully cost-effective. Why is this so?

Let's take a look at two scenarios:

- **When usage increases**: When the usage increases, the need for extra capacity arises. A business is not going to wait until its servers are used to their limits, risking heavy throttling and bottleneck issues, before starting to expand its capacity. Although the risk of full saturation of its servers is hereby avoided, the computing and storage capacity is never fully made use of. While usage can grow linearly or exponentially, costs will rise in discrete increments, referring to distinct expansions of server capacity.

- **When usage decreases**: When the usage decreases, the additional capacity is simply standing there, unused. Even if the decrease in usage lasts for longer periods of time, it is not that simple to just sell the hardware, free up the physical space, and get rid of the extra maintenance personnel. In most situations, this results in costs remaining unchanged despite the usage.

Cloud computing usually follows a **pay-as-you-go** (**PAYG**) business model. This solves the two challenges of cost optimization during variable usage. PAYG allows businesses to match their costs to their usage, avoiding disparities, as can be seen in the following diagram:

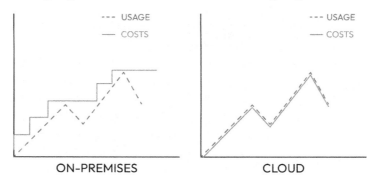

Figure 1.4 – Cost patterns depending on usage for on-premises and cloud infrastructure

Let's cover the next challenge now.

## Agility

In contrast to whether it is possible to make a certain change, agility refers to the speed at which businesses can implement these new changes. Expanding or reducing capacity, changing the types of processing power, and so on takes time in an on-premises environment. In most cases, this involves the acquisition of new hardware, installing the new compute, and configuring security, all of which can be extremely time-consuming in a business context.

Here, cloud architectures benefit from far superior agility over on-premises architectures. Scaling capacity up or down, changing memory-optimized processors for compute-optimized processors: all of this is performed in a matter of seconds or minutes.

## Flexibility

The challenge of flexibility can be interpreted very broadly and has some intersections with the other challenges. Difficulties with scalability and agility can be defined as types of flexibility issues.

Apart from difficulties regarding scalability and agility, on-premises servers face the issue of constant hardware modernization. In this case, we could compare on-premises and cloud infrastructure to a *purchased* car or a *rental* car respectively. There is not always the need to make use of cutting-edge technology, but if the need is present, think about which option will result in having a more modern car in most situations.

In other cases, specialized hardware such as **field-programmable gate arrays** (**FPGAs**) might be required for a short period of time—for example, during the training of an extraordinarily complex ML model. To revisit the car example, would you rather purchase a van when you occasionally have to move furniture or rent a van for a day while moving?

Let's summarize the chapter next.

## Summary

In this chapter, we first discussed how to extract value from your data by asking the right analytical questions. Questions may increase in complexity from descriptive, diagnostic, and predictive to prescriptive but may also hold more value. A complexity-value matrix is necessary to prioritize data projects and build a data roadmap. A crucial thing to remember is to capture data as soon as possible, even if you don't have a data strategy or roadmap yet. All data that you do not capture now cannot be used in the future to extract value from. Next, we introduced a reference architecture diagram. Over time, you will get familiar with every component of the diagram and how they interact with each other.

Four layers of cloud architectures were explained. The ingestion layer is used to pull data into the central cloud data platform. The storage layer is capable of holding massive amounts of data, often in a tiered system, where data gets more business-ready as it moves through the tiers. In the serving layer, the data warehouse is located, which holds data with a strictly enforced schema and is optimized for analytical workloads. Lastly, the consumption layer allows end users and external systems to consume the data in reports and dashboards or to be used in other applications.

Some components of the data platform span across multiple layers. Data orchestration and processing refers to data pipelines that ingest data into the cloud, move data from one place to another, and orchestrate data transformations. Advanced analytics leverages Azure's many pre-trained ML models and a data science environment to perform complex calculations and provide meaningful predictions. Data governance tools bring data asset compliance, flexible access control, data lineage, and overall insights into the entire data estate. Impeccable security of individual components as well as the integrations between them takes away many of the worries regarding harmful actions being made by third parties. Finally, the extensive monitoring capabilities in Azure allow us to get insights into the health and performance of the processes and data storage in the platform.

Finally, we discussed the drawbacks that on-premises architectures face, such as scalability, cost optimization, agility, and flexibility. These challenges are often conveniently dealt with by leveraging the benefits of cloud-based approaches.

In the next chapter, we will look at two Microsoft frameworks that ease the move to the cloud.

# 2

# Preparing for Cloud Adoption

We discussed the challenges of on-premises architectures in the last chapter, but it turns out that for the majority of businesses, moving to the cloud can be greatly beneficial. However, organizations that do not have experience with the cloud can struggle with finding their way as they lack the required skill sets in their teams.

Apart from you helping them out after finishing this book, there are a few other resources these businesses can leverage to ease their journey to the cloud. For this, Microsoft has two frameworks in place:

- Azure's **Well-Architected Framework (WAF)**
- **The Cloud Adoption Framework (CAF)**

This chapter provides an overview of the WAF, curated for the cloud data architect. We will look at the pillars on which the framework is built and which parts are most relevant to a data architect.

Next, we will explore the concept of landing zones – more specifically, the data management landing zone and the accompanying data landing zones. These landing zones are part of the CAF and encompass pre-built architectures for rapid cloud data platform development according to best practices.

## The Azure WAF

The Azure WAF is a framework created by Microsoft for architects, as a result of being a global leader in cloud architecting for years. The framework is designed to guarantee highly qualitative cloud architectures in accordance with proven best practices.

WAF does not only cover data and analytics but can also be used for any workload in the cloud, such as website hosting or application development. However, many of its core principles trickle down into data architectures as well.

The framework is extensively documented, yet the goal of this chapter is to provide you with the core principles and learnings in a bite-sized format and curate the content that is most relevant to the role of a data architect.

The Azure WAF is built upon the following five pillars:

- Reliability

- Security

- Cost optimization

- Operational excellence

- Performance efficiency

We will take a look at each pillar and how it translates into the responsibilities of a cloud data architect. For the complete framework (which also includes many things irrelevant to a data architect), refer to `https://learn.microsoft.com/en-us/azure/architecture/framework/ services/networking/azure-application-gateway`.

## Reliability

Despite the wish for everything to run smoothly all the time, in reality, systems break, processes fail, and databases will have downtime. It is the responsibility of the cloud architect to design with system failures in mind and always have a backup plan ready. The pillar of reliability revolves around the concepts of **high availability (HA)** and **disaster recovery (DR)**.

HA refers to the redundancy and rapid response of failover systems. This is to ensure that the system will either keep running or have minimal downtime, thereby limiting the impact on end users.

DR, on the other hand, encompasses the backup procedures that are in place for when things go south. It is more about preventing or limiting permanent damage or loss of data after a catastrophe.

According to the Azure WAF, reliability comes down to the following principles:

- Design for business requirements

- Design for failure

- Observe application health

- Drive automation

- Design for self-healing

- Design for scale-out

We will summarize the key takeaways of each design principle next, starting with business requirements.

## Designing for business requirements

Reliability can be tracked in many ways, and the business will want to see some metrics to quantitatively evaluate this. **Service-level agreements (SLAs)** come into play here, often regarding the uptime of a system. For example, an SLA of 99.9% uptime comes down to a maximum downtime of less than 9 hours per year for the system.

Usually, the more critical a system is to the health and performance of the business, the higher the required minimal uptime will be. The stricter the SLA, however, the more expensive the solution becomes. An SLA of 99.99% can be significantly costlier than an SLA of 99.9%, as the maximal yearly downtime must be decreased tenfold.

Downtime can be minimized by adding redundancy in the solution – for example, by having multiple instances of the same component in parallel. Another thing to keep in mind is the number of unique (critical) components of the data platform. Every component comes with its own SLA. The more unique components (that can break the entire solution) there are, the higher the downtime will be. Therefore, limiting components and distinct services used in the solution to a minimum is vital for HA.

## Designing for failure

Hope for the best and prepare for the worst. Expecting all components to be running smoothly is dangerously naïve. Moreover, have a plan ready when certain components do not even reach their promised SLA in terms of uptime.

Good preparation counts for both HA and DR. An in-place failover plan will greatly increase availability by switching the workload to redundant instances of the failed component. To prevent loss of data during the downtime of a data platform, have backups of your internal data and think of workarounds for ingestion processes to prevent missing out on external data.

## Observing application health

Observing application health or, in our case, the health of the data platform, comes down to making use of the extensive monitoring services on Azure. Monitoring the data platform and its components is crucial to measuring performance, evaluating SLA adherence, detecting fluctuations and failures, and keeping an eye on capacity usage.

Monitoring can be performed through the evaluation of system metrics and the querying of diagnostic logs. In a later stage, alerts can be added that are triggered by either the metrics or logs, allowing for rapid action in case of a system failure.

## Driving automation

Automation removes the need for manual work, thereby removing the chances of users making mistakes. Especially in situations of low complexity and with few edge cases, automation can be a quick win, both in terms of cost and reliability. Of course, this only counts if the automation processes are rigorously tested for any possible scenario. Poor testing may lead to even lower reliability.

### Designing for self-healing

Self-healing can be seen as a form of automation, but more specifically designed to get a component or the platform up and running again without human intervention. Self-healing features are usually nice to have but not vital to a data platform. Therefore, they are best implemented in the later stages of the data platform development.

### Designing for scale-out

HA does not only come down to preventing or anticipating failures. A system can be unavailable for some users when overall usage hits capacity limits. That is why the architect should design with scalability in mind. For example, SQL compute can be scaled when many users are running queries, database capacity can be scaled when the data volume reaches unseen heights, and clusters can be scaled up right before large data transformation workloads are performed.

In situations with vast and rapid fluctuations in usage, autoscaling becomes a necessity. Luckily, nowadays, most services come with autoscaling out of the box, greatly lowering the barrier to implementing scaling capabilities into the solution.

Now that we have covered reliability, we move on to the next pillar: security.

## Security

Security is always a big topic in technology, especially when it concerns (often sensitive) data, and even more so if the data tends to be highly classified or sensitive. Most data platforms hold data that can be very harmful to the business or others when exposed.

Azure data platforms already benefit from the immense investments Microsoft makes in securing its cloud every year. On top of that, much of the complexity of cybersecurity is abstracted away, and many features can be provisioned in a managed way. This makes it considerably more attainable to build a data platform that is impenetrable to malicious actors.

The Azure WAF recognizes the following principles in terms of security:

- Plan resources and how to harden them
- Use automation and the **principle of least privilege (PoLP)**
- Classify and encrypt data
- Monitor system security and plan incident response
- Identify and protect endpoints
- Protect against code-level vulnerabilities
- Model and test against potential threats

Let us take a look at how each of these is relevant to a cloud data architect.

### Planning resources and how to harden them

The framework strongly recommends always keeping security in mind when planning workloads or resources. Hardening resources requires broad knowledge as security features of platform components can differ vastly. For example, a data lake is secured in different ways compared to a database or data warehouse, data orchestration tools require their own security considerations, and so on.

### Use automation and the PoLP

As mentioned before, security is not a simple concept in terms of a data platform and needs to be configured and optimized on a service-by-service basis. Every service on Azure is equipped with **identity access management** (IAM) and **role-based access control** (RBAC). However, distinct services often have their own unique roles.

The different roles are often subsets or supersets of each other. Typically, owner roles can do everything a contributor role can do and more. According to the PoLP, we strongly advise that user or user group permissions are strictly limited to the bare minimum that is required to perform their work. This is a simple but effective method to minimize the impact of actions taken by insiders with bad intentions.

Furthermore, as was the case with increasing reliability, security benefits from automation. Automating security processes with the use of DevSecOps reduces the chance of vulnerabilities due to human error.

### Classifying and encrypting data

Data classifications are implemented to signal the confidentiality or sensitivity level. The more harm that external sharing of the data can do to the business, the higher its confidentiality level. Data can also be sensitive, referring to the amount of harm it can cause to the data subject when shared. Think of credit card data, social security numbers, or biometrics.

Having these classifications in place allows appropriate security measures to be taken according to their level. High-confidentiality data will typically require more permissions to be accessed and may be stored more securely, at a cost. Highly sensitive data might require compliance with certain regulations such as the **General Data Protection Regulation** (GDPR) in Europe. This data will, among other things, need different retention periods to comply.

Data governance tools such as Microsoft Purview remove much of the complexity and easily allow governing teams to apply these data classifications in a highly automated way.

Data encryption is another complex topic, but with the current Azure features, this has become very trivial. Data should be encrypted both at rest (in a database or the like) and in transit (while moving the data from one place to another). The data can then be decrypted using keys or certificates.

### Monitoring system security and planning incident response

Monitoring data platform security (or more specifically, database security) can be done via audits such as **vulnerability assessments (VAs)**. SQL databases on Azure benefit from the SQL **VA** service, which allows administrators to get insights into current threats on a regular basis. These assessments can also be useful for complying with security requirements or data privacy regulations.

Incident response comes down to having a pre-defined plan and the necessary resources ready to act swiftly when security incidents occur. This plan should be optimized to protect the targeted data while trying to restore everything back to its normal state in the fastest way possible.

### Identifying and protecting endpoints

A mature data platform will have many endpoints that need to be identified, monitored, and secured. Some examples are the following:

- Data lake endpoints for reading/writing data to the data lake
- Data warehouse endpoints for reading/writing data to the data warehouse
- Deployed machine learning model endpoints for inferencing
- Endpoints for triggering data pipelines or machine learning pipelines
- External endpoints such as data sources

Many services come equipped with features for easy endpoint protection, such as firewalls or the ability to create private endpoints. On top of these, API tokens and keys need to be managed and regularly refreshed to optimize security.

### Protecting against code-level vulnerabilities

Compared to application development, data platforms tend to have fewer code-level vulnerabilities. However, they can be just as harmful. Identifying and protecting yourself from these vulnerabilities is vital. The most common example is SQL injection, which can have disastrous consequences for databases. Luckily, it is fairly easy to protect yourself from these types of attacks by sanitizing your database inputs.

### Modeling and testing against potential threats

Without testing the security of the data platform, it is impossible to determine whether the previous principles are implemented as they should be. Just like with any type of development, testing is just as important within of security to identify vulnerabilities. Various methods such as penetration testing, static code analysis, and code scanning can be used to both discover current vulnerabilities and prevent future security issues.

With this, we have covered everything regarding security. The next pillar is cost optimization.

# Cost optimization

As organizations shift their IT systems from on-premises to the cloud, costs shift from **capital expenditure (CapEx)** to **operational expenditure (OpEx)**. This means there are no upfront costs anymore for IT infrastructure. Instead, cloud services follow a consumption-based model. Another way to look at cloud computing is that you're renting compute and storage power from someone else's data center. When you don't use the resources anymore, you release them, hence the term *pay-per-use*.

The benefit of pay-per-use models is that you can plan and manage your operational costs and scale resources up and down when business needs change. Pay-per-use models ideally reduce expenditure but can also lead to huge costs when architected poorly. Think of idle resources that are not stopped or resources that have autoscaling enabled without any spending limit.

In this section, we'll look at ways to reduce unnecessary expenses and improve operational efficiencies.

## Capturing clear requirements

Before designing an architecture, you need to know what the organization wants to achieve and what the business goals are. Try to make the requirements as concise as possible before you start designing the architecture. Data requirements can be concerned with, but are not limited to, the following topics:

- Does data need to be consumed in real time or in a batch?
- What are the data retention policies?
- Does the data need to be highly available?
- What kind of analytics need to be done on the data?
- Are there any reporting requirements?

It is also important to ask about budgeting requirements. A cost-effective design stays within a given budget while achieving the business goals and projecting a successful return on investment.

## Choosing the correct resources

The resources chosen during the design phase should be able to satisfy the captured business requirements without "overachieving" and generating too many costs. For example, storing data across multiple regions when HA is not a requirement will increase costs without any business justification. Keep in mind the flexibility of the chosen resources to address future needs.

Whenever possible, look for cloud-native offerings to offload your workloads. **Software-as-a-Service (SaaS)** and **Platform-as-a-Service (PaaS)** resources are in general more cost-effective than **Infrastructure-as-a-Service (IaaS)** resources as the running and maintenance costs are included in the price.

If the business already has a data estate in the cloud and you're not architecting a greenfield project, identify any existing resources that could be shared to save costs. Be wary of the impact the new project may have on the existing resources in terms of increased load.

### Determining where the resources should be hosted

Azure resources can be hosted in different Azure regions and the cost for the same resource can vary across regions. Also note that not all functionalities of the resource may be available in every region and will therefore have no price listed. Ideally, resources are located in the same region to reduce latencies. Choosing the cheapest region per resource may result in resources not being in the same region, which may increase network ingress and egress costs.

Sometimes, we are constrained when choosing the locations of our resources due to compliance reasons. Compliance may dictate that data has to be stored in a specific country and data cannot leave this country. For high compliance and security needs, there are specialized Azure regions, such as Azure Government USA, which provides an isolated instance of Azure, or Azure Germany, which meets certain privacy certifications. Specialized regions are more expensive. Regular compliance and security needs don't require specialized regions and can be met with Azure Policy, which is free.

### Choosing the billing model

Cloud services are normally offered as consumption-based models where you pay for what you use. Resources can be allocated and deallocated when needed, minimizing costs. Costs can also be saved with autoscaling, scaling down automatically when peak loads have ended. During peak loads, it is recommended to scale out rather than up. It is easier to horizontally add more nodes and minimize downtime than to vertically increase the capacity of one node. Adding small nodes horizontally is often cheaper and reduces the risk of a single point of failure.

In some cases, commitment tiers are also offered where you pay a fixed price for a service, whether you use it or not. Commitment tiers make sense in large volumes as the discounts get bigger for higher commitments.

## Estimating the initial costs

The Azure pricing calculator allows you to estimate the cost of your architecture once you know the resources, location, and billing model you are going to use. You can choose in which currency to display the costs and export them to Excel to share with the business stakeholders.

There is another calculator called the Microsoft Azure **Total Cost of Ownership** (TCO) calculator, which is used for migration projects. It allows you to calculate the cost savings of moving your solution to Azure compared to hosting it in your on-premises data center. Use this calculator in combination with Azure Migrate to evaluate the current on-premises workloads, get Azure replacement suggestions, and provide cost estimates.

*Considering the cost constraints*

The lowest-cost design is often not the optimal design. Trade-offs are made between security, scalability, resilience, operability, and minimizing cost, which may lead to poor design choices. These can result in security risks or unreliable uptimes. Whenever cost-cutting is needed, prioritize the design areas your solution needs to focus on and minimize the costs in areas with the lowest priority.

The following are some examples of cost constraints to consider:

- What is the budget of the project set by the business?
- Are there any policies for budget alerting?
- Identify acceptable boundaries for scale, redundancy, and performance against costs.
- Identify unrestricted resources that need to scale and consume more costs with demand.

*Planning a governance strategy*

When you create a resource, Azure allows you to add resource tags. These tags can logically group the resources to create custom cost reports. The cost can be reported to an owner, application, business department, or project initiative.

Use Azure Policy to enforce compliance and identify cost boundaries. Azure Policy allows you to set rules on management groups, subscriptions, and resource groups, which can prevent the provisioning of expensive resources. Set quotas, limits, and budget alerts in an Azure subscription to prevent unexpected costs.

Next, we will dig into operation excellence, the fourth pillar of the WAF.

## Operational excellence

Operational excellence is concerned with the efficiency of your operational processes to run data pipelines and solutions in production. This includes automated deployment, **continuous integration/ continuous delivery** (CI/CD), unit testing to validate the quality of new code deployments, and many more.

Improving operational efficiency is important to not slow down the release of new features. You also want to be able to roll back as quickly as possible when bugs are discovered in new updates. In this section, we will describe how to create fast and routine deployment processes but also prevent introducing new bugs in updates.

### *Optimizing build and release processes*

There are a couple of ways to optimize and automate release processes. You can provision resources as Infrastructure as Code. This can be done with **Azure Research Manager** (**ARM**) templates, YAML files, or Azure Bicep. You can also create different environments for developing and testing your data platform before releasing it to the business. These environments are called **development, test, acceptance, and production** (**DTAP**) and work hand-in-hand with CI/CD pipelines. The next step is to try and automate the testing method with a unit test. These methods enable consistency, repetition, and early detection of issues in the data platform.

### *Understanding operational health*

Once your data platform is running, the health of processes and workloads needs to be monitored. Most Azure services have a monitoring dashboard to check on the status and health of pipelines or can work with Azure Monitor and Log Analytics.

Monitoring allows you to observe issues and proactively resolve them. It is critical for the business stakeholders to know when services are down to communicate with the end customers.

### *Rehearsing recovery and practicing for failure*

Running DR drills and testing out HA and failovers is especially important for databases. With this, you validate the effectiveness of the recovery process and ensure data is still available for querying and no new incoming data is lost.

### *Using loosely coupled architecture*

Try to use modern architectural patterns, which include microservices, loosely coupled components, and serverless to enable teams to build and deploy services independently and minimize the impact if there is a service failure.

Now, we have one more pillar to cover, which is performance efficiency.

## Performance efficiency

Optimizing the overall performance of a data platform is one of the most technically complex challenges that a cloud data architect will face, both during development and while maintaining the platform.

In short, this comes down to identifying bottlenecks, evaluating potential throttling issues, and finding ways to fix them. A good data management strategy goes a long way in optimizing performance.

The Azure WAF has many suggestions when it comes to performance efficiency and data management. We have curated the most impactful and relevant ones for a cloud data architect here:

- Adopt a data-driven approach
- Use data partitioning
- Consider denormalizing data
- Handle data growth and retention
- Optimize and tune SQL queries and indexes

Every single one of these actions will impact performance. Some actions might have more impact than others, but in the end, every little bit helps. Given that no extra resources or funding is used, increased performance will result in lower costs and increased value gained from the data platform.

### Adopting a data-driven approach

The various processes and storage solutions in the data platform generate heaps of data. Storing this data will allow the business to gain insights into certain performance trends over time. Leverage this data to substantiate decisions taken when adjusting the data platform by either adding new components or substituting components for more fitting alternatives.

### Using data partitioning

Data partitioning is a key concept for any data engineer or data architect. Partitioning can be performed in a few different ways:

- **Horizontal partitioning** (also known as *sharding*): Separating rows into different partitions
- **Vertical partitioning**: Separating columns into different partitions
- **Functional partitioning**: Partitioning based on, for example, data access speed (read-write data in one partition, read-only data in another partition)

The theory of optimal data partitioning strategies is extensive but will be explored in detail in later chapters. Well-thought-out data partitioning strategies can have a tremendous impact on query performance.

### Considering denormalizing data

Data in data warehouses is often normalized to decrease the data volume by avoiding duplicate data. However, it can be beneficial to have data stored in duplicates if this can speed up queries. Because normalized data is split into many tables, queries requiring data from multiple tables will need a lot of join operations. This can slow down performance considerably. In short, normalizing data typically makes storage more cost-effective, while denormalizing increases query performance.

### Handling data growth and retention

Expect data in the data warehouse to grow exponentially over time. Keep an eye on future-proofing the data warehouse by always keeping scalability in mind. When the data volume grows larger, query performance will drop.

A good way to solve this is by using good data partitioning. Another way is by looking at data retention policies. Think about what data is not being processed frequently and consider moving it to a lower, often cheaper, access tier. Azure Storage solutions have three access tiers:

- Hot tier
- Cold tier
- Archive tier

Normally, data that is often analyzed is stored in a hot access tier. Moving this data to the cold tier will decrease storage costs but increase read and write costs. This makes it perfect for infrequently accessed data. Contrary to popular belief, data in a cold tier is not significantly slower to access than data in a hot tier. Data in the archive tier will even further decrease storage costs, but this will vastly increase data access speed.

By splitting infrequently used data into different storages with different access tiers, the solution will become both more performant and more cost-effective.

### Optimizing and tuning SQL queries and indexes

It is straightforward that writing queries in an optimal way will greatly impact performance. When writing ad hoc queries or stored procedures, avoid unnecessary data type conversions and needlessly large WHERE clauses.

Indexing the data warehouse correctly improves performance as well. Indexing done well will organize the data in such a way that it becomes many times easier to search through.

## Data landing zones

Moving to the cloud can be a daunting task for a business. The Azure Cloud allows the provisioning of hundreds of unique services. Without the knowledge of an experienced architect, starting cloud-based projects can quickly become overwhelming. This counts for both greenfield and brownfield development.

> **Note**
> Greenfield development refers to projects built up from scratch, whereas brownfield development uses existing components of a solution to upgrade or revamp a solution.

To lower the barrier of businesses moving their data and infrastructure to the cloud, Azure provides landing zones, as part of the Microsoft CAF. A landing zone is a pre-composed set of services and configurations allowing for simple and fast migration. The architecture of these landing zones is the result of Microsoft's experience with assisting in thousands of cloud migrations, making them a proven and robust approach. Landing zones can be leveraged in two ways, either starting small and planning to scale up later or going for an enterprise-scale landing zone straight away.

## Fundamentals of Azure core services

Before diving deeper into the architecture of an Azure data landing zone, we must introduce a few core Azure concepts:

- Subscriptions
- Resource groups
- Management groups

The three concepts in the previous list are closely related to each other. Management groups, subscriptions, and resource groups form a hierarchy. Each level holds a one-to-many relationship with the level that is below it in the hierarchy, as can be seen in the following figure:

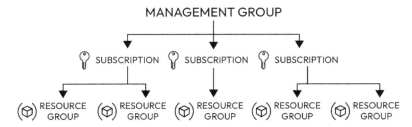

Figure 2.1 – A management group can have multiple subscriptions, which in turn can hold multiple resource groups; the hierarchical structure makes the inheritance of permissions and roles remarkably convenient

All services on Azure, including management groups, subscriptions, and resource groups, come with RBAC. This allows administrators to grant roles to specific users or user groups in the **Azure Active Directory** (**AAD**) of the business. One advantage of the preceding hierarchy is the inheritance of roles and permissions. Even more so, the roles that are granted at the resource group level will trickle down to the distinct resources in that group.

Subscriptions can be interpreted as a grouping of Azure services and come with certain boundaries. Some resources, such as **virtual networks** (**VNets**), are not able to span across multiple subscriptions.

Resource groups are mere logical groupings of resources. In contrast to subscriptions, resource groups do not limit the resources they contain in any way. They are often used to group different services for a specific project with a similar life cycle. Resource groups allow for easy cost analysis, management, and deletion of services.

Management groups provide a higher level of management, as they can group different subscriptions. Management groups make life easier from a governance perspective, making it convenient to filter down policies, RBAC, and blueprints.

## Data management landing zone architecture

The data management landing zone can be deployed as a blueprint on Azure. This means it comes with a subscription, a set of policies, RBAC configurations, and **ARM** templates. ARM templates are essentially JSON files containing a deployment configuration for a specific Azure resource and can be used for fast and standardized provisioning of Azure services.

The data management landing zone is focused on governance. It consists of two major areas: one for platform operations and one for data platform operations. The latter encompasses many master data management services, a data catalog, data quality management, data sharing options, and more. This will serve as the governance and compliance hub for data landing zones. The platform operations domain holds general services for networking, security, and monitoring. The architecture of the data management landing zone is quite extensive and may be hard to clearly visualize in this book. For a cloud data and AI architect, it is not crucial to know about, but if you are interested, the full architecture of the data management landing zone can be found at `https://learn.microsoft.com/en-us/azure/cloud-adoption-framework/scenarios/cloud-scale-analytics/architectures/data-management-landing-zone`.

## Data landing zone architecture

After the data management landing zone is in place, one or more data landing zones can be provisioned. These are connected with the central data management landing zone through a **VNet** peering.

The landing zone architecture is visualized in *Figure 2.2*.

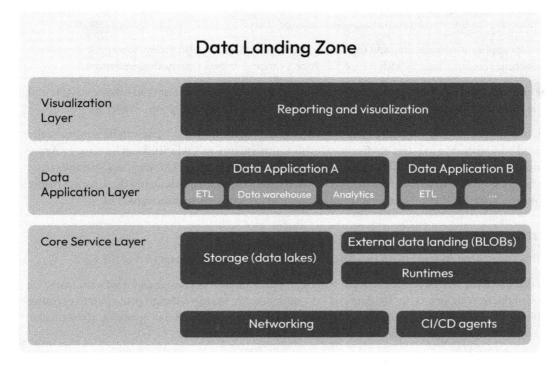

Figure 2.2 – An overview of the data landing zone in Azure

The data landing zone consists of the following:

- A core services layer
- A data application layer
- A visualization layer

For every layer, some example resource groups with their deployed resources are displayed, as well as the collaborators working in that respective layer. The services themselves will be explained further in future chapters. Services shown in color are mandatory for the landing zone, whereas services that appear in gray are optional.

The platform operations team deals with security, governance, and monitoring in the core services layer. Azure uses public links by default to communicate between services, but confidential data may need to be transferred inside a VNet or with private endpoints.

The data platform operations team deals with setting up and maintaining core storage services such as data lakes, storage accounts for your data warehouse (raw, enriched, and curated), and compute services such as integration runtimes, which may be shared by multiple data factory instances.

The data application teams may add their own core data services and also create data applications such as machine learning models with Azure Machine Learning or data warehouses in Synapse.

The end users will use the output of data applications in the visualization layer to extract insights and value from data. A service we often see used here is Microsoft's reporting tool, Power BI.

Often, multiple landing zones are created for the DTAP environments. These can be automatically created and pushed to the next environment with Infrastructure as Code. This can be done in Azure using ARM templates, YAML files, or Azure Bicep. When creating new ARM templates, (default) static names are used to create resources with code. We strongly recommend changing these names before deploying your ARM templates as you will not be able to change them afterward.

## Summary

In this chapter, we zoomed in on two Microsoft frameworks, the WAF and part of the CAF.

We discussed the five pillars of the WAF. Although this framework is designed for all workloads, we curated the relevant principles for data and AI workloads. We explored design principles to optimize reliability, build airtight security, architect for cost-effectiveness, maximize operational excellence, and boost the performance efficiency of an Azure data solution.

Next, the concept of landing zones was introduced, as part of the CAF. After an introduction to some fundamental Azure concepts, such as subscriptions and resource groups, we examined both the data management landing zone and the data landing zone. Leveraging these landing zones is a great way to get started quickly with any data solution at scale on the Azure cloud.

In the next chapter, we will focus on data ingestion into the cloud.

# Part 2:
# Data Engineering on Azure

This part focuses on the data engineering aspects of a full-scale data platform – data ingestion, mass storage, and transformation processes. You will learn different methods and architectural patterns for ingesting data in the cloud. You will also learn how to move and transform data and perform ETL and ELT processes using data pipelines. Finally, you will find out how to get maximum value from implementing a highly scalable data lake as a primary point of storage on your data platform.

This part has the following chapters:

- *Chapter 3, Ingesting Data into the Cloud*
- *Chapter 4, Transforming Data on Azure*
- *Chapter 5, Storing Data for Consumption*

# 3
# Ingesting Data into the Cloud

Ingesting data into the cloud is a key step in any data pipeline and can greatly impact the efficiency and scalability of your data processing and analysis. This is why it is critical for any cloud data architect to have a deep understanding of data ingestion techniques and architectures on Azure. In this chapter, we will dive into the world of data ingestion on Azure, focusing on the key concepts of batch ingestion and data streaming, as well as various ingestion architectures.

We will begin by discussing the differences between batch ingestion and data streaming, and when to use each method. We will also explore the benefits and limitations of each approach and provide examples of use cases for each method.

Next, we will explore data ingestion architectures on Azure. We will introduce **Azure Data Factory** and **Azure Synapse pipelines** for designing and implementing data pipelines on Azure. **Azure Data Lake Storage (ADLS)** is introduced for permanently storing a variety of data formats. We will also discuss how to use **Azure Event Hubs** and **Azure IoT Hub** for streaming data into the cloud in real time.

More specifically, this chapter will look at the following topics:

- Batch and streaming ingestion
- ADLS for raw data ingestion
- Batch ingestion architectures
- Streaming ingestion architectures

First, let's explore the concepts of batch and streaming ingestion.

# Batch and streaming ingestion

Regardless of the type (batch or streaming), data ingestion is located in the first layer of the data architecture, as seen in *Figure 3.1*:

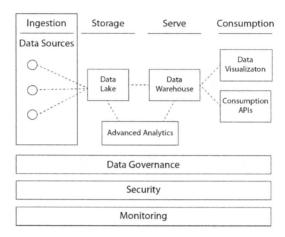

Figure 3.1 – Reference diagram for cloud data architectures: the ingestion layer (on the left) forms the first layer of the architecture

The ingestion layer forms the front door for the solution. Here, we pull in data using data pipelines and, in enterprise-level solutions, commonly have it land in a massive-scale, unstructured storage service such as a data lake.

The type of ingestion plays a key role in the design of a cloud data architecture. Batch ingestion was, and in most cases still is, the norm for ingesting data into the cloud. A batch approach refers to the periodical ingestion or processing of (usually large) bulks of data. Streaming ingestion, as the name suggests, involves continuous streams of data.

In general, batch ingestion and processing have long been the far more prevalent type of the two. However, as the technology in connectivity is advancing fast, with current developments in 5G, for example, streaming data is gaining popularity rapidly.

> **Note**
>
> Although often intertwined, mind the difference between ingestion and processing. Batch ingestion typically means that batch processing is used in a later stage of the data's journey throughout the different layers of the architecture. Adding a very low-latency processing service while ingestion happens periodically just does not make sense and is a waste of expensive resources.
>
> Streaming ingestion, on the other hand, is more flexible. Streaming ingestion will often result in stream processing for fast delivery to end users, or a combination of both streaming and batch-based methods is used. The reason for this will be addressed later. However, in rare cases, some data sources only allow for real-time ingestion as they cannot store data on their own. If there is no valid justification for real-time consumption in this case, batch processing can be used in combination with streaming ingestion.

The two approaches come with clear differences, but either of these can bring immense value to a solution if the use case plays into its strengths. So, when should batch ingestion or streaming ingestion be used? Or even a combination of both? Let's find out.

## Why batch ingestion?

The main reason architects opt for batch-based architectures is cost optimization. Batch ingestion is usually many times cheaper than streaming data. This is the main thing holding back the wider adoption of data streaming. Also, contrary to the constant ingestion of most streaming sources, batch processes can be scheduled during times of low activity, mostly at night, to ease the stress on the system. This helps to avoid overloading the solution during peak times.

Another case is when businesses prioritize data volume over speed. Although data streaming can also handle large data, batch processing is often used because, as mentioned previously, the costs of the solution would otherwise skyrocket. In the end, the choice for batch ingestion simply comes down to costs.

Batch ingestion and processing are preferred in solutions where there is no reason to view or consume the data in (near) real time. However, batches can be ingested in short intervals if action needs to be taken fairly quickly. Running batches every 15 to 30 minutes is still considerably cheaper than having a continuously active stream of data.

Here are some common use cases for batch ingestion:

- Pulling data from other internal databases or silos
- Pulling data from external (SaaS) applications

This results in solutions such as the following:

- Sales and marketing dashboards
- Billing
- Payroll systems

## Why streaming ingestion?

The key strength of streaming is in its latency, often referred to as (near) real time. Streaming allows end users to consume the ingested and processed data in a matter of (milli)seconds.

As previously discussed, this reduction in latency usually comes at a steep cost increase. This is something that most organizations new to these architectures often do not keep in mind. We strongly advise having a good reason for this far more expensive approach. Is the reduction in latency valuable enough to the business performance to justify the extra cost?

Streaming ingestion is always implemented in use cases with stream processing (meaning solutions that need very low latency for consumption) but can also be used with batch processing.

Here are some common use cases for streaming ingestion:

- Ingestion of **Internet of Things** (**IoT**) data such as sensors and wearables for smart home devices
- Logs and metrics from systems or components
- Video feeds, audio streams, and so on
- Stock market data
- Credit card transactions

This results in solutions such as the following:

- Monitoring and alerting for (critical) systems and components
- Stock trading algorithms
- Fraud detection
- Predictive maintenance

We will elaborate further on this in the *Streaming ingestion architectures* section of this chapter.

## When to use both batch and streaming ingestion?

If a streaming data source is included, most data platforms, where the primary goal is to centralize data from a wide range of sources in a central data warehouse, will commonly use a combination of both batch and streaming ingestion. This is decided on a source-by-source basis.

When some data sources are stream-ingested, and their data is processed in real time, this live stream of data is often enriched with batch-ingested metadata from other sources. In most of the preceding use cases on streaming ingestion, this is the case.

Let us look at the example of fraud detection. Transactional credit card data is ingested as a stream, due to rigorous latency requirements. A transaction needs to be canceled in a matter of seconds when fraud is suspected. Meanwhile, this stream of transaction data is enriched with more metadata on cardholders, which is fetched from the central data warehouse. This customer data was previously batch ingested from the customer database of the bank.

# ADLS for raw data ingestion

Before diving deeper into ingestion architectures, we need to introduce the fundamentals of data lakes, where the ingested data will land in the majority of cases.

A data lake can be seen as a mass storage with support for all kinds of data. It does not enforce specific file types or data types, which makes it a remarkably good landing zone for ingestion. The more rules that are enforced—as is the case in structured databases, for example—the likelier it becomes that data ingestion pipelines will break if the file type or schema changes.

On the Azure cloud, a data lake is a specific version of the **Azure Storage account**. Therefore, we will first introduce this service and its features.

## Azure storage accounts

Azure storage accounts can be used to store all kinds of data objects. They provide four distinct types of storage, as follows:

- **Binary Large Object (Blob)** storage
- File storage
- Queue storage
- Table storage

### Blob storage

In data platforms, blob storage is by far the most used feature out of all four. Luckily, thanks to the pay-as-you-go model for Azure services, the other storage types do not incur extra costs if we do not use them.

Blob storage comes with one extra level of management in the hierarchy, namely containers. Containers can be seen as a directory for blobs. There are no limits on the number of containers in a storage account or the number of blobs in a container, as this is designed for massive-scale storage. You see an illustration of this in *Figure 3.2*:

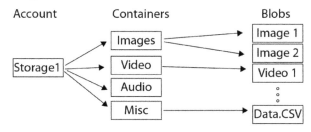

Figure 3.2 – A storage account consists of one or multiple containers,
which in turn can hold multiple blobs

Inside blob containers, it is by default not possible to create folders. However, it is possible to have a virtual folder structure by imitating folder paths using prefixes in filenames.

The blobs themselves are divided into three distinct categories, as follows:

- **Block blobs:** In data projects, block blobs are the most common and versatile. They can hold any text or binary data, which is split into one or more blobs according to the size of the object.

- **Append blobs:** Append blobs are specialized block blobs with enhanced append operations, which can be very useful when writing incoming data streams to blob storage.

- **Page blobs:** Finally, page blobs are used for storing virtual hard drive files, which allow them to serve as disks for **virtual machines (VMs)** on Azure.

### File, queue, and table storage

Next to blob storage, Azure storage accounts provide features for file, queue, and table storage. However, these often fall outside of the scope of most data platform projects, so they will not be discussed in much depth.

Azure Files follows the principles of a file share (that is, storing a file on one computer and sharing it with users and applications running on other computers), but it does so on a cloud-based network. This allows sharing files to scale well as the number of users and their locations increase. Up to 2,000 concurrent connections are allowed per shared file. A file can have a maximum size of 1 TB, and Azure Files can store up to 100 TB with a single storage account.

Azure Queue Storage allows you to store a large number of messages. This message queue can be used in an asynchronous way to communicate between application components via HTTP or HTTPS. A message can have a maximum size of 64 KB, and the number of messages in the queue is only limited by the total capacity limit of the storage account.

Azure Table storage uses a NoSQL approach to store data and uses tables with key-value pairs. These are not tables like in a relational database, however. There is no concept of relations or foreign keys. Each row has a unique identifier called a key, and the value consists of a number of columns that can vary in length. Therefore, the data these tables hold is considered to be semi-structured data.

## ADLS

Data lakes on Azure are provisioned as a specialized variant of the default BLOB storage. The **ADLS Gen2** service is essentially a BLOB storage, giving you the cheapest storage in Azure, combined with a hierarchical namespace from ADLS Gen1. The hierarchical namespace allows for the implementation of a hierarchical folder structure. Compared to BLOB storage, data lakes are vastly more capable of handling big data analytics.

## Redundancy

Most storage services, storage accounts being one of them, can be configured for various levels of redundancy. Ranked according to increasing level, these include the following:

- **Locally redundant storage (LRS)**
- **Zone-redundant storage (ZRS)**
- **Geo-redundant storage (GRS)**
  - **Read-access geo-redundant storage (RA-GRS)**
- **Geo-zone-redundant storage (GZRS)**
  - **Read-access geo-zone-redundant storage (RA-GZRS)**

Any data in Azure storage accounts or databases will be stored as at least three copies. The first two options, LRS and ZRS, store all copies in a single, primary region. LRS will keep the three replicas in the same data center in a single region. ZRS will store a copy in three distinct Azure availability zones, still in the same region.

Availability zones are groupings of multiple data centers, each having an independent power supply, cooling, and networking. This minimizes the risk of a single disaster affecting multiple data centers in the same availability zone. Regions are larger and tend to cover (sub)continents, such as East US or West Europe.

GRS and GZRS make use of multiple, paired regions. GRS will provide LRS in a primary and secondary region, whereas GZRS provides ZRS in both paired regions.

When working with redundancy over multiple regions, we also have the option to configure the secondary region to be read-only to save some costs. This can be useful for specific use cases. A commonly used example of this is the product data of a global web shop. When users browse product information on a website outside of the primary region, they will encounter high latency, which can then be easily solved by adding read-only redundancy to the (secondary) region of interest.

The trade-off regarding redundancy is fairly simple: the higher the level of redundancy, the more expensive the storage becomes. It is one of the responsibilities of the data architect to determine the most cost-effective redundancy for the right use cases.

## Access tiers

Another way of optimizing costs for data lake storage is by leveraging the most efficient access tier for every data asset. Azure storage features three distinct access tiers, as follows:

- **Hot tier**
- **Cold tier**
- **Archive tier**

> **Note**
> When used correctly, the Archive tier will be the cheapest, with the Hot tier being the most expensive. However, there is some elaboration required.

Hot-tier storage is ideal for data assets that are frequently accessed, by either read or write operations. The hot tier comes with the highest storage costs and the lowest access costs, along with very low latency.

Cold-tier storage is often used for infrequently accessed data. Contrary to popular belief, data stored in the cold tier can still be accessed with the same, very low latency as hot-tier storage. The difference lies in the distribution of costs. Storage is less expensive, and access is more expensive compared to the hot tier. Therefore, poorly configured cold tiers can turn out to be more expensive than hot tiers, given that the cold tier contains frequently used data.

Archive-tier storage is designed for long-term storage. This tier features the lowest storage costs and the highest access costs. Contrary to the low-latency access tiers, retrieval of data stored in the archive tier can take hours. *Figure 3.3* shows a representation of the different access tiers:

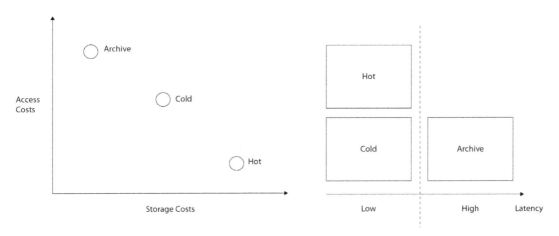

Figure 3.3 – The choice of storage tier is a trade-off between storage costs and access costs; only the archive tier has a higher latency for data retrieval

**Example of access tiers**

Hot-tier storage is typically used for daily or weekly retrieved data, often originating from operational systems. Think of the current year's sales data, payroll data, and so forth. This data will be accessed frequently for analytics or quarterly reporting. On the other hand, sales data from 2 years ago will be analyzed more infrequently. Therefore, we can configure this to be stored in the cold tier.

Lastly, we will make use of the archive tier to store all data that is hardly ever accessed or does not come with low-retrieval latency requirements. This can be old data that must be kept for extended periods of time for compliance reasons, or secondary backups of critical components.

## Why data lakes?

Traditional and small-scale business data platforms often feature a structured data warehouse for reporting, to put it briefly. Data is often ingested directly into the data warehouse, with data being processed to a further stage of business readiness inside the warehouse. Why would this be a bad idea?

In the last few years, the adoption of data lakes has skyrocketed. Apart from being a convenient storage method for unstructured data (video, audio, images, and so on), they are also used for structured business data. For the latter, the data lake serves as the front door of the data warehouse, as it is implemented as an extra layer between the data sources and the data warehouse.

Take a look at *Figure 3.4*:

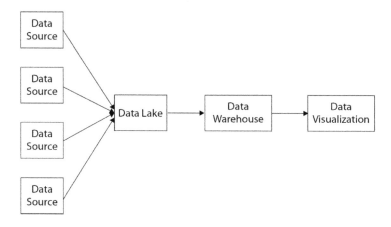

Figure 3.4 – The data lake typically forms the first centralized point of storage, from where data moves downstream to data warehousing and reporting tools

The preceding diagram is a simplified version of the most common yet scalable and reliable data platforms. We strongly recommend following the best practice of implementing a data lake layer in the architecture for the following reasons:

- To optimize reliability and **high availability (HA)** of core components
- To optimize cost efficiency
- As a storage location for unstructured and semi-structured data
- For the storage of big data

First, data lakes are suited to any type of data, having little to no enforcement on file formats or data types. In contrast, data warehouses enforce strict data schemas to guarantee high data quality when performing analytics. However, this enforcement can be detrimental to the reliability of ingestion pipelines. If the data schema in one of the data sources changes, the ingestion pipelines will break. Depending on the data source, this could mean that data is permanently lost.

Using a data lake as an ingestion landing zone solves this problem. Without enforcement, data pipelines have a much higher chance of success, minimizing the amount of potentially lost data.

Secondly, data processing was traditionally often performed in the data warehouse, reading data from one place, transforming it, and writing it back to a different place in the warehouse. This meant there were multiple versions of the same data, with different levels of processing. However, it is only our fully processed data that is usually used for analytics and reporting (data science is an exception to this).

Data lakes are a cheap method of storing massive amounts of data, compared to a data warehouse. Therefore, it would be smart to move the raw and not fully processed data to a data lake to save storage costs. This is where the concept of data lake tiers comes from.

Traditional data warehouses are often built in SQL databases as they only cover structured data. However, SQL databases are relatively limited in size. An Azure SQL managed instance can go up to 16 TB while an Azure SQL Database instance can go up to 100 TB with hyperscaling. This causes problems as data volumes are ever-increasing and data is not always structured. Besides supporting unstructured and semi-structured data, ADLS can store petabyte-scale data with no problem, making it an ideal storage service for big data.

## Data lake tiers

Data lakes are often implemented with a three-tier system. The number of tiers is not enforced and can be altered, but this is the most common implementation. It's important to note that data lake tiers are not a built-in feature, but rather a concept. They could refer to the following:

- Different top-level directories in a data lake container
- Different containers within a single data lake
- Different data lakes all together

The main factors for choosing between these methods are the capacity limits of the service and access control. As the vast majority of corporations around the world will have trouble coming anywhere near the capacity limits of a data lake, we would advise sticking to either directories or containers to be used for the tiering system.

There is no single correct naming convention for these tiers, but commonly used naming conventions are provided here:

- Raw – enriched - curated
- Bronze - silver - gold

The latter originates from the medallion structure, introduced by Databricks. We will use this pattern for the following examples, as it clearly shows the order of the layers.

The bronze layer is meant to store raw data. When leveraging the data lake as a first location to centralize data, the bronze layer is meant to be an exact copy of the data sources. This means absolutely no transformation is happening when ingesting the data, so the ingestion pipeline is simply copying data from the source and placing it into the bronze layer. In this way, we can maximize the reliability of our ingestion pipelines, again to minimize the risk of permanent data loss. If ETL pipelines in later processes fail due to for example schema changes, we can always retroactively process the data in the bronze layer, after repairing the pipeline.

In later stages, ETL pipelines will read data from the bronze layer, perform transformations, and write them to the silver layer. The silver layer can be seen as a location for semi-processed data.

This process will then happen again to have data land in the final gold layer. The goal of the gold layer is to have the data ready to be ingested into the data warehouse. This means (at least a primitive version of) a data model must be in place and data types must be correctly set. For the latter reason, it is recommended to make use of data type-enforcing file types in the gold layer, Parquet files being a common example.

*Figure 3.5* illustrates the process:

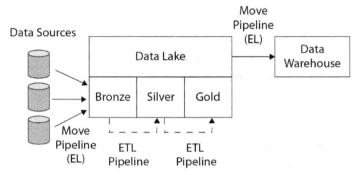

Figure 3.5 – For ETL pipelines, we want to minimize the number of transformations in the first and last pipeline in this diagram; for optimal reliability, most transformations should happen in between data lake tiers

With data lakes covered, we can now take a closer look at batch and streaming ingestion architectures.

## Batch ingestion architectures

The simplest form of ingestion architecture is a use case where data is only ingested in batches from other cloud-based sources (no sources residing on-premises). In this case, we will use data pipelines to periodically fetch large amounts of data and write them to the bronze layer in the data lake. Note that we restrain from performing any kind of transformation in this initial pipeline.

We will look at ingesting data from the following sources:

- Cloud sources
- On-premises sources

Let's first look at how to ingest data from cloud-based sources.

# Ingesting data from cloud sources

When ingesting data from other cloud sources, the connection is often more convenient, Also, we can make use of Azure-hosted **integration runtimes** (**IRs**). This will serve as the compute for the pipeline orchestration in either Azure Data Factory or Azure Synapse pipelines. Other Data Factory components will be more elaborately discussed in the next chapter.

Now, we will look at a typical batch ingestion pipeline design for both **Azure Data Factory** and **Azure Synapse** pipelines (as part of **Azure Synapse Analytics**).

## *Cloud batch ingestion with Azure Data Factory pipelines*

Azure Data Factory is an ideal service to leverage in this scenario. It is meant to orchestrate data movements and/or transformations. After registering our data sources and destination (that is, the data lake instance) as linked services, we can set up an ingestion pipeline, as illustrated in *Figure 3.6*:

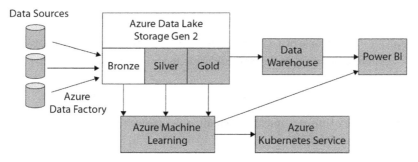

Figure 3.6 – Azure Data Factory is a great tool for ETL pipelines; in this chapter,
we focus on the first pipeline: the data ingestion pipeline

In their simplest form, ingestion pipelines can consist of a single activity—a **Copy** activity. An activity here refers to a single step in the pipeline, represented by a single block in the drag-and-drop GUI. However, some common use cases can make use of slight modifications to the pipeline to increase efficiency, reliability, and security.

## Ingestion from an SQL source

When a data ingestion pipeline fetches data from an SQL database, we can make use of linked services for connecting to the data source. First, we can create a linked service pointing to the SQL database using the credentials. The linked service is used to securely store this connection information. This means we will not have to fetch secrets from an Azure Key Vault in this case, which might differ when accessing external (non-Azure) APIs.

Then, we can start designing the ingestion pipeline. If we want to read multiple tables in the database, a *Lookup* activity can be used to fetch all table names. We can then iterate over the output of this activity to perform Copy activities in a `ForEach` loop.

The pipeline will then look similar to the one shown in *Figure 3.7*:

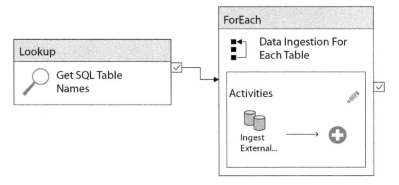

Figure 3.7 – An example of a data ingestion pipeline that loops through all table
names and copies the data for every table into the bronze tier of the data lake

In short, the ingestion pipeline will typically consist of the following activities:

- The Lookup activity (for example, to fetch all table names to loop the Copy activity, if the source is an SQL database)

- A `ForEach` loop (to iterate over the table names found in the Lookup activity)

- The Copy activity inside the `ForEach` loop (to move the data from the source to the data lake)

### Ingestion from external APIs

When ingesting data from external APIs, such as SaaS applications, we adjust the ingestion pipeline in different ways. First, we need to provide a specific endpoint. This can be done by creating an *HTTP-linked service* for the endpoint.

Usually, APIs will need some form of credentials in order to access them. This is often in the form of bearer tokens or keys. We would strongly recommend storing this token securely in an Azure key vault. Any secret can be fetched from a linked Azure key vault using a *Web* activity.

The process is shown in *Figure 3.8*:

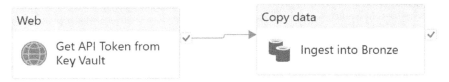

Figure 3.8 – A simple ingestion pipeline that fetches a secret (API token)
from the Azure key vault and retrieves data from an external API

When we have the credentials and endpoint, we can use a Copy activity, in combination with the output of the two Web activities, to perform the actual GET request. The result will look similar to *Figure 3.8*.

> **Pagination**
>
> Some APIs, especially SaaS applications with large databases, make use of pagination to ease the load on their systems by limiting the number of results per request. Much like scrolling through images, pagination allows us to "scroll" through results. In Azure Data Factory or Synapse pipelines, this functionality is built into the **Copy** activity and will require no additional custom coding.

**Incremental ingestion**

If we would like to perform incremental loads and the source accepts datetime parameters for selecting data, we can add the following to existing pipelines:

1.  Define an SQL table for storing the successful run datetimes.

2.  After the Copy activity, write the trigger time of the pipeline along with information on the data source to this table. This can be done using a *Stored Procedure* activity. This activity should run if the Copy activity succeeds.

3.  Add an extra Lookup activity at the start that fetches the latest successful pipeline trigger time from the table and uses this as a parameter when fetching data with the Copy activity.

We can add this approach to any existing pipeline.

*Figure 3.9* shows an example where we added the incremental approach to the previous ingestion pipeline for external APIs:

Figure 3.9 – An example of an incremental loading pipeline, by adding a Lookup
and Stored Procedure activities to the simple ingestion pipeline

## Cloud batch ingestion with Azure Synapse pipelines

We can architect a solution for the previous use case in a very similar way using Synapse pipelines. Synapse pipelines, as part of the Synapse Analytics suite, are similar to Azure Data Factory pipelines in many aspects. The GUI and the underlying code base are mostly the same.

*Figure 3.10* illustrates Synapse pipelines:

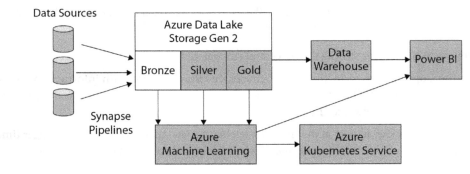

Figure 3.10 – Synapse pipelines are very similar to Azure Data Factory pipelines,
and form a great alternative when using the Synapse suite

However, as the name suggests, Synapse pipelines integrate a lot better with the rest of the Synapse workspace. Whether to use Data Factory pipelines or Synapse pipelines is part of a higher-level discussion—namely, when deciding to build a data platform using Azure Synapse Analytics or using separate services such as Azure Data Factory, Azure SQL Database, and so on. We will come back to this later in the chapter on data warehousing. For now, we just remember that we have two services for ETL pipelines, which are very similar in this early stage of the architecture.

# Ingesting data from on-premises sources

There are numerous methods of ingesting or migrating data from on-premises sources. The most important ways of doing this are set out here:

- Using pipelines
- Using **AzCopy**
- Using Azure Data Box

Let's find out when to use which method.

## Batch ingestion from on-premises sources with pipelines

On-premises sources are data sources that reside in our own environment. The data is stored on local computers or on the servers of the company itself. Common use cases for batch ingestion from on-premises sources are presented here:

- Ingestion of Excel, `.csv`, and `.txt` files in a file share
- Ingestion of a SQL database's tables from an on-premises SQL server

On-premises sources are different in nature from cloud services. While cloud services can communicate with each other, access to a company's laptops or server is often not allowed. For this reason, Data Factory and Synapse use **self-hosted IRs (SHIRs)**.

IRs are compute infrastructures that allow you to run Copy activities to ingest data. There are three types of IRs—namely, Azure IRs, SHIRs, and **Azure-SQL Server Integration Services (Azure-SSIS)** IRs. These will be further discussed in the next chapter. For now, it's enough to know the IRs described in the previous paragraphs are Azure IRs. Among other things, they run Copy activities between cloud data stores and are hosted by Azure.

SHIRs run Copy activities between a cloud data store and a data store in a private network. These can be computers or servers inside an on-premises network or a VM inside a cloud-based **virtual network** (**VNet**) (such as an Azure VNet or an Amazon **virtual private cloud** (**VPC**)). A SHIR means the compute infrastructure is hosted by the computer or the server of the company. After downloading, the SHIR acts as a gateway and will be able to communicate with Azure and ingest data. In fact, the SHIR used to be called the "data management gateway".

One SHIR can be used for multiple on-premises data sources, but you can only install one instance of a SHIR on any single machine. *But what if you need to ingest data from this machine across multiple data factories?*, you may ask. For this reason, Azure Data Factory allows you to share IRs between Data Factory instances. Using only one IR also means a reduction in cost and fewer management concerns. Note that IR sharing is not yet possible with Synapse pipelines.

To ingest data from an on-premises SQL server, create a SQL server-linked service as normal, but connect via the SHIR. To connect to on-premises files in a folder, use the **File system** linked service, as illustrated in *Figure 3.11*:

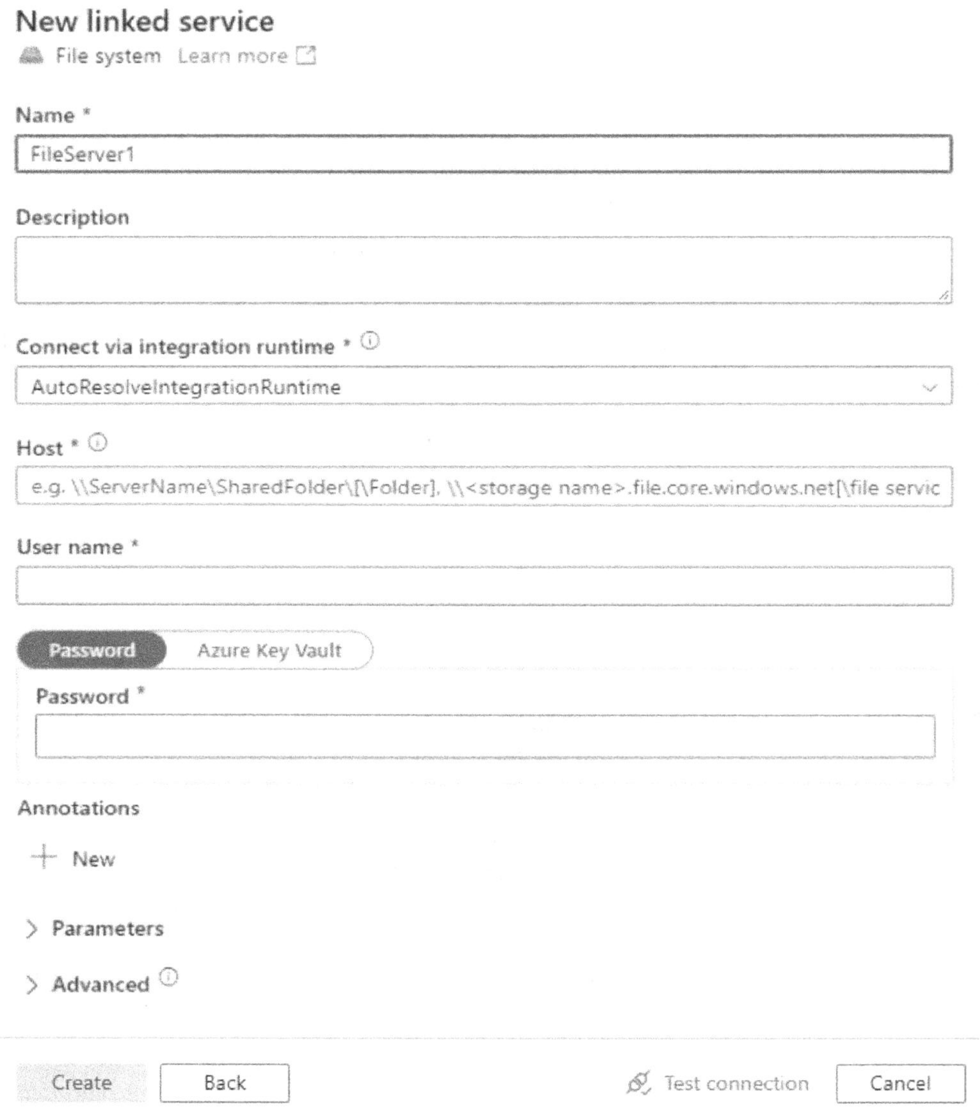

# New linked service
File system    Learn more

Name *

FileServer1

Description

Connect via integration runtime *  ⓘ

AutoResolveIntegrationRuntime

Host *  ⓘ

e.g. \\ServerName\SharedFolder\[\Folder], \\<storage name>.file.core.windows.net[\file servic

User name *

Password    Azure Key Vault

Password *

Annotations

+ New

> Parameters

> Advanced  ⓘ

Create    Back                    ✏ Test connection    Cancel

Figure 3.11 – A screenshot of the linked service registration screen

Pipelines are a great way of easily ingesting data from on-premises, but code-first options such as AzCopy are viable as well.

### Batch ingestion from on-premises sources with AzCopy

Alternatively, AzCopy can be used to ingest data from on-premises sources. AzCopy is installed on-premises as a command-line tool. The commands are designed for optimal performance and allow data to be copied to an Azure storage account. AzCopy is often used as a one-off load of a noticeably big data source or an initial test of data ingestion. Although it is possible to create a scheduled task or cron job that runs an AzCopy command script, it lacks the monitoring (as well as management of linked services) from Data Factory or Synapse pipelines. You will not be able to see the status of pipelines in Azure or why the scheduled job failed as this is all run with a script on-premises. For mature scheduled data ingestion, use Data Factory or Synapse pipelines.

### Batch ingestion from on-premises sources with Azure Data Box

Azure Data Box is a physical storage box that companies can bring to their own server or data center to upload data to, and then ship it to an Azure data center to be ingested in Azure. Although it seems very cumbersome to transfer data this way, Azure Data Box is great in very specific cases, such as the following:

- Sometimes, data will just be too big to send over the network, making previous data ingestion techniques expensive

- In locations where signal strength and upload speed are poor

- When certain security requirements need to be met or to prevent listeners or interceptions on transferred data

Data Box can be used in combination with other ingestion techniques where the initial bulk transfer would be provided by Data Box and incremental loads are done through Data Factory or Synapse pipelines.

The offline data transfer box comes in three formats, as follows:

- **Data Box** with a capacity of 100 TB

- **Data Box Disk** for projects that require a smaller form factor with a capacity of 8 TB or 40 TB per pack of 5

- **Data Box Heavy**, targeted to large-scale projects with a capacity of 1 PB and a weight of over 500 lbs

In general, batch ingestion is immensely popular due to its cost efficiency. Depending on the technical requirements, however, it might be too slow. Let's now take a look at how we can minimize latency by using streaming ingestion.

## Streaming ingestion architectures

While batch ingestion architectures are designed to receive a collection of data at once, streaming ingestion architectures receive data in real time, as soon as a new event occurs in the streaming data sources. Examples of streaming data sources are given here:

- IoT sensors in a manufacturing process
- Server and security logs
- Click-stream data from apps and websites
- Stock values
- Live sport updates
- Real-time traffic updates

Having a real-time data source does not necessarily mean you need a streaming ingestion architecture to ingest the data. Data can also be buffered at the source and ingested in batches. This could be more cost-effective as streaming ingestion architectures tend to be more expensive. Streaming ingestion architectures are recommended when the volume and velocity of data are too big to handle at the source or in use cases where decisions need to be made in real time. Examples of such use cases are given here:

- Machine failures
- Security risks or downtime
- Real-time advertisement on website clicks
- Selling and buying stocks
- Real-time betting systems
- Traffic navigation

Streaming ingestion architectures have key differences from batch ingestion architectures. Reliable delivery needs to be implemented as messages are sent individually and can get lost. Mechanisms also need to be in place to ensure subscribers receive events at least once or exactly once. Messages are received at different times, so the order must be guaranteed, and messages need to be queued to ensure solutions can read the messages at their own pace.

Often, a buffer, also called a message queue, is implemented to retain messages so that solutions can read them at their own pace. The retainment policy determines how long messages are buffered for as streaming ingestion services are not considered to be storage services. If you want to permanently store messages for doing historical playbacks or complex transformations, sink them to a separate storage service such as ADLS. This is referred to as a cold path, which is implemented alongside a hot path for real-time purposes.

## Lambda architecture

A lambda (λ) architecture, as its Greek notation suggests, creates two separate paths for the hot and cold paths. When working with large data volumes, transforming the real-time data can take up a lot of time. For this reason, the cold path stores the raw messages in a data lake and performs batch processing on the data. The cold path is sometimes also referred to as the batch layer. The hot path, also called the speed layer, transforms data in real time, at the expense of accuracy. Both paths come together in reports or applications in the serving layer, showing real-time data as well as historical data.

Stored messages in the batch layer are immutable. This means messages are appended to the existing data and no existing data is ever changed. Assume, for instance, that the messages contain status updates of the same object, then all status updates are stored as separate records rather than overwriting the object record. This allows for the replay of messages but increases the volume of data being stored.

*Figure 3.12* shows a visual overview of a lambda architecture:

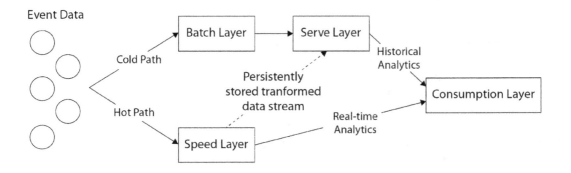

Figure 3.12 – An example of a lambda architecture

## Kappa architecture

The downside of creating two separate paths is that the architecture becomes complex and redundant. The two paths use different frameworks and resources, and both must be maintained. Additionally, the processing appears in both paths and may lead to duplicate transformation logic.

A kappa (κ) architecture tries to achieve the same goals as a lambda architecture but combines all data flows into a single path. There is no need for a batch layer as all processing is done in the speed layer alone. To allow complex transformations on historical data as well as historical playback, all data needs to be kept in the message queue. When historical data is requested, the message queue replays the events from a given time window.

*Figure 3.13* shows a visual overview of a kappa architecture:

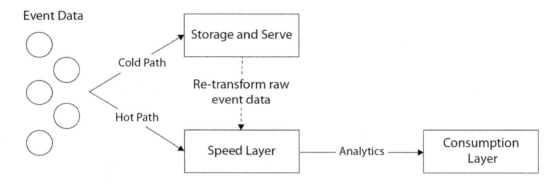

Figure 3.13 – An example of a kappa architecture

## Delta lake architecture

The downside of a kappa architecture is that it does not use a data lake for batch processing at rest but rather misinterprets the message queue as permanent storage. Moreover, messages in the kappa architecture are still immutable, just as with the lambda architecture. A delta (Δ) lake architecture uses a data lake for permanent storage and, as the name suggests, processes incoming data as delta records rather than append-only records. This means that existing data stored in the data lake can be changed with new incoming events. It also brings data warehouse-like capabilities to the data lake (such as **atomicity, consistency, isolation, and durability** (ACID) transactions, data modeling languages, and indexing technologies for datasets). Delta lake architectures unify all data flows in a single path, just as with kappa architectures, but with more performant storage and (using Databricks) more performant processing.

*Figure 3.14* provides us with a visual representation of the structure of a delta lake:

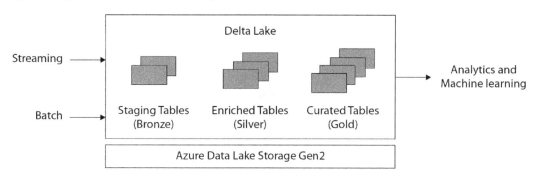

Figure 3.14 – An overview of the architecture of a delta lake

## Streaming ingestion with Event Hubs

Event Hubs is an example of a streaming ingestion service in Azure. It is designed for big data event streaming, scalable up to terabytes of data and millions of events per second. Event Hubs is designed with reliability in mind, preventing data loss and being agnostic to failures. Moreover, it supports multiple protocols to receive events from event producers such as HTTPS, **Advanced Message Queuing Protocol 1.0 (AMQP 1.0)**, and Apache Kafka (1.0 and above). Normally, you would need to spin up a Kafka cluster to be able to read messages produced by an Apache Kafka application.

As Event Hubs supports the Kafka protocol, there is no need for this. Event Hubs contains the following key components:

- **Partitions**: A partition is a specific subset of the message stream. An event hub consists of 1 to 32 partitions, and you cannot change the number of partitions after creation. Messages sent to Event Hubs will be load balanced across those partitions. Equal utilization of partitions cannot be guaranteed, so expect partitions to grow at different rates. Each partition is ordered, but the order cannot be guaranteed across partitions. If you want to make sure to read all messages in the right order, send them to a single partition using a partition key.

- **Consumer groups**: A consumer group is able to listen to a certain subset of the event stream. Using this functionality, different receivers, such as applications or processes, can get a distinct view of incoming events.

- **Capacity units**: Depending on the tier, these can be called either throughput units, processing units, or capacity units. Regardless of the name, we have an abstract measurement to simplify the capacity configuration.

- **Event receivers**: An application, platform, process, or anything similar that receives events from the event hub.

*Figure 3.15* shows the Event Hubs stream processing architecture:

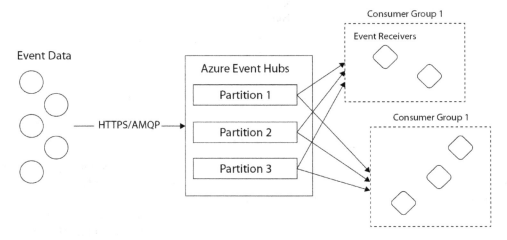

Figure 3.15 – Data is ingested and partitioned in Azure Event Hubs. Consumer groups
(of event receivers) each have their own view of the Azure Event Hub

When you create an event hub in the Azure portal, you're first asked to create a namespace. A namespace or service bus is a logical container for multiple topics called event hubs. Each event hub contains a unique stream of data but shares the same location, pricing tier, and throughput capacity, as these are properties set at the namespace level. You can set the throughput units of a namespace to auto-inflate, which enables you to scale up the throughput units automatically to meet usage needs and scale down when idle, reducing costs.

After creating a namespace, event hubs can be created. When adding an event hub, the Azure portal asks to specify the partition count (remember—this cannot be changed after creation), the message retention, and whether to enable **Capture**.

Messages can be retained or buffered in Event Hubs for a period as short as 1 day (24 hours) up to a maximum of 7 days. The retention period can be extended up to 90 days for Event Hubs **Premium** and **Dedicated**. Changing the retention period applies to all events, including ones that are already in Event Hubs. Once the retention period has passed, messages are deleted from Event Hubs and can't be restored.

If, for any reason, the retention period is not long enough, consider persistently storing these events in ADLS or Azure Blob Storage. This is done fairly simply by leveraging the built-in **Capture** feature inside Event Hubs. From the storage account, these events can be further analyzed using conventional analytical processes. Allowed formats for the content of events include TXT, JSON, XML, and more, but the size of an event sent to Event Hubs must be limited to 1 MB. Events can be sent to or read from Event Hubs using the following languages:

- .NET Core
- Java
- Spring
- Python
- JavaScript
- Apache Kafka
- Apache Storm (receive events only)
- Go

## Streaming ingestion with IoT Hub

IoT Hub is another streaming ingestion service for big data, but more tailored to IoT devices. This service is recommended in use cases where sensor data needs to be pushed to the cloud, such as the following:

- Industry 4.0, which brings analytics, ML, AI, and autonomous systems to manufacturing processes
- Wind turbines adjusting their position to the direction of the wind
- Digital twins, creating a 1:1 virtual representation of a physical object for digital simulations

## Remote asset monitoring

IoT Hub differs from Event Hubs in the sense that it can deliver bi-directional communication, so messages can also be sent from the cloud to IoT devices. Moreover, it stores state information and metadata per IoT device. This is useful when you want to know from which device an event was sent and map it against additional information about the IoT device. Security credentials are used per device for secure communications, and access controls are implemented, as sensors hold sensitive data.

Apart from HTTPS, AMQP, and Kafka protocols, IoT Hub also allows the MQTT protocol to send messages to the cloud. **MQTT** stands for **Message Queuing Telemetry Transport** and is ideal for the transmission of sensor data from remote or inaccessible sources.

An important thing to note is that daily quotas and pricing are calculated per 4 KB (apart from the **free** tier, which is calculated per 0.5 KB). A message sent to IoT Hub that is between 0 KB and 4 KB in size counts as a 4 KB payload. To reduce costs when sending a large volume of small messages, it is recommended to combine messages into one until the size reaches 4 KB before sending. This, however, also delays sending messages, which might not be ideal for all real-time solutions. The maximum size of one message is 256 KB.

## Summary

In this chapter, we provided a comprehensive overview of the various methods and tools available for getting data into the cloud. The chapter started by discussing the differences between batch ingestion and streaming ingestion and when to use each method. It explained the benefits and limitations of each approach and provided examples of use cases for each method.

One of the key tools introduced in this chapter is ADLS. This is a powerful storage solution for big data and allows for efficient and flexible storage of large datasets in the cloud. The chapter explained how ADLS can store data in a variety of formats, including structured and unstructured data. We also discussed access tiers, redundancy, and data lake tiers.

We delved into architectures for both batch ingestion from cloud sources and on-premises sources. Next, we explained streaming architectures, such as lambda and kappa architectures, which are becoming increasingly popular for real-time data ingestion in the cloud. The chapter explained the differences between these architectures, along with their respective advantages and drawbacks. It also introduced delta lakes, a technology that allows for efficient storage and management of streaming data in the cloud.

Finally, the chapter covered the use of Azure Event Hubs and Azure IoT Hub for streaming data into the cloud in real time. These tools can ingest data from a variety of sources, including devices, sensors, and social media platforms. We also explored the best practices for designing real-time data ingestion solutions using these tools.

Overall, the chapter provided a comprehensive understanding of the various methods for ingesting data into the cloud and the tools and technologies that can be used to implement these methods.

# 4

# Transforming Data on Azure

Azure offers a wide range of services for data processing. One of the key features of Azure is its ability to easily transform data from various sources into a format that is suitable for further analysis and reporting.

In this chapter, we will discuss the following:

- Designing data pipelines on Azure
- Transforming data on Azure
- Data transformation architectures
- Data transformations in data lake tiers
- Operationalizing data pipelines on Azure

This chapter will introduce the various tools and services available on Azure for data transformation, including **Azure Data Factory**, (**ADF**) Azure Stream Analytics, and Azure Databricks. We will explore the core features and capabilities of each service, and show in which scenarios they work best. In line with the previous chapter, the focus will be put on both batch processing and real-time processing.

Next, we will look at some example architectures and provide a quick guide on how to select the ideal tool for data transformations in any architecture.

Additionally, we will discuss considerations for operationalizing data transformation solutions on Azure, such as scheduling, monitoring, and CI/CD.

By the end of this chapter, you will have a comprehensive understanding of how to leverage the core transformation tools and services that Azure has to offer, to design efficient and effective data pipelines for your Azure data solution.

# Designing data pipelines on Azure

In the previous chapter, we discussed how ADF and Azure Synapse Analytics fit into a data architecture by providing data pipelines for batch ingestion.

Here, we will look at how Azure Data Factory and Azure Synapse Analytics are used for transformation pipelines. These pipelines will read data from one data lake tier, process it in some way, and write the resulting dataset to the next data lake tier.

> **Types of pipelines on Azure**
>
> Across all Azure services, we can find many different pipelines. However, we can classify these pipelines into three categories; data pipelines (also referred to as ETL or ELT pipelines), machine learning pipelines (also referred to as MLOps pipelines), and release pipelines (also referred to as CI/CD pipelines).
>
> Data pipelines are used for data movements and data transformations, machine learning pipelines are used to (re)train and (re)deploy machine learning models, and release pipelines are used to push code through environments.

The data pipelines are used for the orchestration of processes such as the following:

- Data movements
- Data transformations
- Machine learning jobs

In the previous chapter, we explored how these pipelines are used to ingest data into the cloud, basically moving it from the source to the raw or bronze tier of the data lake while making as few transformations as possible.

In this chapter, we will delve deeper into data transformations. Inherently, this also encompasses data movements, with the difference here being that we perform some transformations after reading the data in one place and writing it to another. This is where the concept of **Extract, Transform, and Load** (**ETL**) originates from. The amount of data transformations happening in pipelines can vary, as seen in *Figure 4.1*.

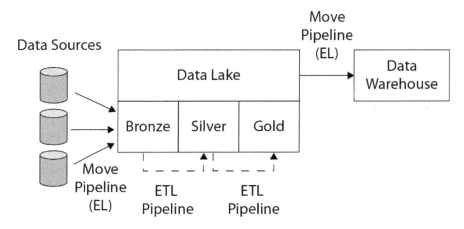

Figure 4.1 – The amount of data transformations in pipelines varies,
with the bulk of it happening between data lake tiers

For clarity, we will distinguish between *ingestion pipelines* and *ETL pipelines*, both being types of data pipelines. In the source-to-data-lake pipeline and data-lake-to-warehouse pipeline, we aim to minimize the amount of data transformations taking place, maximize ingestion reliability, and facilitate data warehousing (off-)loading, respectively. The bulk of data transformations usually happens in pipelines that move data between data lake tiers.

## ETL versus ELT

ETL and **Extract, Load, and Transform (ELT)** are both data integration processes used to move data from one place to another, but they differ in the order in which they perform the three main steps of the process:

- In ETL, data is extracted from one or more sources, transformed to fit the target system's needs, and then loaded into the target system. This process is typically used when the target system is not capable of performing the required transformations, or when the data needs to be cleansed or consolidated before it is loaded.

- On the other hand, in ELT, data is first extracted and loaded into the target system, and then transformed. This process is typically used when the target system has the capability to perform the required transformations, such as a modern data warehouse or a cloud-based data lake.

One of the main advantages of ETL is that it allows for a high degree of data quality control and error checking, as the data is cleansed and consolidated before it is loaded into the target system. This can be important in situations where data integrity is critical, such as in financial or healthcare applications.

On the other hand, ELT has several advantages over ETL. Since the data is loaded into the target system before it is transformed, ELT can take advantage of the processing power of the target system to perform transformations more quickly and efficiently. This can be especially useful in big data environments where the volume and velocity of data can make traditional ETL processes impractical.

## Azure Data Factory versus Synapse pipelines

We can easily simplify the orchestration of data movements and transformations by using the right Azure services. **ADF** and Azure Synapse Analytics (formerly SQL Data Warehouse) are both cloud-based data integration services from Microsoft, running on the same engine and with a similar graphical user interface. Both provide a way to create and manage data pipelines, but they have small differences in use cases and capabilities.

ADF is a fully managed ETL service that allows you to create data pipelines to move and transform data from various sources to various destinations. It can be used to move data between cloud services, such as Azure Storage and Azure SQL Database, as well as between on-premises and cloud environments. It also provides built-in data connectors and a visual authoring interface for creating and managing pipelines.

Synapse runs on the same engine and interface as ADF, but it is integrated into a bigger OLAP solution. This solution provides a one-stop shop for answering analytical questions such as what happened (descriptive), why (diagnostic) with (data warehousing capabilities),hat will happen (predictive), and how to act upon it (prescriptive) with Spark notebooks for AI and ML. Synapse is thus ideal for greenfield projects.

Although being very similar in capabilities, there are some small differences between ADF and Synapse to be aware of when choosing the right transformation tool. ADF cannot monitor Spark jobs for data flows, whereas this is implemented for Synapse pipelines. Synapse cannot share integration runtimes across Synapse instances or have cross-region integration runtimes in data flows and has no support for Power Query activities or global parameters, whereas this is possible in ADF.

### Datasets in ADF and Azure Synapse Analytics

A dataset represents a collection of data that you can use as an input or output for a pipeline. It defines the structure and schema of the data, as well as the location and connection details of the data source or sink.

A dataset is a JSON file that defines the following properties:

- **Type**: The type of data source or sink, such as Azure Blob Storage or Azure SQL Database
- **Schema**: The structure and schema of the data, including column names and data types
- **Connection**: The connection details for the data source or sink, such as the account name and access key for Azure Blob Storage or the server name and database name for Azure SQL Database

You can create a dataset by using the ADF visual authoring interface, by writing JSON code, or by using ADF SDKs. In Synapse, the creation process is similar. Once you create a dataset, you can use it as an input (source) or output (sink) for a pipeline.

Datasets can be used in combination with linked services, which are also JSON files that define the connection information to the data sources or sinks. So, while a dataset defines the structure and schema of the data, a linked service defines the connection information to the data source or sink.

### Integration runtimes for data pipelines

We touched briefly on integration runtimes in *Chapter 3* to ingest data. Other than ingesting data, these compute infrastructures can also be used to transform data. Integration runtimes run the execution of the following capabilities:

- **Data flow**: Create no-code or low-code transformation with a visual interface. These are executed in a managed Azure compute environment.

- **Data movement**: Convert formats and rename columns in a performant and scalable manner

- **Activity dispatch**: Dispatch transformation activities to other compute services (such as Azure Databricks and Azure SQL Server) and monitor them.

- **SQL Server Integration Services (SSIS) package execution**: Move SSIS packages to the cloud and execute them in a managed Azure compute environment.

There are three types of integration runtime, each with specific purposes and compute resources:

- **Azure integration runtime**: This is used for data flow execution, data movement between cloud data stores, and activity dispatches in a public network. The compute is fully managed, serverless, and can be scaled elastically through data integration units. Activity dispatches are lightweight operations and route the activities to the target compute services (e.g., Databricks or SQL Server).

- **Self-hosted integration runtime**: This is only used for data movements from on-premises or virtual networks or activity dispatches to, for example, on-premises SQL servers. As the name suggests, this integration runtime uses the compute infrastructure of the device it was installed on.

- **Azure-SSIS integration runtime**: This can only run SSIS packages in a managed Azure compute environment. They are executed against a fully managed cluster of Azure virtual machines, which are reserved for running SSIS packages.

# Transforming data on Azure

As datasets continue to grow in size and complexity, it is increasingly important to have efficient ways of manipulating and processing this data. We will cover both batch and real-time transformation options.

For batch transformations, we will discuss the use of the following:

- Mapping data flows
- Spark notebooks
- SQL scripts
- SSIS

These tools can be used for shaping and cleaning large datasets and allow you to define complex data transformations using a visual interface or programming language, making it easy to handle even the most challenging data manipulation tasks.

For real-time transformations, we will look at the following:

- Azure Stream Analytics
- Azure Databricks

Both technologies allow you to process data with remarkably low latency, enabling real-time insights and decision-making. With these tools, you can process data streams from various sources in real time, transforming and analyzing the data as it flows through the system.

After this, we will explain how to decide which transformation component to pick in which situation, as this decision is the responsibility of the data architect.

## Batch transformation – mapping data flows

Mapping data flows, sometimes simply referred to as data flows, provide an easy-to-use, low-code method for performing data transformations. The graphical user interface gives the user the ability to create transformation workflows using simple drag-and-drop functionality.

Under the hood, these data flows run on highly scalable Spark clusters, making them ideal for data operations at scale. The lack of technical skills required to create data flows allow any organization to make use of this method, regardless of the skill sets in the team.

*Figure 4.2* shows what a typical data flow might look like:

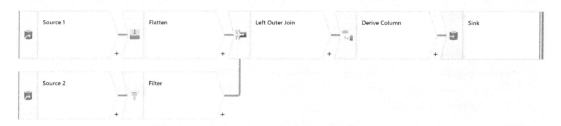

Figure 4.2 – A generic example of a mapping data flow in ADF

Data is fetched from one or more data sources. After reading the data, we can add a wide range of transformation blocks before we write the data to a new location (also called the sink). The transformation blocks at our disposal are listed in five categories:

- **Multiple inputs/outputs**: These blocks contain operations such as splits, joins, unions, and the like.

- **Schema modifiers**: These blocks alter the schema of the dataset by adding or removing columns, pivoting, aggregating, and so on.

- **Formatters**: These blocks get the data in the right shape to perform further transformations by parsing, flattening, or stringifying data.

- **Row modifiers**: These blocks alter rows or the number of rows by filtering on rows, sorting, or making assertions.

- **Flowlets**: (Partial) logic from earlier data flows can be reused in subsequent data flows in the form of a flowlet. A flowlet is a subset of another data flow that can be implemented as a single transformation block.

Data flows come with an array of extra functionalities, which, among other things, allow them to do the following:

- Detect schema drifts between the source and sink.

- Perform auto-mapping, rule-based mapping, or regex mapping on drifted and aggregated columns.

- Preview data and acquire statistics on specific columns while debugging.

- Implement user-defined functions; these are custom expressions that are ideal when you find yourself using the same logic over and over again.

These data flows can be found in both ADF and Azure Synapse. So, whether an Azure data solution is built according to the traditional method or the all-encompassing Synapse approach, data flows are always an available option.

> **Power BI dataflows**
>
> After renaming *mapping data flows* to *data flows* in ADF, this may now cause some confusion with *Power BI dataflows*. Both are tools for transforming data with data pipelines but run on different engines and in different tools.
>
> ADF data flows are a feature of ADF that allows you to create and manage data pipelines in the cloud. It is a visual, drag-and-drop interface that enables you to perform data integration and transformation tasks on large volumes of data, both structured and unstructured, without writing code. ADF data flows allow you to create data flows that can be scheduled and executed on a regular basis and can handle different types of data sources and destinations, including Azure Data Lake, Azure SQL Database, and more.
>
> Power BI dataflows, on the other hand, are a feature of Power BI that allows you to create and manage data pipelines specifically for Power BI data models. They provide a way to transform and shape data in Power BI; you can create a dataflow, which is a reusable transformation that can be used across multiple reports and datasets.
>
> It is recommended to do transformation as far upstream as possible and as far downstream as necessary. This means performing common transformations across the whole data platform in ADF and business-line or department-specific transformations in Power BI.

To conclude briefly, data flows are fast to implement and do not require specific coding skill sets. On the other hand, due to their prebuilt drag-and-drop nature, data flows cannot allow the same flexibility as custom code solutions can.

## Batch transformation – Spark notebooks

When the necessary skill set is present in the development and maintenance teams, code-first solutions are a great way to address complex issues in an efficient manner. In data engineering processes, this often happens in the form of notebooks running on Apache Spark. The main downside of notebooks is the time it takes for development and testing, and the requirement of having one or more data engineers on the team.

> **What is Apache Spark?**
>
> Apache Spark is a framework for processing data in large volumes, often used in data engineering or data science workloads. What really sets Spark apart is its ability to efficiently orchestrate distributed processing of massive datasets. This makes it the perfect asset for data teams looking for scalable solutions. Spark-based workloads are performed on compute clusters with a varying number of nodes, which often feature auto-scaling functionalities. This ensures both small and large data teams can leverage Spark in a cost-effective way.

To create notebooks that we can orchestrate in a data pipeline, we have two options:

- Notebooks in Azure Databricks
- Notebooks in Azure Synapse Analytics

Apart from these two, the Azure Machine Learning workspace also provides the ability to create and run notebooks, but these do not leverage Spark and are therefore not optimized for large-scale data transformations.

The first and foremost reason to pick Synapse notebooks or Azure Databricks notebooks over the other is whether the data solution uses the traditional or Synapse architecture. When using the traditional architecture (i.e., a data solution leveraging ADF, Azure Data Lake, or Azure SQL Database instead of the all-encompassing Synapse workspace), it makes more sense to make use of Azure Databricks notebooks. Connections between resources do not come out of the box anyway, which is one of the main benefits of Synapse, so Azure Databricks is often the preferred option.

When using Synapse architecture, where everything from data transformations to data warehousing happens in a single Synapse workspace, Synapse notebooks are preferred due to their ease of use and built-in connectivity. However, some niche cases may make us reconsider this choice, which we will get to shortly.

Although notebooks in Azure Databricks and Azure Synapse are mostly similar, there are still a few key differences that may weigh on the architect's decision to choose one over the other, such as the following:

- Supported languages
- Connectivity to other Azure resources
- Collaboration
- Strong use cases

Let's dive into each of these.

### Supported languages

Both Azure Databricks and Azure Synapse notebooks support the following languages:

- Python (PySpark)
- R (RSpark)
- SQL (Spark SQL)
- Scala (Spark)
- C# (.NET Spark)

On top of this, Databricks notebooks offer support for one additional language, Java.

Both Synapse and Databricks notebooks will support multiple languages being used in a single notebook, using magic commands. These are commands preceded by a % sign. For example, starting a code cell with the line %python will allow Python code to run in that cell, while the next cell can contain code written in a different language.

### Connectivity to other Azure resources

For quick connectivity to other Azure resources, such as data lakes and data warehouses, Synapse mostly comes out on top. Although most of the connections are also possible to set up using Azure Databricks, they may require some extra work. For instance, Synapse notebooks will have instant access to the data lake (on which the Synapse workspace is placed on top), while access to data lakes in Databricks is only possible after mounting them to the Spark cluster in the Databricks workspace.

### Collaboration

Teams of data engineers working on notebooks in Synapse or Databricks will interact with them in a different way. The main difference to note here is that, in Databricks, different users are able to make real-time changes in the same notebook, whereas Synapse works with a versioning-first approach, requiring saves or commits to update the notebook for all other users.

### Strong use cases

Among the many use cases available, one quick rule of thumb for any Azure data architect is the following:

- **Azure Databricks notebooks**: Databricks will outperform Synapse in any use case requiring real-time data processing. In a real-time use case, we should look at the comparison between Databricks and Azure Stream Analytics instead. The same goes for machine learning use cases. Although Synapse is getting increasingly more machine learning capabilities, for a machine learning use case, the architect should decide between the Azure Machine Learning workspace and Azure Databricks.

- **Azure Synapse notebooks**: Synapse will be the preferred option if the use case is **business intelligence** (**BI**)-focused, and therefore heavily reliant on visualization tools such as Power BI. Power BI reports and dashboards can be created from the same Synapse workspace as where the notebooks are developed, allowing BI developers to easily interact with both.

## Batch transformation – SQL scripts

Besides data transformation using low-code data flows and code-first notebooks, there is one more alternative using SQL, albeit more uncommon. The main reason why an organization may choose SQL-based transformation workflows is mainly due to the available skill sets in the team. If the team is heavily focused on BI, and hence consists mostly of data analysts and BI developers, then this might be a valid option to consider.

In theory, there are three methods on Azure to perform SQL-based data transformations:

- SQL scripts in Azure Synapse Analytics
- SQL in Azure Databricks notebooks
- SQL stored procedures

In the last chapter, we talked about data lake tiers and the benefits of applying transformations while reading and writing data to different tiers of the data lake. For reasons such as cost optimization, we do not want to perform many data transformations in the data warehouse and store different versions of the data there. Stored procedures are still a valid process to integrate into a data solution, but at the data warehouse or database level, not for transforming data in the data lake. We will explore this further in *Chapter 6, Data Warehousing*.

This leaves us with two options: whether to leverage SQL scripts in Synapse or write SQL in Databricks notebooks. The thought process for the data architect here is quite simple. If the team consists mostly of profiles with strong SQL skill sets, then it is more than likely the project is going to be focused on BI. As we have just seen, this is a scenario where Azure Synapse Analytics shines. Therefore, if data is transformed using SQL, it should be done using the SQL scripts in Azure Synapse Analytics.

## Batch transformation – SSIS

**SSIS** is a platform for building data integration and workflow solutions. It is a component of the Microsoft SQL Server database software and is used to perform a wide range of data integration and transformation tasks.

SSIS can be seen as an on-premises tool for data transformations. They are run against an on-premises SQL engine. Often, SSIS is migrated to the cloud and replaced by ADF using the Azure-SSIS integration runtime to execute the SSIS packages. As discussed before, the packages will then be run against a fully managed cluster of Azure VMs, dedicated to running SSIS packages.

SSIS is a product that requires installation and maintenance, whereas ADF is a fully managed service in the Azure cloud. By moving to ADF in the Azure cloud, you don't need to worry about managing and maintaining the service and you only pay for what you use.

## Real-time transformation – Azure Stream Analytics

Azure Stream Analytics allows for the processing of real-time data at a sub-millisecond latency. It comes as a fully managed service, enabling teams to rapidly start up their real-time transformation jobs, wasting little time on setup and development.

Azure Stream Analytics takes two types of input:

- Streaming data
- Reference data

As a real-time processing service, the main goal is to process the streaming data. This data can stem from IoT devices (ingested by Azure IoT Hub) or from Azure Event Hubs. It is also possible to stream data for Azure Data Lake Storage or Blob Storage into Azure Stream Analytics.

The data stream input can be enriched with reference data. This reference data is data in persistent storage, such as Azure Data Lake Storage, Blob Storage, or Azure SQL Database. Another option for enriching the data stream is by leveraging trained machine learning models to make predictions on the streaming data. Models deployed through Azure Machine Learning can easily integrate with Azure Stream Analytics through the use of **user-defined functions** (**UDFs**).

In terms of output, there is a wide range of options. It is possible to output data to multiple outputs at the same time. For example, in Lambda architecture (introduced in the previous chapter), we can output data to a Power BI dashboard for real-time analytics, while also sending the data back to Azure Data Lake Storage for persistent storage. Azure Stream Analytics supports many outputs such as data lakes and Blob Storage, SQL Database, Azure Event Hubs, Azure Cosmos DB, **Azure Data Explorer** (**ADX**), and more. Azure Cosmos DB and ADX will be further discussed in the next chapter.

Stream Analytics comes with its own query language, called **Stream Analytics Query Language** (**SAQL**), which is a subset of the widely adopted **transactional SQL** (**T-SQL**). The following code snippet will give you an idea of what the syntax looks like:

```
WITH filteredData AS (
    SELECT *
    FROM inputSource
    WHERE Temperature > 25
),
enrichedData AS (
    SELECT
        filteredData.*,
        referenceData.DeviceName,
        referenceData.Location
    FROM filteredData
    JOIN referenceData
    ON filteredData.DeviceId = referenceData.DeviceId
)
SELECT
    enrichedData.DeviceId,
    enrichedData.DeviceName,
    enrichedData.Location,
```

```
    AVG(enrichedData.Temperature) AS avgTemperature,
    COUNT(*) AS eventCount
INTO
    powerBIOutput
FROM
    enrichedData
GROUP BY
    enrichedData.DeviceId, TumblingWindow(second, 10)
```

The preceding SAQL query ingests both streaming data (`filteredData`) and reference data (`referenceData`). It enriches the data stream with the reference data. Next, it groups the data using one of the many windowing functions available in Stream Analytics. Finally, it streams the data into a Power BI dataset, allowing for real-time data visualization.

## Real-time transformation – Azure Databricks

Although less common than Azure Stream Analytics, Azure Databricks provides an alternative solution for performing real-time processing of data. It can take in data stream services such as Azure Event Hubs or Kafka, among many others. Data transformations can then be performed using the *Structured Streaming API* from Spark. From there on, results can be written to a Delta Table, as discussed in the previous chapter. To compare Azure Databricks and Azure Stream Analytics, we refer to *Table 4.1*:

| Feature | Azure Databricks | Azure Stream Analytics |
|---|---|---|
| Flexibility | + | - |
| Development efforts | - | + |
| Language support | + | - |
| Input connectors | + | - |
| Output connectors | - | + |
| File formats | + | - |

Table 4.1 – A simplified comparison of strengths between Azure Databricks and Azure Stream Analytics

The following elaborates on the comparison in *Table 4.1*:

- Azure Databricks will provide more flexibility, allowing both declarative and imperative inputs, but will typically require more development time in terms of coding.

- Compared to Azure Stream Analytics, Azure Databricks will offer support for more languages, as mentioned earlier in the section on Spark notebooks.

- On top of the shared compatible data sources (Azure Event Hubs, Azure IoT Hub, and Azure Blob Storage or Data Lake), Databricks will provide additional support for Kafka and **Hadoop Distributed File System (HDFS)**. Azure Stream Analytics will also be able to transform data from Kafka, but it will go through an Azure Event Hubs instance first for ingestion.

- Azure Databricks does not support as many outputs as Azure Stream Analytics. There are no built-in connectors to instantly stream data to Power BI datasets, Azure SQL Databases, Azure Service Buses, or Azure Functions.

- While Azure Stream Analytics can only take in Avro, JSON, or CSV file formats, Azure Databricks is able to process any file format due to its custom code nature.

Now that we have discussed the most important services for data transformation, both batch and real-time, let's explore what influences the decision-making process of the architect when designing data transformation architectures.

# Data transformation architectures

We have explored and discussed the different tools for data transformation. Next, it is time to indicate where they fit in the overall architecture of an Azure data solution. We will look at batch transformation and stream transformation architectures separately.

## Batch transformation architecture

For a solution only making use of batch processing, this is straightforward. The transformation is performed in the ETL pipelines, which push the data through the different data lake tiers. The following figure shows an example architecture of batch processing:

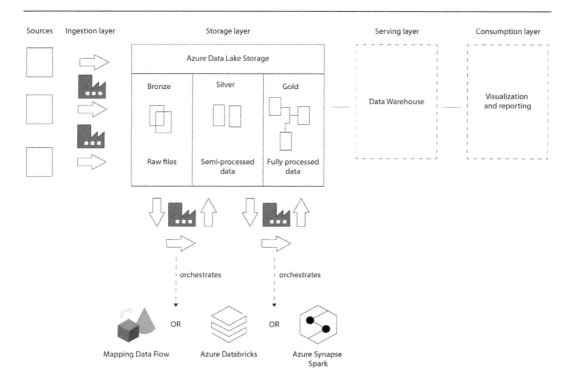

Figure 4.3 – Batch transformations are orchestrated by data pipelines
between data lake tiers in modern cloud architectures

The ADF or Synapse pipeline will call upon the transformation workflow in the form of a pipeline activity. Both ADF and Azure Synapse Analytics have built-in activities for calling mapping data flows, Synapse notebooks, and Azure Databricks notebooks from a pipeline.

## Stream transformation architecture

For the streaming architecture, we will go back to the Lambda architecture as an example, which was explained in the previous chapter. The following figure shows a different, yet abstract, perspective of Lambda architecture:

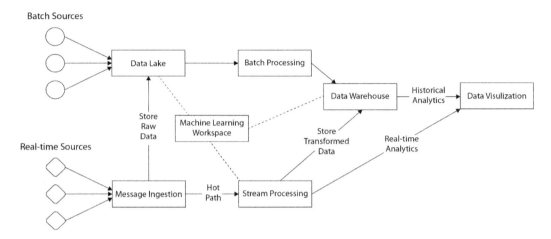

Figure 4.4 – Lambda architecture to combine stream and batch processing

In the preceding Lambda architecture, notice the cold path at the top and the hot path at the bottom. In the cold path, data is ingested in batches to data storage, which is often Azure Data Lake Storage or Azure Blob Storage. In this diagram, batch processing is performed after the storage. As we saw previously, this can be done using mapping data flows, Spark notebooks, or SQL scripts.

In the hot path, data is ingested in real time. In the previous chapter, we discussed how both Azure Event Hubs and Azure IoT Hub can be provisioned to complete this task. The output of these message ingestion services is sent to Azure Data Lake Storage for persistent storage (part of the cold path) and is forwarded to a stream processing service. As we have just discussed, we can choose between Azure Stream Analytics or Azure Databricks for this component.

When fleshing out the architecture, it will look like the following:

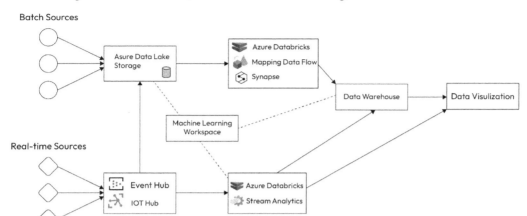

Figure 4.5 – Lambda architecture with the most popular services for each component filled in

Next, machine learning models can be used to enrich both batch and stream processing with predictions. Data is sent to the serving layer – in this case, the analytical data store or data warehouse. Finally, the data continues to the consumption layer to be visualized or used by other systems.

Now that we know which tools exist for transforming data and where they fit in the architecture, the question arises: which transformation tool do we decide on in which scenario?

Let's find out.

## Deciding on the right data transformation service

With the many options available for the architect to choose from, deciding on a transformation tool might be a daunting task at first. To make this more convenient, especially for newer data architects on Azure, we have created holistic flowcharts that visualize the decision process of the architect, for both batch and real-time data processing. Keep in mind that it is not possible to grasp all the complexities of a real-life scenario in a single flowchart, and remember, this diagram is to be used to give a first indication of what tool to dive deeper into.

Let's look at batch transformations first.

## Deciding on a batch transformation tool

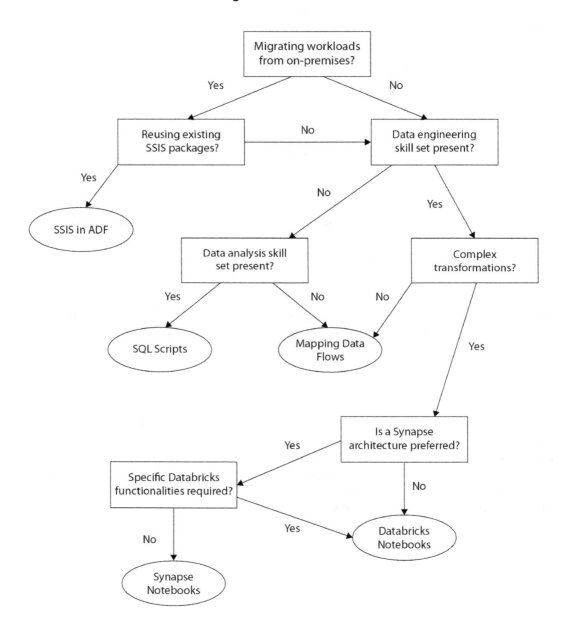

Figure 4.6 – A flowchart of the decision process when deciding on a tool for batch transformations

First, we ask ourselves whether the existing transformational workloads are being migrated from on-premises to Azure. If this is the case and if this involves SSIS packages, we could reuse these packages using the ADF SSIS integration runtime. However, in this case, we can also decide to pick any other tool and develop a more modern transformational workflow.

If we are talking about greenfield development (or brownfield development using cloud-based resources), we will check whether the development and maintenance teams for the solution have sufficient data engineering profiles among them. If this is not the case, we might need to look for a low-code solution.

Before jumping straight to mapping data flows, however, we first check whether the team mainly consists of data analysts with SQL skill sets. This might mostly be the case if the solution focuses heavily on BI. If so, we decide on SQL scripts. If not, we can safely assume that mapping data flows is the preferred tool.

When we do have data engineers at our disposal, there will be more options available. We can still decide between low-code and code-heavy methods. If the required transformations are not very complex, we can opt for mapping data flows as these are fast to develop and easy to maintain. If the complexity is high, we will have to consider Spark notebooks, either in Azure Databricks or Azure Synapse Analytics.

In general, if we are not using most of the functionalities of the Synapse workspace for our architecture (Synapse pipelines, Synapse data warehousing, and so on), we will, by default, choose Azure Databricks notebooks, as Databricks tends to have slightly more functionalities regarding Spark development.

If the Synapse suite is being used, Synapse notebooks will be a good option as they integrate well with the other Synapse components. If, for some reason, a specific Databricks feature is required, we still have the option to switch to Databricks notebooks, at the cost of less convenient integration with other Synapse services.

Next, let's look at the decision-making process for real-time transformations.

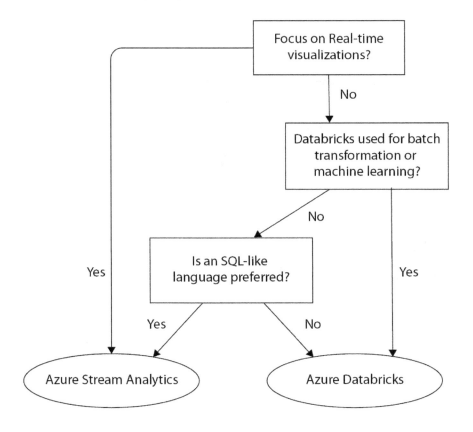

## Deciding on a real-time transformation tool

Figure 4.7 – A flowchart of the decision process when deciding on a tool for stream transformations

As seen earlier, real-time solutions are normally only implemented when the business case justifies the cost. This is because either a system needs to act on the data stream instantly or data needs to be visualized quickly (often allowing a human to take rapid action based on the visualization). In the latter case, we will often prefer Azure Stream Analytics, thanks to its great integration with Power BI for data visualization.

If data visualization is not the primary use case, we have more freedom in terms of choice. Next, it basically comes down to a matter of preference for the developers. If Azure Databricks is already being used for other workloads, such as batch transformations or machine learning, this would be the most convenient option, especially as this means that the development teams have experience with Spark-based programming.

When Databricks is not already being used for other workloads, we can check with the development teams whether they prefer an SQL-like language (which will mostly be the case for data analysts) or Spark-based options (which is mostly part of the skill set of a data engineer), resulting in Azure Stream Analytics or Azure Databricks, respectively.

# Data transformations in data lake tiers

As we saw in *Chapter 3*, we dump raw data into the bronze layer. It serves as the primary source of raw, unrefined data for the warehouse. This layer contains all the original data as it is received from various sources, including transactional systems, log files, and external data feeds. The purpose of the bronze layer is to provide a centralized location for raw data to be stored, and to make it available for further processing in the higher layers of the warehouse. Data is transformed into the silver and gold layers.

## Bronze-to-silver transformations

When moving from the bronze layer to the silver layer, a series of transformations are applied to make the data more usable for analysis. Some examples of transformations that are typically done in the silver layer include the following:

- **Data cleansing**: Removing any duplicates and correcting errors and inconsistencies in the data.
- **Data integration**: Combining data from multiple sources, resolving conflicts, and ensuring data consistency.
- **Data enrichment**: Adding additional information to the data, such as geographic data or demographic data. This is why the silver layer is also called the enrich layer.
- **Data conversion**: Changing data types, formats, or units of measure to make them more consistent and easier to analyze.
- **Data standardization**: Applying a set of standards to the data, such as a common date format or a common currency.
- **Data validation**: Checking the data for logical errors or missing values.
- **Handling missing values**: Filling in missing data with techniques such as imputation or interpolation.
- **Data partitioning**: Splitting data into smaller and more manageable chunks, based on some criteria.

The silver layer can be seen as an intermediate layer for cleansing, standardizing, and enriching data. As the silver layer produces a higher quality of data than the bronze layer, it is often used for data analysis or as a data source for machine learning.

### Silver-to-gold transformations

The gold layer makes the data more usable for reporting. It creates logical business views of the data by aggregating it over periods of time, business units, or countries. It also models the data in a way that is optimized for reporting and analysis. This may include creating fact and dimension tables and calculated columns.

In a modern data warehousing scenario, all layers discussed previously are stored in flexible cloud storage such as Azure Data Lake Storage. This allows us to combine different types of data (e.g., structured, semi-structured, and unstructured data). Before reporting, however, the data of the gold layer is often ingested into a more performant querying service such as a Synapse SQL pool or Azure SQL Database. The data can also be ingested in the semantic layer, where multi-dimensional or tabular models are created from the data for reporting. The semantic layer will be explained in the following chapters.

# Operationalizing data pipelines on Azure

Operationalizing data pipelines on Azure is a process of creating, managing, and maintaining data workflows in the Azure cloud. It involves several key steps, including scheduling data pipelines, monitoring data pipelines, and implementing a **Continuous Integration/Continuous Deployment (CI/CD)** process for data pipelines.

### Scheduling data pipelines on Azure

Scheduling data pipelines on Azure is a crucial step in the operationalization process. It ensures that data pipelines are run at the appropriate times and frequencies, and that data is updated and available when needed. ADF provides several ways to schedule data pipelines, such as triggers, schedules, control flows, and data flows, which offer flexibility in scheduling data pipelines based on time, events, or conditions.

ADF provides two different ways to schedule data pipelines:

- **Triggers**: A trigger is a way to start a pipeline on a schedule or in response to an event. ADF supports several types of triggers such as time-based, event-based, and dependency-based triggers. For example, you can schedule a pipeline to run daily at a specific time, or you can trigger a pipeline to run when a file is added to a specific Azure Blob Storage container.
- **Schedules**: A schedule is a way to run a pipeline on a recurring basis. ADF supports several types of schedules such as daily, weekly, and monthly schedules. You can also set a specific start and end date for the schedule.

## Monitoring data pipelines on Azure

Monitoring data pipelines on Azure is another important step in the operationalization process. It allows you to keep track of the pipeline's execution and view the pipeline status and execution history. ADF provides several monitoring capabilities such as pipeline and activity run history, log streaming, and email notifications. It also allows you to set up alerts for specific events or conditions, and you can use Azure Monitor for more advanced monitoring and logging capabilities.

## CI/CD for data pipelines on Azure

CI/CD for data pipelines on Azure is the process of automating the deployment and testing of data pipeline changes. This allows you to quickly and safely make changes to your data pipelines and deploy them to production with minimal downtime. ADF provides the ability to create and manage data pipelines as code, which allows you to version-control and automate the deployment process. Additionally, Azure DevOps can be used to implement CI/CD for data pipelines, which provides a unified platform for managing and automating the pipeline build, test, and deployment processes.

Unit testing with ADF is a process of testing individual units of code or functionality within an ADF pipeline to ensure that they are working as expected. This can include testing the functionality of specific activities, such as data flow transformations or custom activities, as well as testing the logic of control flow activities.

Unit testing is important for several reasons:

- It helps to ensure that individual units of code are working as expected, which can help to identify and fix bugs early in the development process
- It allows for more efficient debugging and troubleshooting, as it is easier to isolate issues and identify the root cause when testing individual units of code
- It helps to increase the overall quality of the pipeline and reduce the risk of introducing errors into the production environment
- It helps to improve the maintainability of the pipeline by making it easier to update or refactor the pipeline without introducing new errors
- It facilitates the development of a CI/CD process for data pipelines by providing automated testing for pipeline changes

In order to perform unit testing with ADF, you can use a combination of tools such as Azure DevOps, MSTest, and NUnit. Azure DevOps provides a way to version-control the pipeline and manage the CI/CD process. MSTest and NUnit are unit-testing frameworks that can be used to create and execute test cases for ADF pipelines.

# Summary

To recap, data pipelines in Azure are a set of tools and services that allows for the efficient movement and transformation of data. One of the concepts covered in the chapter is the difference between ETL and ELT pipelines. In this book, we will focus mostly on ETL. The chapter also covered the differences between data pipelines in ADF and data pipelines in Azure Synapse Analytics.

We described various tools and technologies available for data transformation in Azure, including mapping data flows, Spark notebooks, SQL scripts, and SSIS packages for batch processing, and Azure Stream Analytics and Azure Databricks for real-time processing.

Next, we looked at an example architecture for both batch and stream processing, providing a high-level overview of the components and technologies involved. Later parts of the architecture remain abstract for now. We introduced a holistic flowchart to map the decision-making process when choosing one of the transformation tools discussed.

We explored which types of transformations are performed between the different tiers of a data lake. This gives a better idea of what the semi-processed and fully processed data will look like.

Finally, in terms of operationalizing data pipelines on Azure, we explored different options to consider such as scheduling pipelines, monitoring and alerting, implementing CI/CD processes, and unit testing. Additionally, version control is an important aspect to ensure the integrity of the pipeline and to maintain a history of changes made to the pipeline.

In the next chapter, we will cover different methods of storing data. We have already seen Data Lake Storage, but Azure provides many other options to meet the requirements for different use cases.

# Storing Data for Consumption

This chapter will explore the critical topic of early data orchestration and storage design. As companies gather increasingly massive amounts of data, it becomes more important to establish best practices for managing and storing that data efficiently.

We will begin by examining how to classify data as structured, semi-structured, or unstructured, and how to determine its use case. We will also determine how data will be used and the differences between ACID transactions and non-ACID transactions, SQL and NoSQL databases, and OLAP and OLTP systems. Additionally, we will focus on when to choose which storage service in Azure, such as **Azure Cosmos DB**, **Azure SQL Database**, or **Azure Blob Storage**, based on your data platform's specific functional and technical requirements.

By the end of this chapter, you will have a firm grasp of the fundamental principles of data storage design, as well as the tools and techniques available for constructing a robust and scalable data platform.

We will be covering the following topics in this chapter:

- Classifying the data type
- Determining how the data will be used
- Choosing the right storage solution in Azure

## Classifying the data type

First, we will explore how the architect can classify different types of data. Data can be classified into three different types:

- Structured data
- Semi-structured data
- Unstructured data

We will also examine various file types associated with each type of data, as different file formats have their own characteristics, benefits, and drawbacks. For each data type, a solid understanding of these file types and their features can help to optimize storage costs, retrieval speeds, and scalability.

Note that there can be some ambiguity on which file format falls under which data type. In particular, file formats such as CSV and Avro are often classified as either structured or semi-structured, depending on whom you ask and what their exact definition is. However, this exact classification is not of importance to the data architect. What is important is knowing which file type is optimal in which scenario.

## Structured data

Structured data is often associated with tabular datasets. This type of data is dependent on a certain schema, with a fixed amount of columns or features. A fixed, tabular structure has the advantage of being incredibly robust and considerably easier to query than semi-structured or unstructured data. On the other hand, this trait also decreases flexibility as part of the trade-off.

Commonly used file formats for structured data are as follows:

- **Parquet**
- **Avro**
- **Excel**

Let's look at each of them in detail, discuss their attributes, and give a few examples of where this type of data might originate from.

### *Parquet*

Parquet files come in a columnar storage file format that is designed to be highly efficient for both storing and querying large datasets. It is commonly used in data warehousing and big data systems.

One of the key benefits of using Parquet files is that they are optimized for columnar operations, meaning that only the relevant columns of data are read and processed when performing a query. This can significantly improve the performance of read-heavy workloads; think tasks such as data analytics and reporting. Additionally, Parquet files are highly compressed and support a variety of encoding schemes to further reduce storage costs.

Parquet files also support a number of advanced features such as nested data structures, complex data types, and predicate pushdown. These features allow for more efficient querying of complex datasets and can help to reduce the amount of data that needs to be read and processed.

Parquet files are also able to enforce schemas and data types. This can make them very useful for data stored in the gold tier of the data lake where we want the data in a strict format, ready for importing into the data warehouse. Another example use case for Parquet files is a lake database, which will be elaborately explained in the next chapter.

Hence, these file types are often the result of data transformations. As such, transformational tools discussed in the previous chapter, such as mapping data flows and Spark notebooks, will typically write their output in Parquet format.

## Avro

Apache Avro is an open source data serialization and exchange service. Avro files are used to store data in a compact binary format, which makes them well suited to storing large amounts of data. This type of file is typically used in services such as **Apache Hadoop** and **Apache Kafka**.

A key benefit of using Avro files (and the reason why they can be classified as structured) is that they have a built-in schema. The schema is stored with the data, which allows for easy evolution of the data over time. Where the data itself is stored in binary, the schema is stored as a JSON. Thanks to this semi-structured schema, new fields can be added to the schema without the need to update all the existing data. Additionally, Avro files support a number of advanced features, such as nested data structures and complex data types.

Avro files are highly compressible and support a variety of compression codecs. This makes them highly efficient in terms of storage and network transfer.

Depending on the definition, Avro can also be seen as semi-structured data.

> **Avro versus Parquet**
>
> In contrast to a columnar storage format such as the previously mentioned Parquet, the Avro format is a row-based storage format. This means Avro will outperform in use cases where, for instance, all columns of a single row need to be retrieved, whereas Parquet is able to quickly look up specific column values. Further, Avro can deal with changing schemas better than Parquet. Parquet, on the other hand, will be more performant in storing nested data and generally has faster compression times. Finally, all things combined, Avro will be better for write-heavy use cases (such as transactional workloads), whereas Parquet will shine in read-heavy scenarios (such as data analytics).

## Excel

Excel (.xlsx) is the file type that stems from Microsoft Office spreadsheets. Although Excel sheets are something we usually do not want to have in the curated tiers of our data lake, they may be prevalent in the bronze or raw layers. Depending on the use case, Excel sheets may still be a major part of ingested data to this day. This is especially the case when working with more traditional, less data-driven organizations. The first thing we should do with these sheets is transform them into a different format, CSV being a convenient option here.

## Semi-structured data

Semi-structured data does not conform to a fixed schema and is therefore not tabular. Still, semi-structured data has some form of structure, which sets it apart from unstructured data formats. These forms of structure can include tags, key-value pairs, and methods of incorporating a hierarchy into the data.

A semi-structured format can have a wide variety in the number of features. This means semi-structured data could be stored in a structured, tabular format. However, as the number of possible features increases, it will become less and less efficient, as a column (often sparsely filled) will have to be added for every possible feature.

Commonly used file formats for semi-structured data are as follows:

- JSON
- XML
- CSV
- TSV

Let's start with the most prevalent one, which is JSON.

### *JSON*

**JavaScript Object Notation (JSON)** is a widely used data format consisting of hierarchical key-value pairs. It has the advantage of being lightweight and easily readable by humans. Despite its name, JSON can be used with many programming languages nowadays. Among a vast variety of use cases, it is often used for systems communicating with each other through APIs, storing configuration files, or when exporting data.

For this reason, JSON files will be encountered frequently when importing data from external data sources and, therefore, will be extensively present in the bronze tier of the data lake. If the goal is to push this to a data warehouse later on, it will need to somehow be transformed into a structural format, the complexity of which may vary, as seen earlier.

### *XML*

**Extensible Markup Language (XML)** is meant for the storage, transmission, and reconstruction of data. Compared to other file types mentioned in this chapter, it may be becoming outdated, but is still quite ubiquitous.

XML consists of hierarchical tags allowing for a variety of features, but is quite verbose in writing as it makes use of start-tags and end-tags to define its hierarchy. The usage of XML has received some criticism throughout the years, as other file types such as JSON provide simpler alternatives.

The use cases for XML are somewhat similar to JSON, but JSON is more widely adopted for most of these nowadays. However, we want to point out a use case where XML can still have the edge, which is schema validation. As XML files come with a schema describing the document, recipients of these files can verify the correctness of this schema.

### CSV

**Comma-separated values** (CSV) files are plain text files containing tabular data. For this reason, many definitions classify CSV files as structured data. However, compared to Parquet, Avro, or Excel files, CSV files do not include data types for their columns, which is why they can be classified as semi-structured. Despite their name, columns in CSV files can use delimiters other than commas, the most common alternative being semicolons.

CSV files are commonly used to store or transport tabular data as they are very lightweight. They are very common in the raw data tier since many data sources will export their tabular data using the CSV format. However, due to their lack of data type enforcement, we would not recommend them in later tiers of the data lake.

### TSV

**Tab-separated values** (TSV) files are very similar to CSV files but use tabs as delimiters. Despite being theoretically more efficient than CSV files due to fewer characters being used on average, TSV files have not seen the same level of adoption that CSV files have.

## Unstructured data

Unstructured data does not follow any data model or schemas and has no built-in hierarchy whatsoever. Think of data such as the following:

- Text
- Images
- Video
- Audio

If we go back a little over a decade ago, it would often not have been possible to analyze this data at scale. Rule-based approaches were used in the early stages but resulted in poor performance. The rise of deep learning in the 2010s and the resulting low-code and pre-trained tools from the last few years have now made it possible and convenient for any organization to start getting insights from unstructured data.

Unstructured data has to be stored in NoSQL storage, as it cannot adhere to the strict rules of a relational database. In reality, most of this data sits in data lakes, often to be consumed by data scientists to extract insights from it.

Contrary to how we looked into structured and semi-structured data, here we will focus on specific sources and how to process the data instead of discussing specific file types.

## Video

Video data is relatively costly in storage due to its volume, and is often industry-specific. Some organizations might not have any video data, while others have enormous amounts. Video data stems from sources such as the following:

- Production-line cameras
- Security cameras
- Virtual meeting recordings
- Drone footage

Video data analytics can be automated in a variety of ways, leveraging the rapid development in trends such as computer vision. In Azure, we can make use of computer vision models in **Azure Cognitive Services** (a collection of pre-trained models) or custom-built models in **Azure Machine Learning** to perform tasks such as the following:

- **Video classification** (for example, classifying videos where viewer discretion is advised)
- **Object detection**, counting, and tracking (for example, counting and tracking cars on a highway)
- **Semantic segmentation** (for example, clustering all pixels related to a specific fruit)
- **Face detection** and **facial expression recognition** (for example, extracting emotions from video)
- **Stereovision** (for example, using multiple cameras to create a 3D representation of a scene)

We will dive deeper into specific machine learning services and APIs in *Chapter 9, Advanced Analytics Using AI*.

Furthermore, video data can easily be converted into images and audio files without the use of any machine learning models.

## Images

Data sources generating image data are quite similar to video data sources. Along with image data originating from converted video files, some examples of typical image data are as follows:

- Product images
- Satellite imagery
- Microscopic imagery

- Medical imaging
- Text-to-image data (generative AI, using models such as **Dall-E** in **Azure OpenAI Service**)

Images are analyzed in similar ways to video files, involving methods such as image classification, object detection, and semantic segmentation.

From images, we can extract text data using the **optical character recognition** (**OCR**) API and digitalize documents using the **Form Recognizer** API (which is built on top of the OCR API) in Azure Cognitive Services.

## Audio

Apart from extracted audio from video files, audio data typically includes the following:

- Interview recordings
- Phone recordings
- Audiobooks
- Podcasts

Using pre-trained deep learning models, we can analyze audio files in the following ways:

- **Speech-to-text** (**STT**)
- **Speaker recognition** (for example, recognizing who in a meeting is speaking)
- **Voice cloning** (for example, creating a synthetic voice similar to one in a recording)
- **Audio denoising** (for example, removing background sounds from a recording)

A considerable amount of audio files in an organization today originate from **text-to-speech** (**TTS**) machine learning models. With Azure, TTS and STT can also be found in Azure Cognitive Services. With advancements in features such as neural voices, the quality of TTS output is increasing fast.

## Text

Text files are the most common type of unstructured data. This type of file is considerably less industry-specific than video, image, or audio data. Every business has text data, from sources such as the following:

- Emails
- Notes
- Reports
- Contracts

- Web pages
- Customer reviews
- Text-to-text (generative AI, using models such as **GPT** in Azure OpenAI Service)

In the world of data science, there is an entire discipline dedicated to the understanding of human language: **natural language processing (NLP)**. NLP models can be used to extract all kinds of things from text data at scale, many of which are also integrated into Azure Cognitive Services and Azure OpenAI Service. This allows for use cases such as the following:

- **Named entity recognition** (for example, extracting person names from text)
- **Sentiment analysis** (for example, analyzing the positivity of a review)
- **Summarization** (for example, summarizing entire documents in a few paragraphs)
- **Translation** (for example, translating from English into French)

Finally, *Figure 5.1* summarizes the different methods of converting unstructured data that we have just discussed:

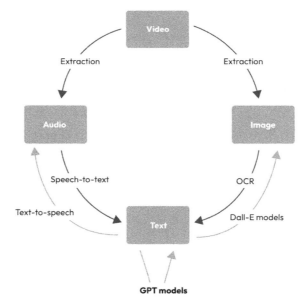

Figure 5.1 – An overview of models or processes to be used when going
from a certain input format to a certain output format

To briefly conclude, images and audio files can be extracted from videos. Text and audio files can be generated from each other. From images, we can extract text in the image. On the other hand, we can also generate images by providing a description of the image to an Azure OpenAI model. Lastly, we can generate new or longer text by providing prompts to another Azure OpenAI model.

# Determining how the data will be used

The aforementioned data types are stored in either a data lake or a database. How the data will be used will determine in which service the data needs to be stored.

As described in the previous chapters, a data lake is a centralized repository that allows data to be stored in its raw format without the need for predefined schemas. Data lakes are often used for big data and analytics workloads, as they enable storing and processing large amounts of data from various sources in a flexible way.

A database, on the other hand, can store structured (and, in some cases, semi-structured) data that is organized in a specific way, typically with a defined schema and defined relationships between the data. This form of organization makes it easy to search, sort, and manipulate the data, and is often used for transactional workloads.

## Relational databases

Structured data is often stored and queried using relational databases. These databases utilize tables to represent entities such as customers, products, or sales orders. Each occurrence of an entity is assigned a unique primary key that is used to reference the entity in other tables. For instance, a sales order record may reference a customer's primary key to indicate which customer placed the order. This use of keys to connect data entities allows for the normalization of the relational database, which includes the reduction of duplicate data values. The details of an individual customer, for example, would only be stored once and not for each sales order. The management and querying of tables are conducted using the **American National Standards Institute** (**ANSI**) standard **Structured Query Language** (**SQL**), which is similar across multiple database systems.

*Figure 5.2* depicts an example of a relational database:

Figure 5.2 – An example of relationships between tables in a database

## Non-relational or NoSQL databases

**Non-relational databases,** also known as **NoSQL databases,** are data management systems that do not rely on a relational schema for organizing data. Some more modern NoSQL databases may support a variant of the SQL language. This has led to what is seen as the meaning of NoSQL for some: *not only SQL,* indicating its abilities to handle both SQL and non-SQL retrieval methods.

There are four common types of non-relational databases in use:

- **Key-value databases,** in which each record comprises a unique key and an associated value that can be in any format.

- **Document databases,** which are a specific form of key-value databases in which the value is a JSON document optimized for parsing and querying.

- **Column-family databases,** which store tabular data comprising rows and columns, but the columns can be divided into groups known as **column families.** Each column family holds a set of columns that is logically related to each other.

- **Graph databases,** which store entities as nodes and use links to define relationships between them. These are optimal for use cases regarding (physical or semantic) network analysis.

Next, we will look at two big areas of data processing: fast-paced online transactional processing (OLTP) and **online analytical processing (OLAP)** for analytics at scale.

## Online transactional processing

A transactional data processing system is a crucial component of business computing, as it is responsible for recording and tracking specific events that occur within an organization. These events are known as transactions and can encompass a wide range of activities, such as financial transactions, retail sales, or inventory management. These transactions are considered small, discrete units of work, and are essential in maintaining accurate records of business operations.

Transactional systems are often high-volume, handling millions of transactions per day, and this high volume of data requires a system that can process data quickly. This type of work is referred to as **OLTP** and is a critical component in maintaining the smooth functioning of business operations.

To handle the demands of OLTP, a system must have a database that is optimized for both read and write operations. This is necessary to support transactional workloads, which include **creating, retrieving, updating, and deleting** data records (**CRUD** operations). To ensure the integrity of the data in the database, OLTP systems enforce transactions that follow ACID semantics:

- **Atomicity:** Each transaction is treated as a single unit, and must either be completed successfully or fail completely

- **Consistency:** Transactions can only take the data from one valid state to another

- **Isolation**: Concurrent transactions cannot interfere with each other and must result in a consistent database state

- **Durability**: Once a transaction is committed, it will remain committed even if the system is turned off

OLTP systems are typically used to support live applications that process business data, also known as **line-of-business (LOB)** applications. These applications include financial management systems, inventory management systems, retail systems, and other similar applications that are critical to the day-to-day operation of businesses. These systems are designed to handle high-volume transactions and provide quick access to data, making it possible for businesses to make real-time decisions that can have a significant impact on their bottom line.

In summary, transactional data processing systems play a vital role in the smooth functioning of business operations by recording and tracking specific events, handling high-volume transactions, and ensuring the integrity of data stored in the database. They are typically used to support live applications that process business data, such as financial management systems, inventory management systems, and retail systems.

## Online analytical processing

Where OLTP systems are perfect for frequent and simple queries such as small reads and writes, a more performant system is necessary to ask analytical questions, which are mostly complex and infrequent queries.

**OLAP** systems are designed for analytical data processing and store vast volumes of historical data or business metrics. They are optimized for read-only or read-mostly operations and are used to support reporting, data visualization, and data analysis. They are strategic systems that provide insights into business performance and trends over a period of time.

An OLAP system typically includes the following components:

- Data files stored in a central data lake for analysis. This allows for the storage of large volumes of unstructured data from various sources and enables data scientists to explore and model data.

- An **extract, transform, and load (ETL)** process that copies data from files and OLTP databases into a data warehouse that is optimized for read activity. This process ensures that data is cleaned, transformed, and structured in a way that can be used for analytical purposes.

- A data warehouse schema based on fact tables that contain numeric values for analysis and dimension tables that represent the entities by which to measure them. This schema is designed to support reporting, data visualization, and data analysis by providing a flexible, high-performance data model. Data warehouses will be explained in depth in *Chapter 6, Data Warehousing*.

- An OLAP model or cube that stores aggregated numeric values for intersections of dimensions from dimension tables, as part of the semantic layer. This allows for quick querying and drilling up and down to view aggregations at multiple hierarchical levels. This topic will be explored in *Chapter 7, The Semantic Layer*.

- The ability to query the data lake, data warehouse, and analytical model to produce reports, visualizations, and dashboards. This enables business users to access and consume the data in a way that is meaningful to them. We will go deeper into this in *Chapter 8, Visualizing Data Using Power BI*.

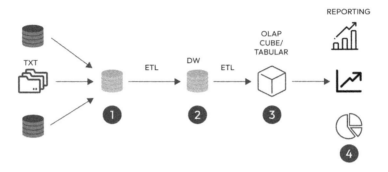

Figure 5.3 – The different components of an OLAP platform

In an OLAP system, data is stored in a multidimensional schema and the data is pre-aggregated across different dimensions, allowing for quick querying and drilling up and down to view aggregations at multiple hierarchical levels. OLAP systems are commonly used by data scientists, data analysts, and business users to gain insights from large datasets. It enables them to analyze business performance and trends, identify patterns and anomalies, and make data-driven decisions. This helps organizations to develop strategies, improve operations, and gain a competitive advantage.

## Choosing the right storage solution on Azure

Now that we've reviewed various storage concepts, let's examine the Azure storage options available to the cloud solution architect and how they correspond to OLTP, OLAP, and NoSQL.

### Azure OLTP services

For OLTP scenarios, we will discuss the following:

- **SQL Server** on Azure virtual machines
- **Azure SQL Managed Instance**
- **Azure SQL Database**

Briefly put, choosing an OLTP service on Azure comes down to deciding on the right SQL option. The level of manageability is a key difference between options, with SQL Server on virtual machines being an **Infrastructure-as-a-Service (IaaS)** solution, while Azure SQL Managed Instance and Azure SQL Database come as **Platform-as-a-Service (PaaS)** solutions. The differences are captured in *Figure 5.4*:

Figure 5.4 – The difference in the level of management between the three cloud-based SQL options

As with any IaaS versus PaaS situation, it comes down to a trade-off between flexibility and management efforts. We will discuss this in more detail shortly.

Let's start with exploring when to use SQL Server on Azure virtual machines.

### SQL Server on Azure virtual machines

As an IaaS solution, SQL Server on VMs provides great flexibility. Compared to the other two Azure SQL options, organizations have their own control over things such as the operating system, the database engine, and **high availability/disaster recovery (HA/DR)**.

In terms of operating systems, SQL Server can run on either Windows Server or Linux Azure virtual machines. On top of this, it is also flexible toward older versions of SQL Server (all the way back to 2008). This allows an organization to easily recreate its current on-premises database landscape in the cloud. Therefore, SQL Server on Azure virtual machines is best suited to lift-and-shift scenarios.

> **Lift-and-shift**
>
> Lift-and-shift is a migration strategy that involves transferring an existing solution (databases, applications, and so on) from one environment to another while trying to keep modifications to a minimum. The objective is to maintain the existing functionality and simplify the migration process, thus reducing the time, effort, and cost involved in migration. This strategy is often used to move workloads from on-premises to the cloud, where they can benefit from increased scalability, reliability, and security.

Having full control over HA/DR means the organization can decide for itself when to start maintenance or patching. Disaster recovery can be facilitated by using **point-in-time restore (PITR)** in **Azure Backup**. This regularly creates a complete database backup along with log backups and differential backups with the option of geo-redundancy, allows for restoration to new databases, and has the possibility of long-term retention of up to ten years.

Furthermore, when using the IaaS SQL Server as an application database, it is possible to have the application hosted on the same host for fast and secure connectivity.

In terms of storage capacity, this option falls in between the two others, with the ability to store up to 256 TB of data per instance.

To summarize, SQL Server on Azure virtual machines is an IaaS solution that excels in database and application migration scenarios, granting great flexibility at the cost of extra management.

### Azure SQL Managed Instance

Azure SQL Managed Instance and Azure SQL Database come as PaaS solutions. Things such as the underlying operating system and HA/DR are outsourced to the cloud provider (Microsoft). Both PaaS solutions feature different deployment options and service tiers.

The SQL Managed Instance deployment options are the following:

- **Single instance**
- **Instance Pool**

A single instance comes as a fully managed service, which makes it a perfect solution for migrating and modernizing existing databases. The number of virtual cores can range anywhere from 4 to 80 **virtual cores (vCores)**, while storage limits depend on the service tier, which will be explained soon.

When working with many smaller SQL server instances, an Instance Pool becomes an interesting option to consider. Instance Pools have a total of between 8 and 80 virtual cores. These cores can then be distributed between instances within the pool. Contrary to a single instance, the Instance Pools allow instances to be created with 2 virtual cores, making them economically viable for smaller SQL servers. In terms of storage, capacity can range from 32 GB all the way up to 8 TB per instance in the pool (apart from 2 and 4 vCore instances, which have a lower upper limit).

*Figure 5.5* provides an example of an Azure SQL Managed Instance Pool:

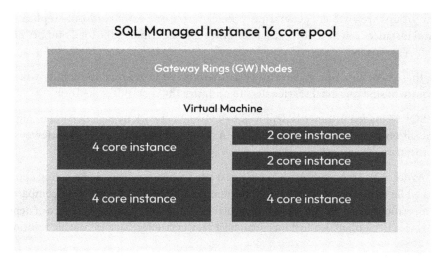

Figure 5.5 – Visual overview of an Azure SQL Managed Instance Pool

Note that instances inside the pool can differ in storage capacity and the number of virtual cores to meet the exact requirements of each migrated database.

As well as the deployment options (single instance or Instance Pool), we will decide on one of the following service tiers:

- **General-purpose**
- **Business-critical**

A single instance can be deployed using either service tier. An Instance Pool requires all instances in that pool to match the service tier of the pool itself. At the time of writing this book, only general-purpose is available for Instance Pools, but both service tiers should be applicable to Instance Pools in the future.

In short, the general-purpose tier is suited to most conventional workloads. Compared to the general-purpose tier, instances with a business-critical service tier will have the following:

- **Lower latency**
- **Faster recovery**
- **Read-only secondary replica**

When failover groups are enabled, general-purpose can have one extra read-only replica, whereas business-critical instances can have two extra read-only replicas, bringing the total number of replicas to two and four respectively.

Nevertheless, these benefits come at an extra cost. Therefore, it is essential to identify which OLTP workloads require business-critical service tiers to optimize the costs of the solution.

Lastly, Azure SQL Managed Instance is deployed in a virtual network by default. When migrating to Azure, this means on-premises servers will require **Azure ExpressRoute** or **VPN Gateway** to access the managed instance.

To conclude, Azure SQL Managed Instances are best used when modernizing existing applications and databases while migrating to the cloud, unburdening a lot of the management compared to the lift-and-shift migrations using an SQL server on virtual machines. With the right choice of deployment options and service tiers, managed instances can be a very cost-effective and reliable solution.

### Azure SQL Database

Azure SQL Database is a second PaaS option for Azure cloud databases, yet this one is more targeted toward application innovation instead of migration.

Compared to the other options, Azure SQL Database is the most scalable solution. It has the option to hyperscale to a capacity limit of 100 TB, instead of the usual 2 TB.

Much like SQL Managed Instance, choices must be made in terms of service tiers and deployment options. Although the naming is different, the deployment options for Azure SQL DB remain roughly the same, which are as follows:

- **Single database**
- **Elastic pool**

The single database will have the aforementioned option to hyperscale and comes with a serverless compute. The latter makes manageability and cost optimization significantly more convenient.

The elastic pool leverages principles of economies of scale. By combining the resources for multiple databases into a pool, fluctuations in usage and capacity can often cancel each other out. Although the approach is different, the benefits stay the same: simple management and easy cost optimization.

Looking at the service tiers, Azure SQL DB has three options:

- General-purpose
- Business-critical
- Hyperscale

The difference between general-purpose and business-critical does not change much compared to SQL Managed Instance. The big difference is the addition of hyperscale.

Next to the increased volume capacity, hyperscale can make rapid database backups and restores (using file snapshots), increase the transaction log throughput, and decrease the commit time per transaction, and it offers the ability to scale multiple read-only replicas and compute resources.

Lastly, Azure SQL DB does not come with native virtual network integration like SQL Managed Instance does, but it can make use of virtual network endpoints.

*Figure 5.6* provides an easy-to-follow flowchart to assist in making the right choice for any given solution:

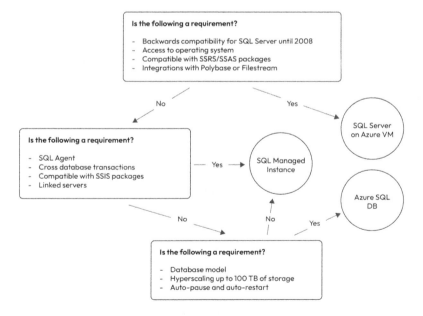

Figure 5.6 – Flowchart to help guide the architect to the right Azure SQL offering

# Azure OLAP services

Online analytical processing is an approach to answering analytical questions efficiently. Analytical questions are often complex, infrequent queries that are run against big data.

OLAP systems were traditionally built using the same SQL databases that OLTP systems were built on. This had several drawbacks. Often a copy of the database had to be created, as building the OLAP system on the database of the OLTP system would increase the load and slow down performance. Moreover, SQL databases only allow structured data to be queried, have rather expensive storage, and can only hold up to 100 TB with hyperscale enabled. Also, SQL databases are not optimized to run complex queries.

Popular choices for modern OLAP systems often perform distributed query execution to deliver fast results for complex analytical queries. They are often built on top of data lakes to allow cost-efficient storage of big data. Apart from structured data, the data lake also allows semi-structured and unstructured data to be stored. Services for OLAP systems are often accompanied by ETL tools to transform data and machine learning capabilities to also ask predictive and perspective questions.

For OLAP scenarios, we will look at the following services:

- **Azure Synapse Analytics**
- **Azure Databricks Lakehouse**
- **Azure Analysis Services**
- **Power BI**
- **CosmosDB analytical store**

## Azure Synapse Analytics

One of the key features of Azure Synapse Analytics is its ability to handle big data. It can ingest and process large volumes of data from various sources, including structured, semi-structured, and unstructured data. This allows organizations to consolidate their data in a single location and perform advanced analytics on it.

Azure Synapse Analytics supports advanced analytics capabilities such as machine learning, which allows organizations to build predictive models and make data-driven decisions. It also provides integration with other Azure services, such as Azure Data Factory, Azure Stream Analytics, and Azure Databricks, to enable end-to-end data processing and analytics workflows.

## Azure Databricks Lakehouse

Azure Databricks Lakehouse is a cloud-based analytics service that combines the best features of a data warehouse and a data lake. It provides a scalable and secure platform for building and managing OLAP systems, allowing organizations to analyze and derive insights from their data.

One of the key features of Azure Databricks Lakehouse is its ability to handle large and complex datasets. It can ingest data from various sources, including structured, semi-structured, and unstructured data, and store it in a centralized data repository that is optimized for analytics. This enables organizations to perform advanced analytics on their data and gain valuable insights.

Azure Databricks Lakehouse also provides integration with other Azure services, such as Azure Synapse Analytics, Azure Data Factory, and Azure Stream Analytics, to enable end-to-end data processing and analytics workflows. It supports advanced analytics capabilities such as machine learning and provides a collaborative environment for data scientists and analysts to work together on data analysis projects.

One of the unique features of Azure Databricks Lakehouse is its ability to provide transactional capabilities on top of the data lake. It provides **Atomicity, Consistency, Isolation, and Durability (ACID)** transactions on the data lake, allowing organizations to perform OLTP workloads and OLAP workloads in a single system.

Overall, Azure Databricks Lakehouse is a powerful and flexible OLAP system that combines the best features of a data warehouse and a data lake. It provides a scalable, secure, and collaborative platform for building and managing advanced analytics systems.

### Azure Analysis Services

Azure Analysis Services is a pay-as-you-go, cloud-based PaaS service that provides a more efficient way of querying data for reporting purposes. It is the successor to the on-premises and license-based SQL Server Analysis Services. The semantic layer, as it's often called, translates underlying data structures into business-oriented data models and includes calculations and aggregations. There are two types of models within the semantic layer: *multidimensional cubes* and *tabular models.*

Multidimensional cubes, also known as OLAP cubes, enable businesses to analyze data across multiple dimensions rather than just view 2D tables in a spreadsheet. For instance, a business unit might request a report on the revenue generated per year by a particular product group in each country. In this scenario, sales data would be aggregated in a revenue cube based on the three dimensions of country, year, and product group:

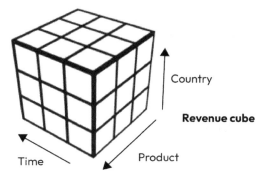

Figure 5.7 – A multidimensional cube, with pre-aggregations on country, product, and time

Although these types of models pre-calculate the aggregations to make reporting faster, loading the pre-aggregations from disk into memory still takes some time. Tabular models have taken over multidimensional models in popularity. They load all data into the memory for fast calculations and aggregations. As memory size is more limiting than disk size, technologies such as **Vertipaq** have been developed by Microsoft to highly compress big data models into memory.

SQL Server Analysis Services primarily supported multidimensional models but later on added support for tabular models. Azure Analysis Services only supports tabular models.

We will dive deeper into the semantic layer in *Chapter 7, The Semantic Layer*.

### Tabular models in Power BI

Just like Azure Analysis Services, Power BI also provides tabular models on top of excellent reporting capabilities. Power BI intends to become a superset of Azure Analysis Services, meaning it will incorporate all the features of Azure Analysis Services. More on this will also be explained in *Chapter 7, The Semantic Layer*, and *Chapter 8, Visualizing Data Using Power BI*.

### Cosmos DB analytical store

The CosmosDB analytical store enables OLAP systems for Azure Cosmos DB without any impact on the transactional workload. It creates a fully isolated column store that can be used to do large-scale analytics. As opposed to Azure Cosmos DB, which is schemaless, the analytical store is schematized to optimize analytical query performance. The column store and the transactional store (which is row-oriented) are stored in different locations within a managed storage account.

## Azure NoSQL services

For NoSQL storage services on Azure, the main options are **Azure Data Lake Storage** and Azure CosmosDB. The latter is a versatile service that can suit many solutions due to its various APIs.

### Azure Data Lake Storage

Azure Data Lake Storage, which was explained in *Chapter 3, Ingesting Data into the Cloud*, is a cheap and scalable option, making it perfect for long-term storage and storage of unstructured data, or as a central storage location for combining data from different data sources and operational silos. For more detailed information, please refer back to *Chapter 3*.

### Azure Cosmos DB

CosmosDB is a highly scalable, globally distributed, multi-model database service on Azure. It is a fully managed service and is mostly seen as low-latency file storage. This makes it ideal to be used for a wide range of applications such as gaming, IoT, and e-commerce.

Cosmos DB focuses on horizontal scalability. This means that data is partitioned or distributed across multiple nodes, with each node being responsible for a subset of the data. This allows for a greater amount of data to be stored and processed while providing better fault tolerance and higher availability, as data can be replicated across multiple nodes.

Using its different APIs, Azure Cosmos DB can support multiple data models, including document, key-value, graph, and column-family data models.

It is most known for its low-latency and high-throughput access to data. Its good partitioning design makes it suitable for read-heavy workloads. However, heavy writes to this service can rapidly become costly due to how the partitioning works. This often results in Cosmos DB finding a perfect fit in some less prevalent use cases requiring either low latency or global scalability.

Cosmos DB provides built-in global distribution, active-active replication, and automatic failover, ensuring that the data is always available and accessible, even in the event of an outage or disaster.

Let us briefly touch on the different Cosmos DB APIs, which are the following:

- Cosmos DB NoSQL API

- Cosmos DB MongoDB API

- Cosmos DB PostgreSQL

- Cosmos DB Apache Cassandra API

- Cosmos DB Apache Gremlin API

- Cosmos DB Table API

Firstly, the **NoSQL API** is the main go-to API for Cosmos DB. This will store data in the document format that characterizes CosmosDB. It allows for data to be queried with SQL (remember, NoSQL stands for *not only SQL*). On top of this, new features will typically be rolled out to the NoSQL API first. This API would be recommended when migrating from databases other than those that have a specific Cosmos DB API, such as MongoDB.

The **MongoDB API** combines the best of both worlds when it comes to migrating data from MongoDB. Users can still make use of the MongoDB ecosystem while benefitting from the scalability, availability, and replicability of Cosmos DB. The **PostgreSQL API** is similar to this, as it combines the open source databases of PostgreSQL with the advantages of Cosmos DB.

The **Cassandra API** provides a scalable datastore based on **Apache Cassandra** using its **Cassandra Query Language** (**CQL**). This stores data in a column-oriented schema and, to put it concisely, also adds CosmosDB benefits to the existing Apache Cassandra ecosystem.

The **Gremlin API**, based on **Apache Gremlin**, is known for its ability to handle graph structures that are typically used in network analysis. Storing data in a graph database is efficient when relationships in the data play a key role in the overall structure. When thinking of use cases here, do not limit yourself to physical networks (such as traffic analysis, molecular analysis, and so on), but also take into account social networks, knowledge graphs, or financial networks.

Lastly, the **Table API** provides a key-value pair storage format and is generally seen as an enhanced version of **Table Storage** in **Azure Storage Accounts**, providing superior performance, latency, and scalability.

## Summary

To summarize, this chapter provided you with valuable skills and lessons related to storage design. We learned how to classify data as structured, semi-structured, or unstructured, which is essential for choosing the right type of storage solution. Next, we determined how the data will be used and covered key concepts such as ACID transactions, SQL and NoSQL databases, and OLAP and OLTP systems. Finally, we learned how to choose which storage service to use in Azure and, in every scenario, whether it requires an OLTP, OLAP, or NoSQL solution. For each of the three, you will have a set of solid and powerful services to choose from.

These skills and lessons are vital for businesses and organizations that manage large amounts of data. By understanding how to classify data and choose the right data serving method, companies can ensure their data platform is efficient, scalable, and capable of supporting their business needs. Choosing the right storage service in Azure can help organizations save costs and improve performance.

Once our data is stored in Azure, we can extract value and insights from it by creating a data warehouse. The next chapter will dive deeper into OLAP systems, the different types of data warehouses, and how to create them with different Azure services.

# Part 3: Data Warehousing and Analytics

In this section, you'll learn what to consider when deciding which data warehousing option will best fit the data platform. You will also learn about scalable and modern techniques of data warehousing in Azure, improving self-service for business users, setting up dashboards that meet business requirements, and performing advanced predictive analytics in the cloud.

This part has the following chapters:

- *Chapter 6, Data Warehousing*
- *Chapter 7, The Semantic Layer*
- *Chapter 8, Visualizing Data Using Power BI*
- *Chapter 9, Advanced Analytics Using AI*

# 6

# Data Warehousing

As businesses collect ever-increasing amounts of data, data warehousing has become a critical component in managing and analyzing data. Cloud-based data warehousing provides a flexible and cost-effective solution for building systems that support data analytics as well as reporting. Here, we'll explore the fundamental concepts of data warehousing, as well as the different approaches to designing a data warehouse.

We will start by discussing the two main approaches to data warehousing: the normalized approach by Bill Inmon (*Inmon, William H. (1992). Building the Data Warehouse. Boston: QED Technical Pub. Group. ISBN 0-89435-404-3. OCLC 24846118*) and the dimensional approach by Ralph Kimball (*Ralph Kimball* and *Margy Ross (26 April 2002). The Data Warehouse Toolkit: The Complete Guide to Dimensional Modeling (Second ed.). Wiley. ISBN 0-471-20024-7*). Inmon's approach emphasizes the importance of data integration and consistency, while Kimball's approach focuses on performance and ease of use. We will dive deeper into these approaches, exploring the different normal forms and dimensions, as well as the star schema, snowflake schema, and **slowly changing dimensions (SCDs)**.

Next, we will shift our focus to building a data warehouse in the cloud. We will explore two popular cloud-based solutions for data warehousing: Azure SQL Database and Synapse. We will discuss how to set up a data warehouse using Synapse dedicated SQL pools and explore the benefits of using a lakehouse with Synapse serverless SQL pools and the medallion architecture.

By the end of this chapter, data architects will have a solid understanding of the concepts and approaches to data warehousing, as well as the practical knowledge to design and build a data warehouse in the cloud. They will be able to make informed decisions on the best approach for their organization and confidently use cloud-based data warehousing solutions.

In this chapter, we're going to cover the following main topics:

- Fundamental concepts of data warehousing
- Approaches to data warehousing
- SCDs
- Building a data warehouse in the cloud

# Fundamental concepts of data warehousing

An (enterprise) **data warehouse**, often abbreviated as **DW** or **DWH**, is a specialized system utilized for analyzing and reporting data. It acts as a centralized hub where data from different sources is consolidated and organized, serving as a vital component of **business intelligence** (**BI**). Businesses need to make informed decisions by learning from data from the past as well as examining present data. To accomplish this, both sets of data are stored in a single location called the data warehouse. Operational systems such as **customer relationship management** (**CRM**) systems (sales) or marketing are often data sources of a data warehouse and may require cleansing and curating before they can be utilized for analysis and reporting.

The design of a data warehouse includes two essential concepts: **extract, transform, and load** (**ETL**) and **extract, load, and transform** (**ELT**). These processes involve extracting data from source systems and transforming it into a data warehouse that acts as a **single source of truth** (**SSOT**) with consistent and qualitative data.

## Database normalization

If the source system is a database, it is often put into a normal form before going into a data warehouse. This process is called database normalization and is a fundamental concept to know about before talking about modeling a data warehouse. Therefore, we will first explain the different normal forms a database can be in.

Database normalization organizes data in a relational database in a way that reduces redundancy (for example, storing the same data in more than one table) and ensures data dependencies make sense (for example, only storing related data in a table). It involves breaking down a database into multiple tables and defining relationships between them. There are several normal forms in database normalization, each with its own set of rules and requirements.

The **first normal form** (**1NF**) requires a database table to follow these rules:

1. Each table holds a set of related data.
2. Every table should have a primary key.
3. No table can have repeating groups.
4. Values stored in a column should be of the same type.
5. All the columns in a table should have unique names.
6. Using row order to convey any information is not allowed.

Let's say we want to create a table of client purchases in a supermarket. Not following 1NF might end up with a table looking like this:

| Client ID | Client Name | Product | Quantity | Product | Quantity | Product | Quantity |
|---|---|---|---|---|---|---|---|
| 142 | Carmen | Onions | 4 | Pasta | 1 | | |
| 389 | Marc | Pasta | One | Tonic | 6 | Coke Zero | 2 |

Table 6.1 – Purchase table not in first normal form

Each row in this table represents a basket of items bought by a client in a supermarket. Although this table holds a set of related data, there are a lot of problems working with this database structure. There is no primary key to uniquely identify a row in the table. A row might be duplicated if one of the clients purchases the exact same items as before. There are repeating (product, quantity) groups in each row, which is not manageable. When a client buys more than three different products, the table schema has to be changed. There are multiple columns with the same name, which leads to ambiguity when selecting a column, and the type of the first **Quantity** column is inconsistent. The column contains both numbers and text, which may cause errors when transforming the data. Changing the table to 1NF gives us the following:

| CheckoutID | ClientID | ClientName | Product | Quantity |
|---|---|---|---|---|
| 1 | 142 | Carmen | Onion | 4 |
| 1 | 142 | Carmen | Pasta | 1 |
| 2 | 389 | Marc | Pasta | 1 |
| 2 | 389 | Marc | Tonic | 6 |
| 2 | 389 | Marc | Coke Zero | 2 |

Table 6.2 – Purchase table in first normal form

The primary key in this table is a composite key, meaning it consists of more than one column—namely, the **CheckoutID** and **Product** columns. Note that the order of the rows does not imply the scan order during the checkout. If we want to convey this information in the table, we should add a separate column.

The **second normal form (2NF)** builds further on 1NF and states the following rules:

- It should be in 1NF
- There should be no partial dependencies

The second rule means each column that isn't (part of) a key must depend on the whole primary key and not just a part of the primary key. Let's say we want to add product categories to our table, as follows:

| CheckoutID | ClientID | ClientName | Product | Product Category | Quantity |
|---|---|---|---|---|---|
| 1 | 142 | Carmen | Onion | Vegetables | 4 |
| 1 | 142 | Carmen | Pasta | Food | 1 |
| 2 | 389 | Marc | Pasta | Food | 1 |
| 2 | 389 | Marc | Tonic | Drinks | 6 |
| 2 | 389 | Marc | Coke Zero | Drinks | 2 |

Table 6.3 – Purchase table not in second normal form

The **Quantity** column depends on the whole primary key as you purchase a quantity of a specific product for a certain **CheckoutID**. However, the **ProductCategory** column depends only on the product and is not specific to a **CheckoutID**. This may lead to all kinds of anomalies. Let's say **Carmen** did not want to buy onions, and the record gets deleted. Now, we've lost the information that onions belong to the **Vegetables product category**. We call this a deletion anomaly. Let's say we update the **ProductCategory** column to include carbs. If by accident we only update one of the **Pasta** rows, we create update anomalies. Let's say we have a new product but there's no record of it as no one bought it yet. This we call an insertion anomaly. To combat this, we split the table into checkout and product tables, as follows:

| CheckoutID | ClientID | ClientName | ProductID | Quantity |
|---|---|---|---|---|
| 1 | 142 | Carmen | 1 | 4 |
| 1 | 142 | Carmen | 2 | 1 |
| 2 | 389 | Marc | 2 | 1 |
| 2 | 389 | Marc | 3 | 6 |
| 2 | 389 | Marc | 4 | 2 |

Table 6.4 – Purchase table in second normal form

A separate product table contains the product categories.

| ProductID | Product | Product-Category |
|---|---|---|
| 1 | Onion | Vegetables |
| 2 | Pasta | Food |
| 3 | Tonic | Drinks |
| 4 | Coke Zero | Drinks |

Table 6.5 – Product table

Note that the `ProductID` column in the checkout table refers to the product foreign table and is therefore considered a foreign key. The `ProductID` column in the product table is a primary key.

The **third normal form** (**3NF**) builds further on 2NF and states the following rules:

- It should be in 2NF

- There should be no transitive dependencies

Transitive dependencies are different from partial dependencies. The second rule means that each column that isn't (part of) a key may not depend on another non-key column, but must depend on nothing but the whole primary key. In our example, the `ClientName` column of the checkout table seems to only depend on the `ClientID` column, which is not the primary key. We should therefore split the table into checkout and client tables, like so:

| CheckoutID | ClientID | ProductID | Quantity |
|------------|----------|-----------|----------|
| 1          | 142      | 1         | 4        |
| 1          | 142      | 2         | 1        |
| 2          | 389      | 2         | 1        |
| 2          | 389      | 3         | 6        |
| 2          | 389      | 4         | 2        |

Table 6.6 – Purchase table in third normal form

Create a separate client table with the **ClientName data**:

| ClientID | ClientName |
|----------|------------|
| 142      | Carmen     |
| 389      | Marc       |

Table 6.7 – Client table

Most databases and also many data warehouses are in 3NF. We will refer to this form throughout the chapter.

There is a slightly stricter version of 3NF called the **Boyce-Codd normal form** (**BCNF**) or 3.5NF. It enforces that each column, non-key or not, should depend on nothing but the entire primary key.

The **fourth normal form** (**4NF**) builds further on 3NF and states the following rules:

1. It should be in BCNF.
2. There should be no multi-valued dependencies (unless they depend on the key).

We call a column A multi-valued dependent on another column B if for a single value of A, multiple values of B exist. Let's say we want to add in which products are sold in which supermarkets. A naïve implementation would change the product table like this:

| ProductID | Product | Product-Category | SupermarketID |
|-----------|---------|------------------|---------------|
| 1 | Onion | Vegetables | 1 |
| 1 | Onion | Vegetables | 2 |
| 2 | Pasta | Food | 1 |
| 2 | Pasta | Food | 2 |
| 3 | Tonic | Drinks | 1 |
| 3 | Tonic | Drinks | 2 |
| 4 | Coke Zero | Drinks | 1 |
| 4 | Coke Zero | Drinks | 2 |

Table 6.8 – Product table not in fourth normal form

Note that the `Product` and `ProductCategory` values of each record are replicated as they are sold in both supermarkets. The `ProductID` value is no longer unique for every row, so the new primary key is (`ProductID`, `SupermarketID`). `ProductID` is multi-value dependency on `SupermarketID`, but `ProductID` is not the key anymore. We fix this by splitting the table, as follows:

| ProductID | Product | Product-Category |
|-----------|---------|------------------|
| 1 | Onion | Vegetables |
| 2 | Pasta | Food |
| 3 | Tonic | Drinks |
| 4 | Coke Zero | Drinks |

Table 6.9 – Product table in fourth normal form

Create a separate table to record which products are sold in which supermarket.

| ProductID | SupermarketID |
|-----------|---------------|
| 1 | 1 |
| 1 | 2 |
| 2 | 1 |
| 2 | 2 |
| 3 | 1 |
| 3 | 2 |
| 4 | 1 |
| 4 | 2 |

Table 6.10 – Supermarket-Product table

The **fifth normal form (5NF)** (or **project-join normal form (PJNF)**) builds further on 4NF and states the following rules:

- It should be in 4NF

- There should be no join dependencies

A join dependency is quite easy to grasp. If we can recreate a table by splitting it and joining the split tables, there is a join dependency. Without join dependencies, we ensure there is no unnecessary duplication of data.

## Data marts versus data warehouses

To avoid some confusion in terminology, let's first explain the difference between a data mart and a data warehouse. Data marts are used in most data warehouse approaches and focus on the data of a specific area, department, or domain of the business. A data warehouse focuses on building an SSOT for all data. A data warehouse can be made up of data marts (bottom-up approach), or data marts can be created from the data warehouse (top-down approach). In either case, data marts are smaller and less complicated than the data warehouse. As they only contain a subset of the data, data marts are often easier and quicker to establish. They are often managed by the departments the data mart focuses on.

The differences between the two can be summarized as follows. In terms of the scope of the data, a data warehouse is focused on an enterprise-wide level, while a data mart has a department-wide scope. The number of subject areas covered in a data warehouse is multiple, whereas, in a data mart, it is limited to a single subject area. The process of building a data warehouse is more challenging, whereas building a data mart is relatively easy. It takes more time to build a data warehouse than a data mart. A data warehouse typically requires a larger amount of memory compared to a data mart, which has limited memory requirements.

## Design methods of data warehouses

A variety of techniques exist for constructing a data warehouse, including bottom-up, top-down, and hybrid. Using the **bottom-up** strategy, the initial step is to generate data marts that are tailored to certain commercial activities to provide analytics for a single business process. Once these data marts are in place, they are then joined together to become a unified data warehouse. To effectively put in place the data warehouse architecture, the **bus matrix** should be employed, which shows which facts and dimensions are shared among two or more data marts. This is important to be able to reuse created tables for new data marts and to know which data marts are impacted by changes to a shared table. An example of this can be seen here:

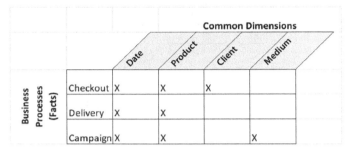

Figure 6.1 – Bus matrix

In contrast, the **top-down** method first builds the complete data warehouse and then derives data marts from it. The data in the data warehouse is stored at the lowest granularity and is normalized, meaning it follows certain rules to ensure the deduplication of data and minimize inconsistencies. Data marts are derived from the data warehouse, tailored to specific departments or business processes.

A **hybrid** method tries to combine the best practices of both the bottom-up and top-down methods. To not invest a lot of time first in building the complete data warehouse, an operational data store is often built first. This contains initial data cleansing and transformations and is updated daily, before permanently storing it in the data warehouse. Just as with the top-down method, the data warehouse is normalized, and data marts can be derived from it.

Both the top-down and bottom-up methods have issues with data changes as the structure of these methods is not flexible or adaptable. When data does not conform, it is cleansed and lost. The data vault method tries to keep all the data all the time by implementing hubs for business keys, links for relationships, and satellites for data changes. In the rest of this chapter, we will only focus on the bottom-up and top-down methods as these are the most popular.

# Data warehouse characteristics

To better understand the different approaches to building a data warehouse, it is best to first understand some characteristics, such as subject orientation, data integration, time-variant data, nonvolatile data, and data granularity, as follows:

| | |
|---|---|
| **Subject orientation** | Refers to structuring data around enterprise-relevant subjects, rather than the database normalization process. Focusing on subjects is useful for reporting and decision-making processes. |
| **Time-variant** | Data in a data warehouse represents a long time horizon, storing historical data for data mining and forecasting purposes. This allows us to find patterns in data over time. |
| **Nonvolatile** | Data is read-only and cannot be created, updated, or deleted, except when required by regulations. |
| **Data integration** | Ensures that data is free from inconsistencies. |

Table 6.11 – Data warehouse characteristics

Additionally, you can aggregate data and perform data virtualization in a data warehouse. Here's what this involves:

- **Aggregation**: Aggregation is an important part of the data warehouse process, allowing for data to be analyzed at various levels of abstraction. Mostly performed in data marts, it allows departments to gain insights into trends and patterns that may not be visible at a more granular level. By beginning analysis at a higher level and then proceeding to lower levels of detail, it is possible to gain a better understanding of the data and its implications. Aggregations in **Structured Query Language** (**SQL**) are often performed by the GROUP BY clause to extract measures such as SUM, MIN, MAX, and so on.

- **Data virtualization**: Data virtualization allows for direct access to data in its original location, meaning there is no need to move or transform the data in order to utilize it. This eliminates compatibility issues and provides real-time access to the most up-to-date information. However, this requires that the connection to the data source remain active at all times, as there is no local copy of the data. Querying external data sources also means latencies may be higher when doing data exploration or analysis. In Azure, data virtualization is often referred to as **PolyBase**.

The following diagram gives an overview of the data virtualization process:

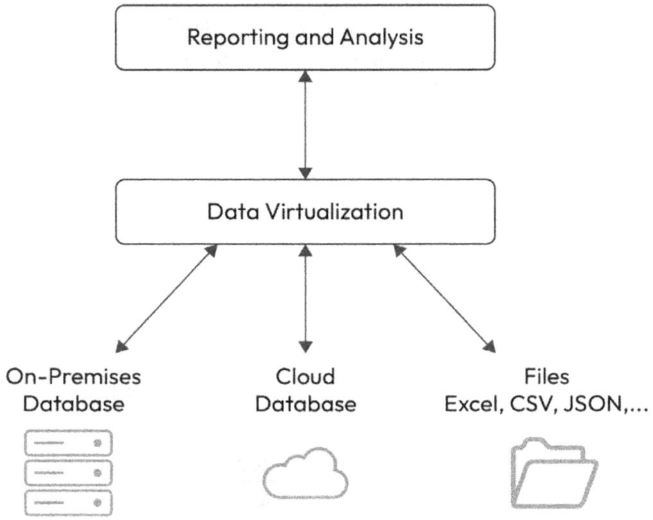

Figure 6.2 – Data virtualization

## Approaches to data warehousing

There are two popular approaches to designing a data warehouse, namely the normalized approach by Bill Inmon and the dimensional approach by Ralph Kimball. In this section, we'll explain the two different approaches further in detail.

### Normalized approach by Bill Inmon

The first approach we would like to introduce is the normalized approach by Bill Inmon. Bill Inmon was one of the first people to define the term *data warehousing* and defined it as a "*subject-oriented, nonvolatile, integrated, time-variant collection of data in support of management's decisions.*" This means a data warehouse focuses on subjects, such as products and customers, and stores historical data for an indefinite time.

The Inmon design approach constructs a logical model for each subject that includes all relevant attributes, relationships, dependencies, and affiliations. This logical model uses a normalized structure (3NF) to minimize data redundancy, which ensures an SSOT and prevents data update irregularities.

It uses a top-down approach, where first, the data warehouse is fully built in its normalized form, and then data marts are built for specific **business units** (**BUs**) to make it easier for them to query data, as depicted in the following diagram:

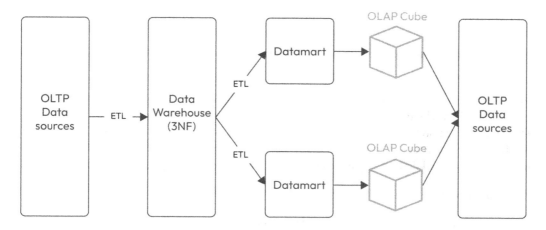

**Normalized approach – Inmon Model**

Figure 6.3 – Normalized approach for data warehousing: Inmon model

## Advantages of the normalized approach

The Inmon method of data warehouse design provides several advantages, including the following:

- Providing an SSSOT for the entire organization, allowing for the integration of all data
- Reducing data redundancy by normalizing the data warehouse, which simplifies the ETL process and reduces the chance of data update errors
- Simplifying business processes by using a logical model that represents detailed business objects
- Offering greater flexibility to adapt to changing business requirements or source data
- Ability to satisfy enterprise-wide reporting requirements

## Disadvantages of the normalized approach

This method has several potential disadvantages, including the following:

- The initial setup and delivery can be really time-consuming as the whole data warehouse has to be built and put in normalized form before deriving data marts from it
- As more tables are added to the data model over time, complexity can increase

- Expertise in data warehousing is necessary, which is both costly and difficult to locate
- Extra ETL processes are required because data marts are established after the creation of the data warehouse
- Effective management of a data warehouse requires skilled experts

## Dimensional approach by Ralph Kimball

Ralph Kimball developed the Kimball model, which takes a bottom-up approach to data warehousing. The first step is to create data marts based on business requirements. Next, the required sources of data are assessed, and an ETL tool is used to extract data and load it into the staging layer in a relational database. Once data is available in the data warehouse staging layer, data is loaded into a denormalized dimensional data warehouse model. This model separates data into two categories: a fact table for numerical transactional data and a dimension table for reference information that supports facts.

### Dimension tables

Dimension tables serve as a way to describe different business entities, including people, places, products, and dates in a data warehouse. Such tables consist of attribute columns for each entity, such as first name, last name, email address, and postal address for a customer entity. Each row in a dimension table is uniquely identified by a key column, which could be a surrogate key assigned by the data warehouse or a natural key that is used in the source system. A surrogate key is a system-generated unique ID assigned to each row in a dimension table within a data warehouse. This surrogate key is usually an increasing integer number, unique to the dimension table, and is created specifically for the data warehouse. An alternate key in a dimension table is typically a natural or business key that is used to identify a specific instance of an entity in the transactional source system. This could be a product code or a customer ID, for example.

In addition to entity-specific dimension tables, a data warehouse commonly includes a time dimension table. The purpose of this table is to allow data analysts to aggregate data over time intervals. The granularity of the time dimension can vary widely, depending on the needs of the analysis. For example, the lowest level of granularity could be times, dates, or even more specific intervals such as milliseconds or nanoseconds.

To ensure the time dimension table is useful for analysis, it must cover the entire time span for any related events recorded in a fact table. This requires having a record for every interval at the appropriate granularity level. By including a time dimension table in a data warehouse, analysts can easily analyze data over time and identify trends or patterns in the data.

## *Fact tables*

A fact table stores data related to specific business processes, such as sales or inventory. It contains columns that store numeric data, which can be aggregated using different dimensions, such as time, location, or product. Along with these numeric columns, fact tables also contain key columns that link the fact table to the corresponding dimension tables. The key columns in the fact table reference the unique keys in the related dimension tables, enabling efficient querying and analysis of the data.

### Star schema

Transactional databases typically use normalization to minimize redundancy. However, in dimensional data warehousing, the data in dimension tables is usually denormalized to simplify data querying by reducing the number of joins required. At the core of the dimensional data warehousing approach is the star schema, which involves a fact table and several dimensional tables. Using Kimball dimensional modeling, multiple star schemas can be constructed to meet different reporting requirements. The star schema structure, presented in the following diagram, provides the benefit of fast query processing for small dimension-table queries:

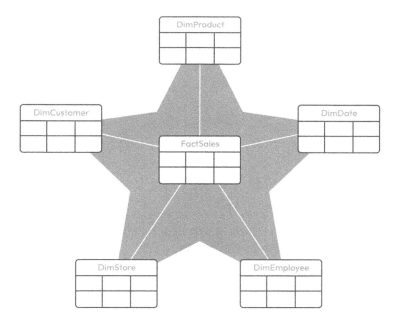

Figure 6.4 – Star schema

In cases where a dimension has a large number of hierarchical attribute levels or when some attributes can be shared by multiple dimensions, using a snowflake schema may be a more suitable approach. A snowflake schema is a variation of the star schema that applies some normalization to the dimension tables, resulting in a more complex but more flexible structure, as depicted here:

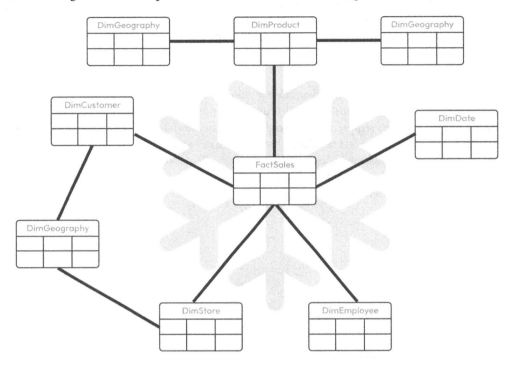

Figure 6.5 – Snowflake schema

The Kimball approach to the data warehouse life cycle involves integrating data by using conformed data dimensions. This involves various fact tables sharing the same dimension table, ensuring that a certain data entity is used consistently over all fact tables.

To support this approach, the Kimball methodology also utilizes the bus matrix, which records facts as rows and dimensions as columns. The matrix shows the construction of star schemas and their usage by different BUs to give priority to which (shared) entities to create first.

Another important aspect of the Kimball approach is the use of conformed facts, which are separately implemented data marts that follow a robust architecture, as illustrated here:

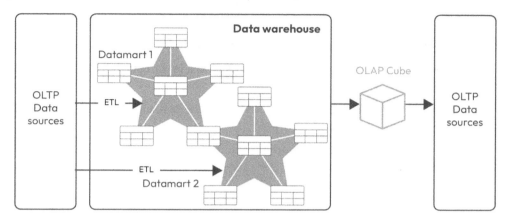

**Dimensional approach - Kimball Model**

Figure 6.6 – Dimensional approach for data warehousing: Kimball model

### Advantages of the Kimball approach

The Kimball data warehousing concept has several key advantages, including the following:

- Dimensional modeling, which is used in the Kimball approach, is quick to implement because it does not involve normalization, resulting in a swift initial construction of a data warehouse.

- A star schema, which is denormalized, is easy to understand for most data operators. This simplified structure facilitates querying and analysis. (Examples of denormalization are having multiple levels of product categories in the product dimension table or having a redundant amount column in the sales fact table, multiplying the unit price and quantity columns, to make querying faster and more suited for reporting purposes.)

- The Kimball approach is built bottom-up per BU, rather than enterprise-wide, resulting in a smaller data warehouse system footprint. As a result, it takes up less space, making management simpler. It also requires a smaller team of data warehouse designers and builders.

**Disadvantages of the Kimball approach**

The Kimball data warehousing design concept has some drawbacks that should be considered, such as the following:

- The idea of an SSOT can be lost as data warehouses are built bottom-up

- With a denormalization technique, redundant data is seen in the data warehouse, which may lead to irregularities and inconsistencies

- The performance of the Kimball architecture may be impacted by adding columns to fact tables as these tables tend to have a lot of rows

- Since the Kimball model uses a bottom-up methodology, it may not be able to handle enterprise-wide requirements

# SCDs

In data warehousing, an SCD is used to manage infrequent changes to the values of a business entity over time, as opposed to changes that occur on a set schedule. Star schema design theory defines various types of SCDs, with *Type 1* and *Type 2* being the most common. In practice, a dimension table may support a combination of SCD types, such as *Type 3* and *Type 6*, for tracking historical changes. Understanding the differences between these SCD types can be useful for designing an effective data warehousing solution.

## Type 1 SCD

A Type 1 SCD design approach updates the dimension table with the most recent changes every time updates in the sources are seen. This method is typically used for storing supplementary values such as email addresses or company names of customers. If a customer's contact information is altered, an update will be made to the dimension table to reflect the changes. The key of the table, such as `CustomerID`, will remain unchanged, ensuring that links in the fact table will point to the updated customer record, as follows:

| CustomerID | FirstName | Email | Company | InsertDate | ModifiedDate |
|---|---|---|---|---|---|
| 142 | Carmen | `carmen@hotmail.com` | Lemworks | 2021-06-01 | 2023-03-26 |
| 389 | Marc | `marc@hotmail.com` | Bally's | 2022-02-10 | 2023-03-26 |

Table 6.12 – Customer table before any changes

Let's see how the table changes in a type 1 SCD after a customer records is updated.

| CustomerID | FirstName | Email | Company | InsertDate | ModifiedDate |
|---|---|---|---|---|---|
| 142 | Carmen | carmen@hotmail.com | Lemworks | 2021-06-01 | 2023-03-26 |
| 389 | Marc | marc@hotmail.com | Bally's and sons | 2022-02-10 | 2023-03-28 |

Table 6.13 – Customer table after change as a type 1 SCD

## Type 2 SCD

A Type 2 SCD allows for tracking updates in dimensions over time by creating a new row for each version. Since the source system often lacks versioning, the data warehouse load process must detect and manage these changes. To accomplish this, a surrogate key is used to uniquely identify each version of the dimension member, while additional columns, such as `StartDate`, `EndDate`, and `IsCurrent`, provide information on the validity and currency of each version. By assigning an empty end date or a specific "`current`" flag to the most recent version, users can easily filter for the latest data, as shown here:

| ID | CustomerID | FirstName | Company | StartDate | EndDate | IsCurrent |
|---|---|---|---|---|---|---|
| 1 | 142 | Carmen | Lemworks | 2021-06-01 | 2023-03-26 | True |
| 2 | 389 | Marc | Bally's | 2022-02-10 | 2023-03-26 | True |

Table 6.14 – Customer table before any changes

Let's see how the table changes in a type 2 SCD after a customer records is updated.

| ID | CustomerID | FirstName | Company | StartDate | EndDate | IsCurrent |
|---|---|---|---|---|---|---|
| 1 | 142 | Carmen | Lemworks | 2021-06-01 | 9999-12-31 | True |
| 2 | 389 | Marc | Bally's | 2022-02-10 | 2023-03-27 | False |
| 3 | 389 | Marc | Bally's and sons | 2023-03-28 | 9999-12-31 | True |

Table 6.15 – Customer table after change as a type 2 SCD

It is crucial to understand that in scenarios where the source data doesn't keep track of versioning, a data warehouse can become the primary system to track changes. When a data warehouse is updated, the existing data must be preserved while changes are detected and recorded. This involves updating the `EndDate` value of the current record and inserting a new record with a `StartDate` value corresponding to the previous `EndDate` value. To retrieve the right dimension record, related facts need to use a time-based lookup.

## Type 3 SCD

A Type 3 SCD is a way of tracking changes to a single key instance of a dimension table over time. Instead of adding extra rows for each change, as in a Type 2 SCD, two columns are used to store the current and previous/original values of the member. This approach is not typically used for multiple members in the same table but is often combined with Type 1 or Type 2 SCDs to provide a more comprehensive history of the dimension's changes. You can see an example of this here:

| CustomerID | FirstName | Current-Company | Original-Company | InsertDate | ModifiedDate |
|---|---|---|---|---|---|
| 142 | Carmen | Lemworks | Lemworks | 2021-06-01 | 2023-03-26 |
| 389 | Marc | Bally's | Bally's | 2022-02-10 | 2023-03-26 |

Table 6.16 – Customer table before any changes

Let's see how the table changes in a type 3 SCD after a customer records is updated.

| CustomerID | FirstName | Current- Company | Original-Company | InsertDate | ModifiedDate |
|---|---|---|---|---|---|
| 142 | Carmen | Lemworks | Lemworks | 2021-06-01 | 2023-03-26 |
| 389 | Marc | Bally's and sons | Bally's | 2022-02-10 | 2023-03-28 |

Table 6.17 – Customer table after change as a type 3 SCD

## Type 6 SCD

A Type 6 SCD is a combination of Types 1, 2, and 3 SCDs. When a change is made to a Type 2 member, a new row is created with the appropriate StartDate and EndDate values. In contrast to the other types, the Type 6 design stores the current value in all versions of the entity, allowing for easy reporting of either the current or historical value. For example, the Type 6 design would split the Company column into CurrentCompany and HistoricalCompany. The CurrentCompany column will always display the most recent value, while the HistoricalCompany column will show the company that was valid between the StartDate and EndDate. In the same customer record, the CurrentCompany column will always contain the latest company value, while the HistoricalCompany column works similarly to the Company field in the Type 2 SCD example. Here's an example of a Type 6 SCD:

| ID | CustomerID | FirstName | Current-Company | Historical-Company | StartDate | EndDate | IsCurrent |
|---|---|---|---|---|---|---|---|
| 1 | 142 | Carmen | Lemworks | Lemworks | 2021-06-01 | 2023-03-26 | True |
| 2 | 389 | Marc | Bally's | Bally's | 2022-02-10 | 2023-03-26 | True |

Table 6.18 – Customer table before any changes

Let's see how the table changes in a Type 6 SCD after a customer records is updated.

| ID | CustomerID | FirstName | Current-Company | Historical-Company | StartDate | EndDate | IsCurrent |
|---|---|---|---|---|---|---|---|
| 1 | 142 | Carmen | Lemworks | Lemworks | 2021-06-01 | 2023-03-26 | True |
| 2 | 389 | Marc | Bally's and sons | Bally's | 2022-02-10 | 2023-03-28 | False |
| 3 | 389 | Marc | Bally's and sons | Bally's and sons | 2022-02-10 | 2023-03-28 | True |

Table 6.19 – Customer table after change as a type 6 SCD

# Building a data warehouse in the cloud

Data warehouses can be built with different Azure services. Traditional data warehouses used to be built on-premises with databases in SQL servers. When moving to the cloud, this changed to either SQL server on Azure VMs (**Infrastructure as a Service**, or **IaaS**) or Azure SQL Database or Managed Instance (**Platform as a Service**, or **PaaS**), depending on how Microsoft-managed the database needed to be. Building SQL databases feel very familiar to building data warehouses as they are also often used operationally as a backend for applications. However, data warehouses are built for analytical purposes, not operational purposes, and thus have different needs, as outlined here:

- Queries against operational databases are often frequent and simple in nature (small reads and writes), whereas queries against analytical data warehouses are infrequent and complex in nature (often with lots of joins and aggregates).

- Data warehouses are often nonvolatile in nature and store as much data as possible for an indefinite time. This can become very expensive very quickly when using SQL databases, which calls for a more cheap storage layer.

- All data can hold value and analytical insights for a data warehouse, independent of how structured the data is. SQL databases can only hold structured data.

Therefore, modern data warehousing was introduced. It often uses distributed compute engines, such as Spark clusters or SQL pools, and uses a data lake as a storage layer. A data warehouse built on top of a lake is often called a lakehouse. The **Azure Data Lake Storage Gen2** (**ADLS Gen2**) service combines the benefits of Azure Blob storage (which is the cheapest storage layer in Azure) with the hierarchical namespaces of the first generation of Azure Data Lake for big data analytics. A data lake can also hold unstructured (images, text) and semi-structured (CSV, JSON) files.

In this chapter, we'll show how to create a traditional data warehouse with Azure SQL Database as well as a modern data warehouse with Synapse serverless and dedicated SQL pools.

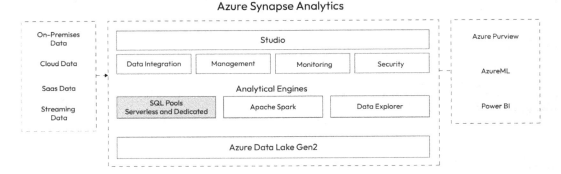

Figure 6.7 – Azure Synapse Analytics: architecture diagram

## Using Azure SQL Database

A data warehouse is often built in three layers, namely the **staging layer**, the **enriched layer**, and the **curated layer**. The staging layer is the initial landing area for incoming data from various source systems. Its primary purpose is to store raw or minimally processed data in its original form. It acts as a temporary storage area before further processing, but can also act as a backup of the source data.

The enriched layer is an intermediate layer wherein data is processed, transformed, and enriched with additional information. It involves activities such as data cleansing, data quality checks, data integration, data consolidation, and the application of business rules or calculations. This layer helps improve the quality, consistency, and usefulness of the data before it is loaded into the curated layer.

The curated layer, also known as the presentation layer, translates the data structures into business-oriented processes. This layer involves activities such as data modeling, data aggregation, and data summarization for efficient querying and analysis.

In a traditional data warehouse, these layers are schemas of the database (for example, `stg.table` for a staging table). Schemas can be created with the SQL statements illustrated here:

```
CREATE SCHEMA stg;
GO
CREATE SCHEMA enr;
GO
CREATE SCHEMA cur;
GO
```

Next, tables can be created for the staging layer. We might have customer information coming from one system that we want to merge with customer address data coming from another system. Ingesting this data from the source systems into the Azure SQL Database data warehouse can be done with Azure Data Factory. In SQL Server, this was often done with **SQL Server Integration Services (SSIS)** packages. In Azure SQL Managed Instance, you could use cross-database queries if the source systems were databases in the same instance, as follows:

```
CREATE TABLE stg.System1DimCustomer
(
    CustomerKey INT IDENTITY NOT NULL,
    CustomerName NVARCHAR(80) NOT NULL,
    EmailAddress NVARCHAR(50) NULL,
    Phone NVARCHAR(25) NULL
);
GO
CREATE TABLE stg.System2DimCustomer
(
    CustomerKey INT IDENTITY NOT NULL,
    StreetAddress NVARCHAR(100),
    City NVARCHAR(20),
    PostalCode NVARCHAR(10),
    CountryRegion NVARCHAR(20)
);
GO
```

It's often easiest to use an IDENTITY column to autogenerate an incrementing surrogate key (otherwise, you need to generate unique keys every time you load data).

In the enriched layer, we'll combine these two tables to form the complete customer dimension table of the data warehouse, like so:

```
SELECT  S1C.CustomerKey,
    S1C.CustomerName,
    S1C.EmailAddress,
    S1C.Phone,
    S2C.StreetAddress,
    S2C.City,
    S2C.PostalCode,
    S2C.CountryRegion
INTO enr.DimCustomer
FROM stg.System1DimCustomer AS S1C
FULL OUTER JOIN stg.System2DimCustomer AS S2C
    ON S1C.CustomerKey = S2C.CustomerKey
```

In the enriched layer, data quality issues and inconsistencies are also addressed. For instance, if we have a sales table, we might convert all sales amounts to the same currency, or deal with negative amounts, which could be returns or discounts.

In the curated layer, we might aggregate some sales statistics over different fiscal years and product groups, as follows:

```
SELECT date.FiscalYear,
product.ProductGroup,
sales.Revenue
INTO cur.FactYearSales
FROM enr.FactSales AS sales
LEFT JOIN enr.DimDate AS date
      ON date.DateKey = sales.DateKey
LEFT JOIN enr.DimProduct AS product
      ON product.ProductKey = sales.ProductKey
GROUP BY date.FiscalYear, product.ProductGroup
```

Let's move on to using Synapse serverless SQL pools.

## Using Synapse serverless SQL pools

Synapse is an example of a modern data warehouse that is built on top of a data lake (ADLS Gen2), which we also call a lakehouse. The idea is to separate the storage and compute layer, storing the data in an optimized file format in the lake and querying it with a distributed query engine. Synapse offers two distributed query engines for data warehousing: Spark clusters and SQL pools. SQL pools allow people coming from traditional data warehousing to use their SQL skills but execute them in a distributed way on a pool of SQL nodes. Even though Spark also offers execution of SQL statements via Spark SQL, SQL pools offer a more familiar experience with Synapse SQL, which can be considered a limited version of **Transact-SQL** (**T-SQL**) (the Microsoft SQL flavor used in SQL Server and Azure SQL services).

SQL pools come in two variants, namely serverless and dedicated. The following table notes the key differences between the two variants:

|  | **Serverless SQL pools** | **Dedicated SQL pools** <br><br>**(Formerly known as Azure SQL Data Warehouse)** |
| --- | --- | --- |
| **Resources (nodes)** | Shared | Reserved |
| **Scaling of compute nodes** | Automatic | Manual |
| **Operations** | Query data from the data lake <br><br>(Write to the data lake but can't perform INSERT and UPDATE T-SQL statements) | Query data from the data lake and ingest data into compute nodes <br><br>(Write to compute nodes with INSERT and UPDATE T-SQL statements) |
| **Cost** | $5 per TB queried (cheaper) | Fixed price; predictable (but more expensive) |

Table 6.20 – Comparison between serverless and dedicated SQL pools

Resources in serverless SQL pools are shared with other Microsoft customers, meaning there are some limitations on the usage of the compute nodes. For instance, queries can't run longer than 30 minutes. With dedicated SQL pools, you reserve the resources. Both SQL pools are distributed computes, but with serverless SQL pools, the scaling of the compute nodes is managed by Microsoft. With dedicated SQL pools, you have 1 to 60 SQL nodes at your disposal. As Synapse uses a data lake as the storage layer, storing operations such as INSERT and UPDATE SQL statements are not normally allowed. With dedicated SQL pools, the data is ingested and distributed across the compute nodes to still allow INSERT and UPDATE SQL statements. This is managed by the **Data Migration Service (DMS)**.

In *Figures 6.8* and *6.9*, you can find the architectures of both serverless and dedicated SQL pools. As they are distributed compute engines, both have a control node to optimize and coordinate parallel queries and compute nodes to do the actual parallel processing. In serverless SQL pools, the control node splits a SQL query into smaller, independently runnable queries that can execute in parallel on the compute nodes. In dedicated SQL pools, the control node transforms the SQL query into queries that run against each distribution in parallel:

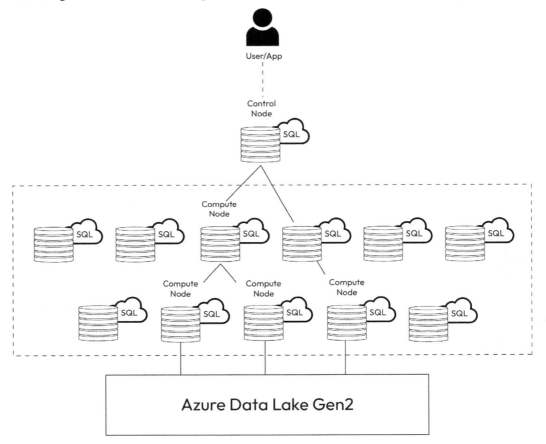

Figure 6.8 – Serverless SQL pool architecture

The dedicated SQL pool architecture uses dedicated compute nodes and a **data movement service (DMS)**.

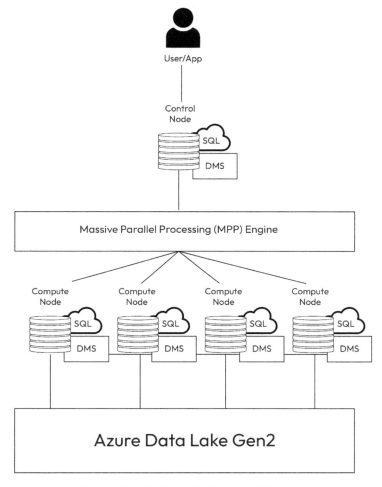

Figure 6.9 – Dedicated SQL pool architecture

The three layers of a traditional data warehouse (staging, enriched, and curated) are kept in the modern data warehouse but stored on the lake (hence the name *lakehouse*) and rebranded as the bronze, silver, and gold layers, as coined by the medallion architecture from Databricks.

As serverless SQL pools cannot use INSERT or UPDATE statements, they write straight to the data lake. This can be done by using Synapse pipelines, which run a (scheduled) SQL script on a serverless SQL pool (with, for instance, the Script activity) to transform the data and sink it to a folder (named bronze, silver, or gold) in the data lake to move the data to the next layer in the lakehouse.

Data can be queried directly from the lake with serverless SQL pools using the OPENROWSET command. In this example, we will query a JSON file from the bronze layer. Let's assume the JSON file has the following format:

```
{
    "customer_key":1,
    "customer_name":"John Doe",
    "email_address":"john.doe@hotmail.com",
    "phone":"+32456789012"
}
```

Then, we can use the OPENROWSET command as follows to query the JSON file with SQL:

```
select JSON_VALUE(doc, '$.customer_key') AS CustomerKey,
    JSON_VALUE(doc,'$.customer_name') AS CustomerName,
    JSON_VALUE(doc, '$.email_address') AS EmailAddress,
    JSON_VALUE(doc, '$.phone') AS Phone,
    doc
from openrowset(
        bulk 'https://datalakename.blob.core.windows.net/public/
bronze/customers.json',
        format = 'csv',
        fieldterminator ='0x0b',
        fieldquote = '0x0b'
    ) with (doc nvarchar(max)) as rows
```

The JSON file is treated as a CSV file with fieldquote and a 0x0b determinator.

## Using Synapse dedicated SQL pools

Dedicated SQL pools allow the usage of INSERT and UPDATE T-SQL statements as with relational databases, but also have a lot of dissimilarities.

### *Data integrity constraints*

Unlike other relational database systems such as SQL Server, Azure Synapse Analytics dedicated SQL pools do not support foreign keys and unique constraints. This implies that jobs utilized for loading data must preserve the uniqueness and referential integrity of keys without relying on the table definitions in the database to perform these functions.

### *Indexes*

Azure Synapse Analytics dedicated SQL pools allow clustered indexes, such as those used in SQL Server, but the default index type is a clustered columnstore. This index type offers a notable performance improvement when querying significant amounts of data in a typical data warehouse schema and should be used whenever feasible. Nevertheless, some tables may contain data types that cannot be included in a clustered columnstore index, such as VARBINARY(MAX). In such cases, a clustered index can be utilized instead.

## Distribution

Azure Synapse Analytics dedicated SQL pools utilize a **massively parallel processing (MPP)** architecture that is different from the **symmetric multiprocessing (SMP)** architecture used in most **online transaction processing (OLTP)** database systems. In an MPP system, data in a table is distributed for processing across a pool of nodes. Azure Synapse Analytics supports three types of distribution, namely hash, round-robin, and replicated. **Hash** distribution assigns rows to a compute node based on a deterministic hash value calculated for a specified column. **Round-robin** distribution distributes rows evenly across all compute nodes. **Replicated** distribution stores a copy of the table on each compute node. The choice of distribution method depends on the table type.

To prevent the movement of data while joining distributed fact tables, use replicated distribution for smaller dimension tables. If the tables are too big to fit on each compute node, utilize hash distribution. For distributing fact tables across compute nodes, use hash distribution with a clustered columnstore index. For evenly distributing data across compute nodes when ingesting, use round-robin distribution for staging tables.

Here is an example of a code to create customer dimension table, created for dedicated SQL pools. The distribution and index strategies are defined with the WITH clause:

```
CREATE TABLE dbo.DimCustomer
(
    CustomerKey INT IDENTITY NOT NULL,
    CustomerAlternateKey NVARCHAR(15) NULL,
    CustomerName NVARCHAR(80) NOT NULL,
    EmailAddress NVARCHAR(50) NULL,
    Phone NVARCHAR(25) NULL,
    StreetAddress NVARCHAR(100),
    City NVARCHAR(20),
    PostalCode NVARCHAR(10),
    CountryRegion NVARCHAR(20)
)
WITH
(
    DISTRIBUTION = REPLICATE,
    CLUSTERED COLUMNSTORE INDEX
);
```

## Summary

In this chapter on data warehousing in the cloud, we covered key concepts and approaches to data warehousing, including the normalized approach by Bill Inmon and the dimensional approach by Ralph Kimball. We also explored building a data warehouse in the cloud using Azure SQL Database and Synapse SQL, including dedicated pools and serverless pools with the medallion architecture.

By the end of this chapter, readers should have a solid understanding of the different data warehousing approaches and the benefits of building a data warehouse in the cloud. They should also be able to build a data warehouse using Azure SQL Database and Synapse SQL. These skills are essential for data architects looking to design and implement data warehousing solutions in the cloud.

The semantic layer is the next logical step in building a data platform after the data warehouse. It enables users to easily access and analyze data without needing to understand the complex underlying data model. The data warehouse stores data in a structured format that is optimized for querying and reporting, but the semantic layer adds a layer of abstraction that makes it easier for non-technical users to access and use the data. The semantic layer also enables users to define their own business terms and hierarchies, which makes it easier to analyze and report on the data in a way that is meaningful to the business to improve productivity and decision-making.

# 7
# The Semantic Layer

Positioned after the data has been modeled in a data warehouse or lakehouse, the semantic layer acts as a performance-enhancing data querying layer for reporting, offering a more efficient and business-friendly view of the data. By employing aggregations, calculations, and business-oriented terms and concepts, the semantic layer simplifies the complexity of technical data structures and caters to the needs of business users. The end result is a well-defined data model that effectively translates the underlying data structures of the warehouse or lakehouse into business-oriented terms. The value of this is to allow reports to more quickly query and visualize data, as well as allow business people to understand the data structures and extract insights from them.

In this chapter, we're going to cover the following main topics:

- Multidimensional versus tabular models
- The VertiPaq engine for tabular models
- Modes in tabular models
- Tools for the semantic layer

You'll learn that a semantic layer can be implemented in two ways, with multidimensional models or tabular models. Tabular models try to fit the semantic layer in memory instead of on disk (like multi-dimensional models), for which a compression engine called the VertiPaq engine is deployed. There are two different ways to connect to data sources in tabular models; the data can be copied to the semantic layer, or the underlying data sources can be queried. Finally, we'll talk about Microsoft's tools that can be used to build the semantic layer, both on-premises as well as in the cloud (Azure).

# Multidimensional versus tabular models

The semantic layer can be constructed using two different approaches: multi-dimensional models and tabular models. Multi-dimensional models, which represent an earlier technique, involve the creation of what are known as **OLAP cubes**. These cubes are designed to capture and express the multidimensional nature of the underlying data. To better understand this concept, one can envision an extension of a two-dimensional table in a spreadsheet, where data can be aggregated across not just two axes but multiple dimensions.

To illustrate the practical application of multi-dimensional models, let's consider a scenario where a data warehouse contains detailed purchase records at the lowest level of granularity. The CEO of the organization wants to translate this data into a structure that allows them to report on revenue trends per country per product. In this case, a multidimensional cube would be created, aggregating the purchase data across three dimensions: **Product**, **Country**, and **Time**. The resulting aggregated data would then be stored on disk in a multidimensional database to be used for reporting purposes:

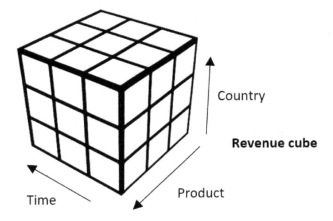

Figure 7.1 – A multidimensional or OLAP cube

Tabular models have emerged as a more modern approach to building a semantic layer. Unlike traditional methods that involve persisting pre-calculated aggregations and calculations on disk, tabular models embrace a different strategy by persisting the entire data model in memory.

In tabular models, the individual rows of data are stored at their lowest level of granularity, ensuring that every piece of information is readily accessible. This enables efficient in-memory processing, allowing for faster data calculations and aggregations. Rather than relying on disk-based operations, the data is manipulated and consolidated in memory, resulting in significant performance improvements.

However, since memory capacity is often limited compared to the storage capacity of disk-based systems, tabular models employ a compression engine known as VertiPaq. This powerful engine optimizes the data model, employing various techniques to compress the data and ensuring that it can fit within the available memory space. Through the VertiPaq engine's compression capabilities, tabular models can efficiently store and manage large volumes of data, maximizing the utilization of in-memory resources.

With data residing in memory, operations such as calculations, aggregations, and queries can be executed rapidly, delivering near-instantaneous results. This real-time processing capability enables businesses to obtain valuable insights and make informed decisions without enduring the delays associated with traditional disk-based operations.

Let's consider the same example where a CEO wants to report on purchase trends across all countries and products. Instead of persisting the aggregation in a multidimensional database like with multidimensional models, tabular models will calculate these aggregations in memory. Let's take a look at the following table as an example of purchases:

| Purchase ID | Country | Product | Revenue |
|---|---|---|---|
| 1 | Belgium | Product A | $13.00 |
| 2 | Ireland | Product B | $20.00 |
| 3 | Belgium | Product B | $7.00 |
| 4 | Ireland | Product B | $10.00 |
| 5 | Ireland | Product A | $15.00 |

Table 7.1 – Purchase table

When reporting, this table is loaded in memory, keeping the purchases at the lowest level of granularity. If we report on the Country column, only unique countries are shown, as follows:

| Country |
|---|
| Belgium |
| Ireland |

Table 7.2 – Unique countries

When adding the **Revenue** column to the report, the report will sum the revenue for each unique country in memory, as shown in *Table 7.3*. This is done by performing an aggregation query to the in-memory database. Queries can, for instance, be written with **Data Analysis Expressions (DAX)**. In the same way as described before, we can also report on the revenue per product.

| Country | Revenue |
|---|---|
| Belgium | $20.00 |
| Ireland | $45.00 |

Table 7.3 – Summarized revenue per country

Depending on the connection to the underlying data sources, the query execution will be different. Please refer to the *Modes in tabular models* section to see a detailed explanation of how the query is executed.

As mentioned earlier, tabular models try to fit the semantic layer in memory. The memory size or RAM of a device is often way smaller than the disk size, thus there is a need for a compression engine to fit everything in memory. This leads us to introduce the VertiPaq engine.

## The VertiPaq engine for tabular models

The VertiPaq engine is an in-memory database engine that is responsible for storing the data model in memory. This engine leverages advanced compression algorithms and memory management techniques to fit the data model in memory:

- **Columnar compression**: VertiPaq stores data in a columnar format, where each column is compressed independently. This allows for efficient compression based on the characteristics of the data in each column. Columnar compression eliminates redundant values and exploits data patterns within a column, resulting in significant space savings.

- **Hash or dictionary encoding**: VertiPaq uses dictionary encoding to compress repetitive values within a column. It creates a dictionary that maps unique values to numeric identifiers, then replaces the actual values with these compact identifiers. As a result, the storage required for repeated values is greatly reduced.

- **Run-length encoding**: This technique is used to compress sequences of repeated values within a column. Instead of storing each individual value, VertiPaq stores the value once and represents subsequent repetitions as a range or count. Run-length encoding is particularly effective for columns with long sequences of repeated values.

By storing data in columns rather than rows, the VertiPaq engine can efficiently aggregate and filter data (from DAX queries, for instance), enabling fast and interactive data exploration.

## Modes in tabular models

By default, tabular models use an **Import mode** to load data into memory. An ETL tool such as **Power Query** extracts the data from data sources, transforms it, and loads it into memory. Afterward, DAX queries can be performed against the in-memory database to calculate and aggregate the data. When tabular models query data residing in memory, processing can be very fast, but the data also needs to be refreshed with the ETL tool every now and then to reflect the most recent changes.

**DirectQuery mode** is very different from Import mode. Queries are run against the underlying data sources instead of the in-memory database. This means the data is always up-to-date and no refreshes of the in-memory database need to be scheduled, but latencies are higher, meaning performance is worse. Another benefit of DirectQuery mode is that the data model can grow beyond the memory size limits as no copy of the data is kept in memory.

When performing a DAX query against a tabular model, a formula engine first processes the request and creates a query plan. Whenever the query plan needs to get data from the tabular model, the storage engine is called. If the data comes from a data source using Import mode, VertiPaq is used to get the data from memory. If the data source uses DirectQuery mode, the query is forwarded directly to the original data source for processing. For example, DAX queries will be translated to SQL syntax to run against SQL databases. *Figure 7.2* depicts how DAX queries are executed:

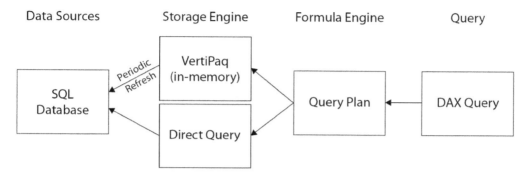

Figure 7.2 – DAX query execution

## Tools for the semantic layer

There are several different tools for implementing the semantic layer, as follows:

- **SQL Server Analysis Services (SSAS)**: SSAS is part of the SQL Server services. It is primarily deployed on-premises, meaning it is hosted within an organization's local infrastructure. SSAS offers a robust and scalable platform for building multidimensional and tabular models. Initially, only multidimensional models were supported, but due to popular demand, tabular model support was added later. Multidimensional models are designed for complex analytical scenarios and support features such as hierarchies, calculated members, and advanced aggregation capabilities. Tabular models, on the other hand, provide a simpler and more intuitive approach to data modeling, allowing users to create analytical models using tables and relationships. SSAS also includes advanced features such as data mining and data visualization.

  The following architecture diagram (*Figure 7.3*) shows a data platform using SSAS as the semantic layer. Various source systems, often OLTP databases that serve as a backend for apps, would be combined in a data warehouse via **SQL Server Integration Services (SSIS)** packages on an SQL server. The data warehouse would then be modeled into a multidimensional data warehouse with SSAS and stored on disk. **SQL Server Reporting Services (SSRS)** would visualize the OLAP cubes in the multidimensional data warehouse via paginated reports. The upside of an on-premises architecture is that you have full control over the system. The downside is a lot of upfront investment in infrastructure (capex); you have to maintain everything yourself, and you need an SQL server license to use the SQL Server services such as SSIS, SSAS, and SSRS.

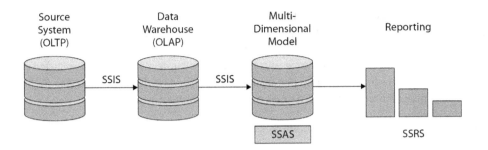

Figure 7.3 – Data platform architecture with SSAS as a semantic layer

- **Azure Analysis Services (AAS)**: AAS is a cloud-based semantic layer tool offered by Microsoft Azure. It operates as a **Platform-as-a-Service (PaaS)** solution, meaning it is hosted in the cloud, eliminating the need for on-premises infrastructure. AAS primarily focuses on providing tabular models for data analysis. Tabular models in AAS offer high performance, scalability, and flexibility, enabling organizations to quickly analyze and visualize large volumes of data. AAS supports advanced features such as row-level security, in-memory processing, and integration with other Azure services. It follows a pay-as-you-go billing model, allowing users to pay only for the resources they consume.

In *Figure 7.4*, we see the same architecture for a data platform as before, but now using AAS as a semantic layer and translating the other services to cloud services. SSIS has been replaced by **Azure Data Factory (ADF)** and SSRS has been replaced by Power BI. These are PaaS services, meaning they are more Microsoft-managed. As they are Azure services, there are pause and resume functionalities for optimizing costs. The downside is that there is no integrated solution here for both the semantic layer and reporting, requiring maintenance and governance in two separate systems.

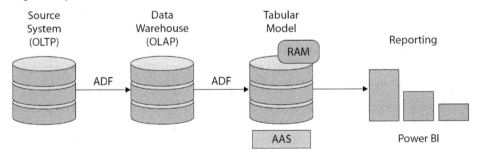

Figure 7.4 – Data platform architecture with AAS as a semantic layer

- **Power BI**: Power BI is a popular cloud-based **Software-as-a-Service** (**SaaS**) tool provided by Microsoft. It combines data visualization, self-service analytics, and collaboration capabilities. Power BI added a semantic layer functionality that is built around tabular models, providing users with a user-friendly and intuitive way to analyze data. Power BI offers both license-based and pay-as-you-go billing options, allowing users to choose between purchasing licenses or opting for a subscription-based model. With Power BI, users can create interactive reports, dashboards, and data visualizations, enabling data-driven decision-making across the organization. Its architecture is depicted in *Figure 7.5*:

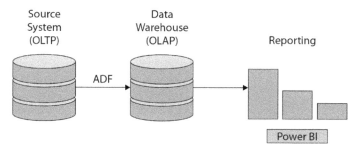

Figure 7.5 – Data platform architecture with Power BI as a semantic layer

Via tabular models in Power BI, we achieve an integrated solution for both the semantic layer and reporting. Tabular models are actually already available in the free version, but sharing reports with those tabular models requires a license. In the following table, we compare the different tools for the semantic layer based on deployment, billing model, and whether they can support multidimensional and/or tabular models:

|  | **Deployment** | **Billing model** | **Models** |
|---|---|---|---|
| **SSAS** | On-premises | License-based | Multidimensional and tabular models |
| **AAS** | Cloud-based (PaaS) | Pay-as-you-go | Tabular models |
| **Power BI** | Cloud-based (SaaS) | License-based (or pay-as-you-go) | Tabular models |

Table 7.4 – Comparison between tools for a semantic layer

Some people still preferred using AAS for their semantic layer as it had more advanced features (such as support for large models) than Power BI. The Power BI product group saw this and started to add more and more of these advanced features to **Power BI Premium** to become a superset of AAS.

## Power BI as a superset of AAS

Power BI has evolved into a leading platform for both self-service and enterprise **business intelligence (BI)**. To meet the growing demands of customers, Power BI is incorporating AAS capabilities, making it a superset of AAS. Notable capabilities inherited from AAS include **XMLA endpoints** for seamless integration, support for large models, object-level security, **Azure Log Analytics** integration, backup/restore functionality, asynchronous refresh, and evaluation of query scale-out.

*Figure 7.6* depicts AAS with its features that were incorporated into Power BI Premium on the left, with additional Power BI Premium features that are not in AAS on the right, thus making it a superset of AAS:

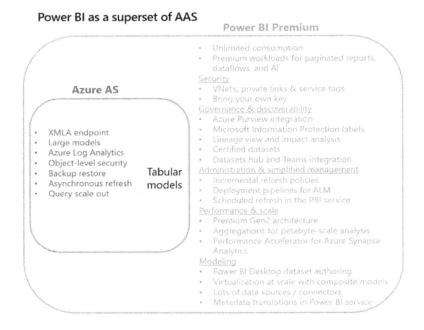

Figure 7.6 – Power BI Premium as a superset of AAS

Let's summarize the chapter next.

# Summary

In this chapter, we discussed how the semantic layer is used to create a more performant layer for reporting. We learned the semantic layer can be implemented using either multidimensional or tabular models. Multidimensional models are based on the concept of cubes and provide analytical capabilities by aggregating the data. Tabular models, on the other hand, utilize a columnar in-memory technology known as the VertiPaq engine, which enables faster processing and compression. Tabular models are well suited for scenarios where fast query performance and self-service analytics are paramount.

The VertiPaq engine was explained as a key component of tabular models and powers their impressive performance capabilities. By leveraging in-memory storage and columnar data structures, the VertiPaq engine optimizes data compression and enables efficient query execution. This engine plays a significant role in the success of tabular models, allowing for interactive and near-real-time data exploration.

To build and manage the semantic layer, several powerful tools were introduced. SQL SSAS is the on-premises, license-based tool that allows users to define and create both multidimensional and tabular models. AAS is the cloud-based variant of SSAS, delivering a pay-as-you-go, **Platform-as-a-Service (PaaS)** offering within Azure. Preference was given to the newer and more performant tabular models as multidimensional models are no longer supported with AAS. Apart from being an excellent reporting tool, Power BI is becoming a superset of AAS. This means tabular models can also be built inside Power BI and all features of AAS are or will become available in Power BI.

In conclusion, the semantic layer holds immense significance in facilitating efficient data analysis and reporting. Through the use of multidimensional and tabular models, and with the support of tools such as SSAS, AAS, and Power BI, organizations can construct a semantic layer that empowers business users to access, analyze, and derive meaningful insights from complex data structures. This bridging of the gap between technical data structures and business needs enhances decision-making and unlocks the full potential of data-driven strategies.

In the next chapter, we will see how the data models of the semantic layer can be used to build reports with Power BI.

# Visualizing Data Using Power BI

Power BI is a powerful **Business Intelligence** (**BI**) tool, made for data visualization, analysis, and reporting. It allows you to generate insights from data and share them with key stakeholders. Power BI is part of the Microsoft Power Platform but goes hand in hand with the Azure data services. Data often comes from Azure or is first processed in a data warehouse in Azure before being ingested into Power BI to report on.

In this chapter, we will explore the basics of Power BI, including how it works, licensing, and how to build reports. We will also go into more advanced topics, such as DevOps, security, and self-service BI.

Following that, we will dive into building reports. We will discuss how to get data into Power BI, including Import mode, DirectQuery, and real-time data. We will also explore how to prepare data using Power Query and DAX Query. Finally, we will look at how to visualize data using reports and dashboards.

After building reports, we will explore how to publish and share your reports with others. We will discuss the different artifacts that can be published, including reports and datasets. We will also look at external sharing options, such as AD B2B sharing and application development.

Once you have published your reports, we will examine how to mature your development process. We will discuss release cycles with apps and deployment pipelines and versioning with XMLA endpoints. Finally, we will look at security, including row-level security and object-level security.

This chapter will cover the following topics:

- Learning how Power BI works
- Choosing the right license and pricing
- Practicing your skills
- Moving to self-service BI

By the end of this chapter, you will understand how to use Power BI to gain insights into your data and share those insights with others. Let's get started!

# Learning how Power BI works

The main usage of Power BI is creating reports that give insights into data. An example of such a Power BI report can be seen here.

Figure 8.1 – An example of a Power BI report

To build and share these reports, Power BI uses multiple tools, such as Power BI Desktop, the Power BI service, and Power BI Report Server. In this section, we try to make sense of the tools and when to use them. We will split up the workings of Power BI into four layers:

- Get data
- Transform and visualize
- Share and collaborate
- Consume

We will give an overview of the layers here, before deep diving in a practical example in the *Practice your skills* section.

The **get data** layer describes connectors for getting data in Power BI. The **transform and visualize** layer uses Power BI Desktop, a free tool that allows you to transform data and develop reports on your desktop computer. Once ready, reports can be published to either the cloud version of Power BI, called the Power BI service, or the on-premises version of Power BI, called Power BI Report Server, to share reports and collaborate with other users. Once shared, other users can consume the reports. For sharing, collaborating, and consuming the shared content, a license is required.

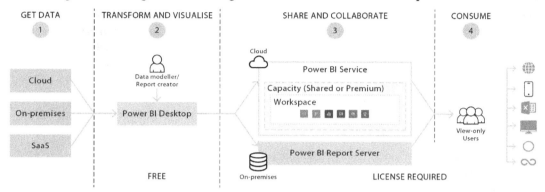

Figure 8.2 – How Power BI works

## Get data

Power BI uses Power Query to connect to data sources. Power Query comes with a graphical user interface to connect to data and allows you to apply transformations *before* loading the data into Power BI with the M language. You might have worked with Power Query before. It is also used to get data in other Microsoft products such as Excel, Azure Data Lake Storage, and Dataverse.

Power Query has more than 150 connectors to get data from on-premises data sources, multi-cloud data sources (including Azure but also other cloud providers such as Amazon Web Services and Google Cloud Platform), and third-party SaaS applications. Common data sources to connect to are SQL Server, Azure SQL Database, Azure Data Lake Storage, and Excel files.

There are two modes to connect to data, called **Import mode** and **DirectQuery**. With Import mode, you import the data inside Power BI. This gives the highest performance for visualizing data as a copy of the data sits right there in Power BI. However, this also means that the copy of data must be refreshed from time to time to show the most recent changes. DirectQuery mode queries the underlying data sources directly. This means slower performance for visualizing the data as the latency to get data directly from the underlying sources is higher. The benefit is that data is always up to date and we don't need to worry about data storage limits in Power BI. There is a final hybrid mode called **Composite mode**, which mixes Import and DirectQuery in the same report. The goal of Composite mode is to combine the benefits of the high query performance from Import mode (e.g. for use with a large chunk of historical data) with the benefits of up-to-date data from DirectQuery (e.g. for use with recent data).

## Transform and visualize

Creating reports on top of these data sources is done using **Power BI Desktop**. This is a free application that you install on your local computer to further transform the loaded data and visualize it.

Transformations *after* loading the data in Power BI are done using **Data Analysis Expressions (DAX)**. This is the same language used in the Analysis service and Power Pivot in Excel. They allow you to enrich the data loaded in Power BI with measures, calculated columns, and calculated tables to answer analytical questions. Measures are formulas for dynamic calculations. This means the result of a measure may change depending on the context. For instance, an aggregation such as COUNT or SUM can be used to create a measure, and the value of that measure may change depending on the filters applied. Calculated columns are columns that can be added to an existing table and for which the values are defined by the DAX formula. For instance, you can create a month column from an existing date column by using the MONTH() operation. Calculated tables are derived from all or parts of other tables.

Before visualizing, we need to model the data. This will define the relationship between the different tables of the loaded data sources, just like linking primary and foreign keys in a relational database. Relationships are necessary to link data in a single visual and apply filters in reports. Let's say we have a dimension table called **Customer** and a fact table called **Purchases**. When we filter a customer in the dimension table, we only want to see the purchases of that customer in the fact table. This modeling results in a data model, which represents the tabular model from *Chapter 7, The Semantic Layer*.

Power BI comes with readily available visuals that can be added with a click of a button. There is also a marketplace to download more visuals created by third parties. If this is not enough, Power BI also allows you to create custom visuals with Python and R scripts. A visual normally has fields in which data columns can be dragged and dropped to visualize. Visuals can be grouped in pages and a report can have multiple pages.

## Share and collaborate

Once the development of the report in Power BI Desktop is done, you can save it locally in a `.pbix` file. When you want to share this report for others to see, you need to publish the report. Publishing can be done to the Power BI service, the cloud version of Power BI, or to **Power BI Report Server**, the on-premises version of Power BI. In both cases, a license is required to share reports and collaborate with others.

The Power BI service allows you to host reports in the cloud. Published reports are split into a report artifact and a dataset artifact, separating the visuals from the data model.

Also, other artifacts can be hosted, such as dataflows, datamarts, and dashboards. When building multiple reports on the same data sources, you don't want to keep creating the same data transformations. Dataflows allow you to define the transformations once and reuse it for multiple reports. The transformations are stored in Power BI or in a provided Azure Data Lake Storage instance and can be imported as any other data source when building reports. A downside is that dataflows can't be queried or explored without a dataset. Datamarts also provide reusable data transformations, but data can be explored with a fully managed SQL database. It allows self-service, user-based data warehousing to sort, filter, or do simple aggregation through SQL expressions or a graphical user interface. Dashboards are single-page canvases with pinned visuals called tiles for storytelling. You can pin and combine tiles from multiple reports, other dashboards, Excel, images, and videos. Let's see the Power BI artifacts in the following figure.

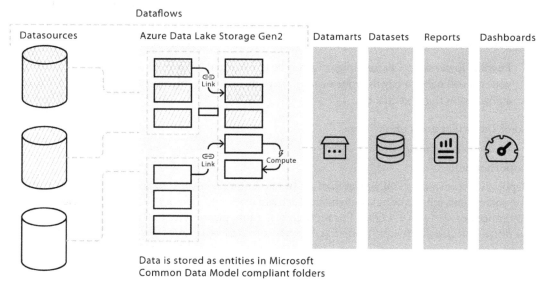

Figure 8.3 – Power BI artifacts

Artifacts are hosted on capacities, which represent a set of resources, such as storage, a processing unit, and memory. Capacities can be either *shared* or *reserved*. The default capacity is the shared capacity. Here, you share the set of resources with other Microsoft customers. This means there will be some limitations imposed on the usage of those services to ensure "fair play." Reserved capacities are also called **premium capacities**. They are more expensive because the resources are reserved for usage by a single customer.

Workspaces are created on capacities and represent containers, logically grouping artifacts. Workspaces come in two flavors, called **My workspace** and **workspaces**. **My workspace** is an individual workspace for any Power BI user where they can work on their own artifacts. This workspace is free to use but cannot be shared with others and is intended to only be used by the individual. When you do want to share and collaborate, use workspaces. You can add colleagues to your workspaces and collaborate on any content, but it requires a license.

Power BI Report Server allows you to host reports on-premises. In terms of features, it is more limited than the Power BI service, but it is actually a superset of **SQL Server Reporting Services (SSRS)**. Anything you can do with SSRS, you can also do with Power BI Report Server. Going on-premises is a good option for Power BI in the following scenarios:

- **Security and compliance concerns**: If your organization has strict security and compliance policies that require data to be stored on-premises, then Power BI Report Server is a good option for you. This is because Power BI Report Server will be installed on-premises, in your intranet.

- **Limited or no internet connectivity**: If your organization has limited or no internet connectivity, Power BI Report Server is a good option as it allows you to host and access reports on-premises.

- **Possibly lower cost**: A license might already be in place to use Power BI Report Server. However, you will still need to pay for your own infrastructure to host the reports. More on this will be explained in the next chapter.

See some important notes on this here.

> **Important note**
>
> Report Server requires a SQL Server instance (minimum version 2012) to host reports. There are also some minimum hardware requirements, such as a minimum memory of 1GB and a minimum x64 processor speed of 1.4 GHz. For more information, please refer to https://learn. microsoft.com/en-us/power-bi/report-server/system-requirements.
>
> Organizations often migrate from SSRS to Power BI Report Server or the Power BI service. SSRS reports can be migrated to Power BI paginated reports, which are available for any paid license in Power BI. There is also a migration tool available on the GitHub page of Microsoft called **RDLmigration**.

## Consume

Viewing reports shared by others also requires a license. A per-user license can be bought, or a Premium license can give free read access to everyone inside the organization. You can also buy a Premium capacity to embed in applications such as internal SharePoint and Teams or your own web app for users outside your organization. Reports can be viewed either on computers or mobile devices, such as smartphones and laptops. There is also an option to analyze the data model in Excel.

We'll go over each sharing scenario in more detail here:

- **The Power BI service**: The primary and most common way to consume Power BI reports is through the Power BI service, also known as the Power BI web portal. Users can access the Power BI service through a web browser on their computers or mobile devices. This cloud-based environment allows authorized users to view and interact with shared reports and dashboards. The Power BI service provides a rich and interactive experience, enabling users to explore the data, apply filters, drill down into details, and interact with visualizations for deeper insights.

- **Power BI mobile app**: To cater to users who are constantly on the move, Microsoft offers a dedicated Power BI mobile app for iOS and Android devices. The mobile app allows users to access their Power BI content from anywhere, making it easier to stay connected to critical business data. Users can view and interact with reports and dashboards seamlessly on their smartphones or tablets, ensuring that they can make informed decisions on the fly.

- **Embedding in applications**: Organizations can embed Power BI reports and dashboards into their internal applications, such as SharePoint sites, Microsoft Teams, or custom web apps. This embedding capability is facilitated by Power BI Premium capacity. By integrating Power BI content directly into other applications, users can access reports without having to leave the familiar environment of the application they are already using, enhancing the overall user experience and increasing data accessibility.

- **Exporting to PowerPoint, PDF, and Excel**: Power BI allows users to export reports and dashboards to other formats such as PowerPoint, PDF, and Excel. This feature is useful when users need to share specific insights or presentations with stakeholders who may not have direct access to the Power BI service or when data needs to be presented offline.

- **Data analysis in Excel**: For advanced users and analysts, Power BI provides an option to analyze the underlying data model directly in Excel. This feature enables users to leverage the full power of Excel's data manipulation and analysis capabilities while working with the data imported into Power BI.

Let's now move on to cover the right license and pricing.

# Choosing the right license and pricing

Licenses are required to publish content for sharing and collaborating with other users and consume shared content. Power BI licensing comes in three flavors: Pro License, Premium Per User License, and Premium Per Capacity license. All prices mentioned are in US dollars.

| Power BI Pro | Power BI Premium | |
|---|---|---|
| Per User | Per User | Per Capacity |
| **$10** | **$20** | **$4,995** |
| Per user/month | Per user/month | Per capacity/month |

Figure 8.4 – Power BI pricing (in USD)

Please refer to `https://powerbi.microsoft.com/en-us/pricing/` for up-to-date pricing.

The Pro License is a per-user license and costs $10 per user/month. This license allows you to publish content to a workspace other than **My workspace** to share and collaborate with other licensed users. It also allows you to consume shared content. The shared content is hosted on a shared capacity, meaning that some limitations will apply to the resource usage. For example, the data model can't be bigger than 1 GB (after compression with Vertipaq), the dataset can't be refreshed more than eight times per day (which of course is only relevant when Import mode is used), the per workspace storage limit is 10 GB, and the per tenant storage limit is 10 GB multiplied by the number of Pro licenses in the organization. Pro licenses are free if an M365 E5 license has been purchased.

The **Premium Per User license** is also a user-based license and costs $20 per user/month. This license can do everything the Pro license can but also gives users individual access to Premium features. Premium features include for instance datamarts and XMLA endpoints. XMLA endpoints will be further explained when talking about DevOps. Access to Premium features is given in Premium Per User workspaces, which are only accessible to those users with Premium Per User licenses. In these workspaces, data models can go up to 100 GB in size and can be refreshed 48 times a day. The per-tenant storage limit of these workspaces combined is 100 TB. If the organization has an M365 E5 license, then Premium Per User licenses are half the price ($10 per user/month).

The **Premium Per Capacity license** also gives access to Premium features but is not a user-based license. Rather, you buy a reserved capacity, only to be used by your organization. The benefit of this is that the consumption of Power BI content is free for your whole organization. So, there is no need to buy user-based licenses to consume content anymore. To publish content, however, you will still need to have a Pro or Premium Per User license. As there is probably a way smaller group of people in the organization that need to publish content rather than consume content, buying a Premium Per Capacity license could be more cost-effective. Let's consider the following example.

There are 600 users in an organization that need a Power BI license to share and collaborate. Buying each user a Pro license would cost $6,000/user per month. However, only 50 of those users will ever publish content to Power BI. Buying a Premium Per Capacity license to give free consume access to everyone inside the organization costs $4,995 per month. Additionally, you buy 50 users a Power BI Pro license, which brings you to $5,495 per month. As we will see in a bit, Premium capacities come in many flavors and $4,995 is just a starting price. Premium capacities also have Premium features that you don't get with Premium Per User licenses, such as multi-geo deployments, **Bring Your Own Key** (**BYOK**), and autoscaling capabilities.

A summary of the features per license can be found in the table at this link, under the heading **Feature availability**: `https://learn.microsoft.com/en-us/office365/servicedescriptions/power-bi-service-description`.

Also, please refer to `https://powerbi.microsoft.com/en-us/pricing/` for up-to-date information on Power BI features per license.

If you want to share and collaborate on-premises with Power BI Report Server, licensing is required. You either need to purchase a Premium Per Capacity license or have a **Software Assurance** (**SA**) benefit through SQL Server **Enterprise Edition** (**EE**) + SA per-core licenses. You also need additional Pro licenses to publish content. However, Power BI Report Server is free to use in Evaluation or Developer mode. The Evaluation installation will expire after 180 days.

| | Evaluation | Developer | Production |
|---|---|---|---|
| Description | Try out the full-fledged Power BI Report Server and evaluate non-production BI solutions. | Also a full-featured edition but intended to develop and test BI solutions. | The Production edition can be used for analytical solutions in production environments or when working with production data. |
| Power BI Report Server License Requirement | Free. Installation expires after 180 days. | Free if not using production data or production environments. | Buy Power BI Premium or use the SA benefit through SQL Server EE + SA per core licenses to get the rights to use this in production. |
| Additional License Requirement | / | / | In order to publish reports to Power BI Report Server, a Power BI Pro license is still required. You don't need any additional license to consume shared reports, though. |

Table 8.1 – Power BI Report Server licensing

To help you choose the right license, we created a licensing flowchart. We first list the Premium Per Capacity only features as this license is a superset of the Premium Per User license, with the exception of publishing content. Then, we list the Premium Per User features as this license is a superset of the Pro license. The flowchart also shows when the Premium Per capacity is more cost effective than a user-based license.

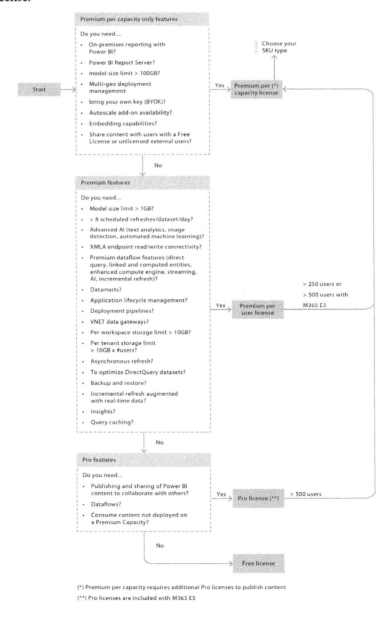

Figure 8.5 – Power BI licensing flowchart

If you landed on the Premium Per Capacity License, you need to choose a certain SKU type of capacity to purchase. There are three SKU types, namely P SKUs, EM SKUs, and A SKUs. P SKUs are offered through Office and have a monthly or yearly commitment. They allow you to embed reports in apps and in the Power BI service.

EM SKUs are also offered through Office. They are a bit cheaper than P SKUs but require a yearly commitment. They also allow you to embed reports in apps but aren't meant to be used in the Power BI service. Instead, they can be used to embed reports in Microsoft applications such as SharePoint and Teams.

P and EM SKUs can both embed reports for your internal organization (that is, including it in the Power BI service or Microsoft applications where *users own the data*) as well as for your external customers (that is, creating a web application where the *app owns the data*). A SKUs should only be used to embed content for your external customers. They are offered through Azure and billed by the hour. Although they are a bit more expensive than their P and EM counterparts, they can pause and resume to regulate costs. A SKUs are also often used during the development or testing of P and EM SKUs, before making a monthly or yearly commitment. The following flowchart helps with choosing the right Power BI Premium Capacity (or SKU) for your needs.

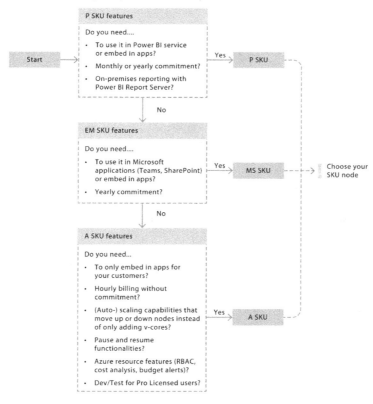

Figure 8.6 – Power BI Premium capacity (SKU) flowchart

If you chose an SKU type for the Premium capacity, you also need to choose an SKU node. SKU nodes determine the set of resources that will be reserved for you.

V-cores are the compute resources. The more v-cores, the more performant the Premium capacity is. The best way to choose the number of v-cores is by testing it out. If you want to test out a P/EM SKU before making a monthly or yearly commitment, you can ask for a trial SKU or test it out on a corresponding A SKU that is hourly billed. V-cores can be combined to create a new SKU node. For example, if you want to upgrade from a P1 SKU (8 v-cores) to a P2 SKU (16 v-cores), you can just buy another P1 SKU and combine the v-cores of the two P1 SKUs to make a new P2 SKU.

The max memory per dataset (also called the data model size limit) varies depending on the SKU node. Datasets can go up to 400 GB in size with these Premium capacities. The max memory limit represents the RAM of the SKU node. It's important to note that the RAM limit specified in the table applies only to a single Power BI artifact (such as a dataset), rather than the combined memory usage of multiple artifacts. However, some memory for a single item will be necessary for data refreshes. The old dataset is kept in memory while data is being refreshed, meaning it is advised to double the amount of RAM to process the refresh. Let's say your dataset is 40 GB; you'll need to choose an SKU node that has a max memory limit bigger than 80 GB, such as the P3 SKU. Remember that this is only relevant for datasets using Import mode where data is copied into Power BI and loaded into memory.

Other limitations include the amount of DirectQuery/live connections per second, the max memory per query, how many data models can be refreshed in parallel, how many dataflow tasks can be run in parallel, and the max concurrent pages for the export API.

It is important to note that SKU nodes with a max memory of above 100 GB are not available in all regions. If you need such SKU nodes for big data models, it is best to contact the Microsoft account manager. At the following link, check out the table under the heading **SKU memory and computing power**, which shows the capacity resources and limits for all SKU nodes: `https://learn.microsoft.com/en-us/power-bi/developer/embedded/embedded-capacity`.

Power BI v-cores are a unit of measure for compute resources in Power BI. They can be used to run a variety of Power BI workloads in parallel. Previously, v-cores would be evenly split between frontend and backend cores (four frontend and four backend cores for a P1 SKU), but now they are called unified v-cores (eight unified v-cores for a P1 SKU).

The max memory is the limit for a single dataset, not the combined size of all datasets. This feature was introduced with Power BI Premium Gen 2. Model refresh parallelism means how many models can be refreshed at the same time, which is important for datasets using Import mode as they hold a copy of the data in Power BI.

The pricing of the SKU nodes can be seen here. EM1 and EM2 are only available through volume licensing, and EM1, EM2, and EM3 SKUs do not include Power BI Report Server. All prices here are expressed in US dollars:

| Node | Price per month | Deployment option |
| --- | --- | --- |
| Power BI Premium EM1 | $625 | PaaS |
| Power BI Premium EM2 | $1,245 | PaaS |
| Power BI Premium EM3 | $2,495 | PaaS |
| Power BI Premium P1 | $4,995 | PaaS |
| Power BI Premium P2 | $9,995 | SaaS or PaaS |
| Power BI Premium P3 | $19,995 | SaaS or PaaS |
| Power BI Premium P4[4] | $39,995 | SaaS or PaaS |
| Power BI Premium P5[4] | $79,995 | SaaS or PaaS |

Table 8.2 – Power BI Premium Per Capacity (P, EM SKU) pricing in USD – purchased through Office

A SKUs are bought in the Azure portal and prices may vary depending on the region:

| Node | Price per month |
| --- | --- |
| Power BI Premium A1 | $750.03 |
| Power BI Premium A2 | $1,494.03 |
| Power BI Premium A3 | $2,994.00 |
| Power BI Premium A4 | $5,994.04 |
| Power BI Premium A5 | $11,994.02 |
| Power BI Premium A6 | $23,994.45 |
| Power BI Premium A7 | $47,988.89 |
| Power BI Premium A8 | $95,977.79 |

Table 8.3 – Power BI Premium per capacity (A SKU) pricing in USD – purchased through Azure

Now that we know about licensing for Power BI, let's actually practice your skills and build some reports.

# Practicing your skills

In this section, we are going to show a practical example of how to build a report using Power BI Desktop. As mentioned in the *How Power BI works* section, we'll use Power BI Desktop to develop a report.

# Getting the data

The first step is to get data. When opening Power BI Desktop, you can connect to data sources by clicking on **Get data** in the **Home** tab, or load some sample data by clicking on **Try a sample dataset** as outlined in the following figure.

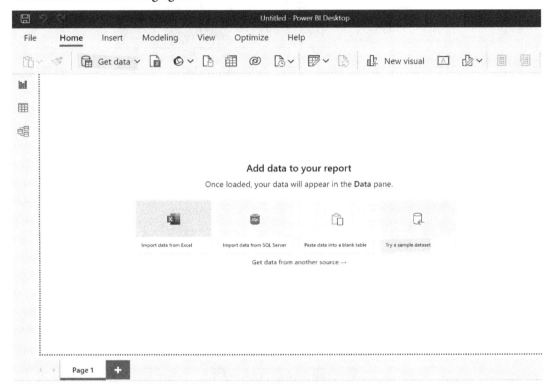

Figure 8.7 – Try a sample dataset in Power BI Desktop

Once you have got the data, we will move on to prepare your data.

# Preparing the data

**Navigator** provides the opportunity to change or import the data, with a preview of the data so you can check whether the data is accurate or needs any adjustment. If you need to make any changes, it is recommended to do it before loading the data. In the following steps, we will demonstrate how to use Power Query to transform data:

1. To make the visualizations more understandable later, it is wise to modify the data now.

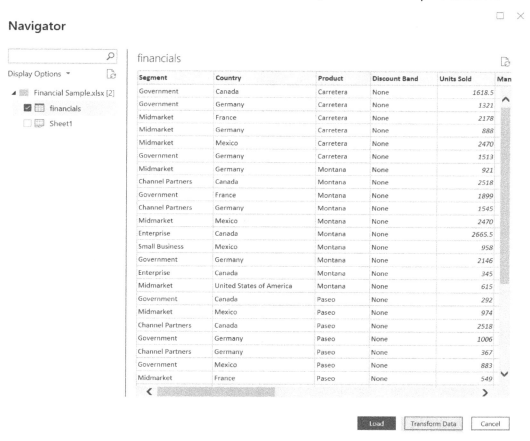

Figure 8.8 – Transforming data in Navigator

2.  Altering the data type is one of the most common transformations users do, but other transformations, such as replacing values or splitting columns, are also possible.

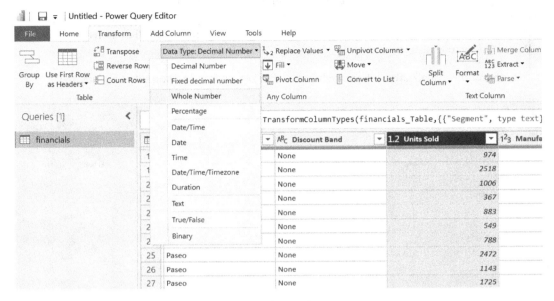

Figure 8.9 – Change data types

3.  Each transformation you do is shown as an **applied step** in the query settings. Power BI will try to do something called query folding, which is combining as many applied steps as possible in a single query to send to the data source to request the data. By doing this, we make sure as few queries as possible are sent to the source data, increasing the data refresh performance for datasets using Import mode and increasing report performance for datasets using DirectQuery. More information on these modes has been discussed in *Chapter 7, The Semantic Layer*. Once you've done all necessary transformations, click on the **Home** tab and then on **Close & Apply** to apply the applied steps.

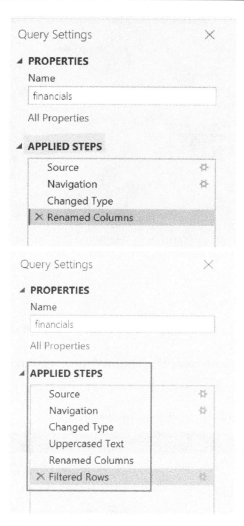

Figure 8.10 – Applied steps in Power Query

Once you're done preparing the data, let's enrich your data with DAX.

## Enriching data with DAX

We can enrich the data by creating measures or calculated columns using DAX:

1. Let's consider an example where we want to create a calculated column to calculate the total sales prices from the unit price column and the number of units sold column. On the **Home** ribbon, select **New calculated column**.

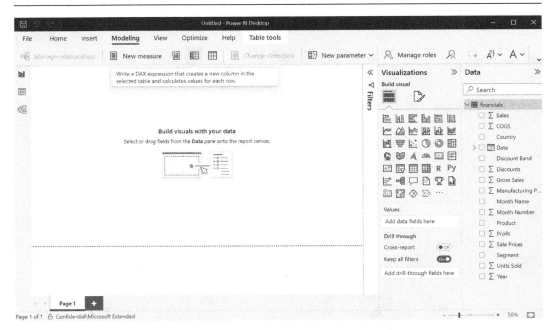

Figure 8.11 – Creating a new calculated column with DAX

2.  You can use this expression to create the calculated column and type it in the expression field:

    ```
    Total Price = financials[Units Sold] * financials[Sale Prices]
    ```

3.  Commit the calculated column by clicking on the check mark.

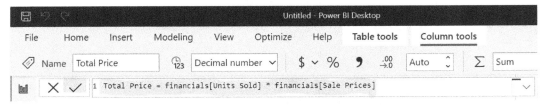

Figure 8.12 – Commiting a measure

Now, we are done with enriching the data with DAX. Let's move on to the next step, that is, modeling the data.

## Modeling the data

Modeling the data defines relationships between tables so that one table can filter and interact with another one. Let's see how we can build such a model in Power BI Desktop:

1.  First, let's click on the data modeling tab to start building our data model.

Figure 8.13 – The data modeling tab

2.  Let's say we want to be able to filter a financial table on different product groups. In that case, we would create a *relationship* by dragging the **Product** field from the **financials** table to the **Product** field in the **Product** table to join the tables.

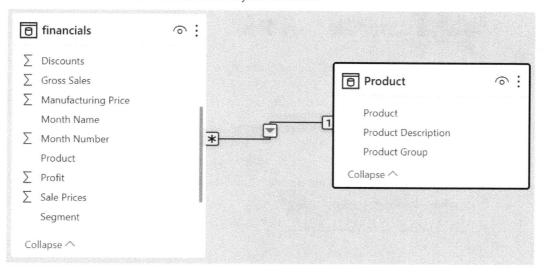

Figure 8.14 – Creating a relationship

Now, let's move on to building your report and creating visuals.

## Creating visuals

Now that you've transformed and loaded your data, let's go ahead to create your report visuals. We will be building the final report, one visual at a time.

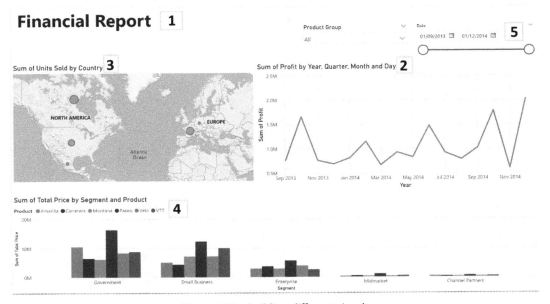

Figure 8.15 – Building different visuals

Let's now get into the details of the visuals by covering each reference number in *Figure 8.16* as follows.

### Creating the page title

1.  Click on **Text Box** in the **Insert** tab. Type Financial Report.
2.  After selecting the typed text, set **Font Size** to 20 and make the text bold.

Figure 8.16 – Add a title to the report page

## Showing the profit per date

To see profit peaks for different months and years, we'll create a line chart. We will create a line chart that will help us to see which month and year had the highest profit:

1. From the **Build visual** pane, click on the line chart icon. This will add a blank line chart visual to the report.

2. Drag the **Date** field to the **X-axis** field of the line chart and drag the **Profit** field to the **Y-axis** field. This will summarize the profits over the dates and will show as **Sum of Profit**.

Figure 8.17 – Build a line chart

Now it is easy to see that December 2014 had the biggest profit peak.

## Visualizing units sold per country on a map

First, go through *Visual 3: Profit by Country/Region* here: https://learn.microsoft.com/en-us/power-bi/create-reports/desktop-excel-stunning-report. Once done, construct a map to compare the profits of different countries/regions:

1. Click on the **Map** visual in the **Build a visual** section.

2. Drag the **Country** column to the **Location** field of the map visual.

3. Drag the **Units sold** column to the **Bubble size** field. This will summarize the units sold across countries.

Power BI will then generate a map visual with bubbles showing the relative profit of each region.

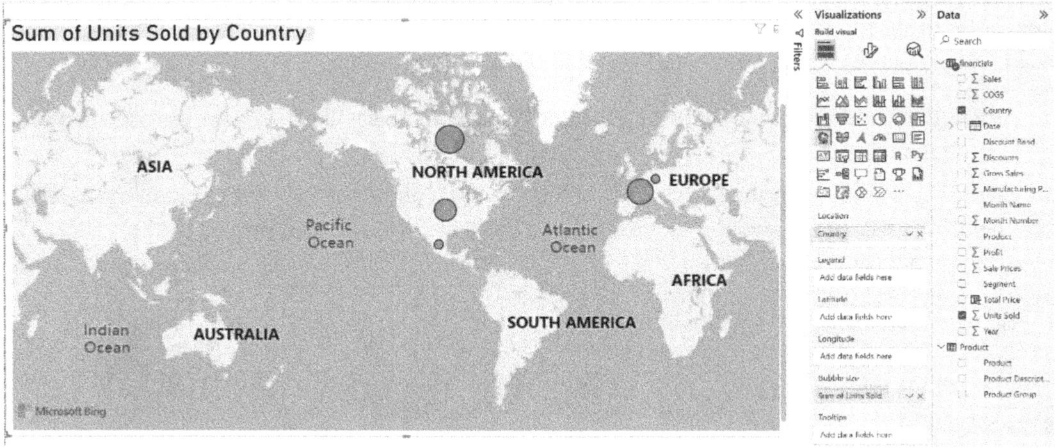

Figure 8.18 – Create a map visual

It looks like more units have been sold in North America than in Europe.

## Total price by segment and product

1.  Select a clustered column chart from the **Build visual** pane.
2.  Drag the **Segment** column to the **X-axis** field.
3.  Drag the **Total price** column to the **Y-axis** field, which will be summarized over the segments.
4.  Drag the **Product** column to the **Legend** field, splitting the bar chart over a group of clustered product bar charts.
5.  Make the chart wide enough to fill the space under the two upper charts.

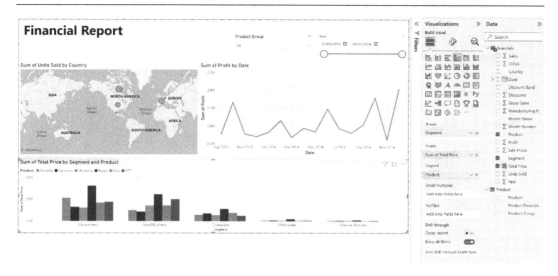

Figure 8.19 – Edit chart width and height

It seems like **Government** is the segment creating the most revenue. The product **Paseo** is the product generating the most revenue.

## Date slicer

Slicers can be used to refine the visuals on a report page to a specific selection. In this example, two slicers can be created to focus on performance for a specific date range and product group. The first slicer uses the **Date** field in the original data table. Let's see how to create such a slicer:

1.  In the **Financials** table, select the **Date** field in the **Fields** pane and move it to the empty space on the left side of the canvas.

2.  Choose **Slicer** in the **Visualizations** pane.

    Power BI will show a numeric range slicer instantly.

Figure 8.20 – Numeric range slicer

3.    You can move the ends of the slicer to filter.

To share your report with your manager and colleagues, you can publish it to the Power BI service. In Power BI Desktop, select the **Publish** option on the **Home** ribbon. You may need to sign in to the Power BI service, or if you don't have an account yet, you can sign up for a free trial. Select a destination different from **My workspace** in the Power BI service to share with others, and then select the report file to publish.

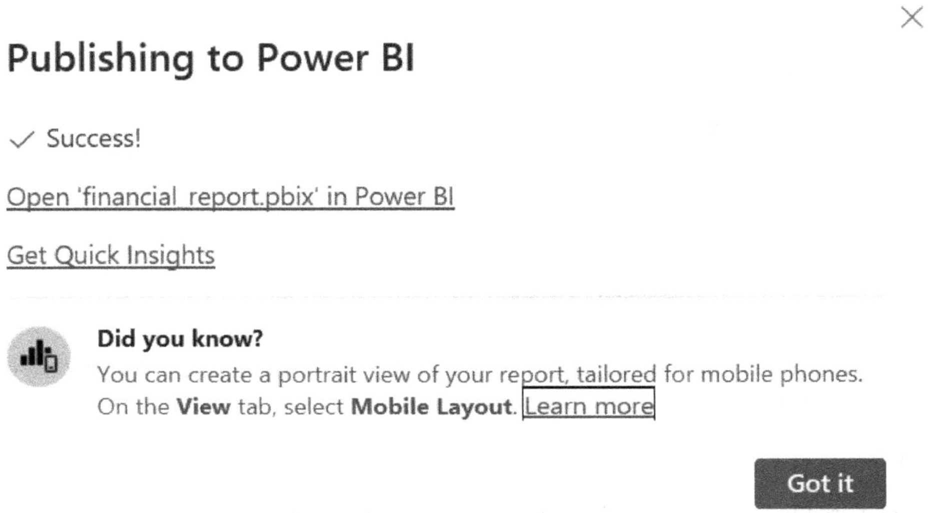

✕

## Publishing to Power BI

✓ Success!

Open 'financial_report.pbix' in Power BI

Get Quick Insights

 **Did you know?**
You can create a portrait view of your report, tailored for mobile phones.
On the **View** tab, select **Mobile Layout**. Learn more

Got it

Figure 8.21 – Publish to the Power BI service

4.    The report can now be opened through the browser.

Figure 8.22 – View the published report

5.  Click on **Share** at the top of the report in the Power BI service to share with others.

Figure 8.23 – Share the published report

Let's move on to cover self-service BI next.

## Moving to self-service BI

Over the years, BI has undergone significant changes, with new generations of BI systems emerging to meet the evolving needs of businesses. The three waves of BI, namely **technical BI**, **self-service BI**, and **end user BI**, are key milestones in the history of BI.

Let's take a look at how each wave changed the way we work in BI:

- **First wave**: Technical BI refers to the early stages of BI when IT staff, developers, and data analysts relied on technical tools to manage and analyze data. These tools were often expensive and required significant technical expertise to use.

- **Second wave**: Self-service BI refers to the emergence of BI systems that provided business users with more accessible tools to access and analyze data without relying on IT staff or data analysts. Power BI is an example of a self-service BI tool that provides drag-and-drop interfaces and data visualizations to make it easier for non-technical users to work with data.

- **Third wave**: End user BI, which is also sometimes referred to as modern BI, focuses on empowering business users at all levels of an organization to make data-driven decisions. Power BI has evolved to become an end user BI tool that is highly intuitive and user-friendly, allowing non-analysts to explore data, build reports and dashboards, and gain insights from data. Power BI includes features such as natural language processing and machine learning, making it easier for business users to interact with data and gain insights quickly.

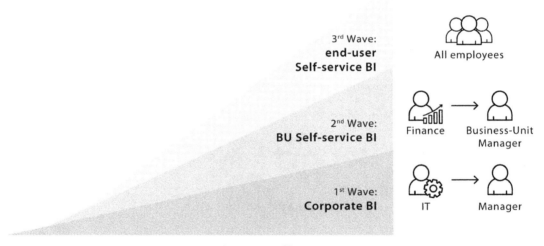

Figure 8.24 – BI waves

The scenarios presented here aim to support self-service BI activities, where individuals from various areas of the organization are responsible for analytical tasks. Additionally, these scenarios also include aspects of self-service BI in content collaboration and delivery. The purpose of this collection of scenarios is to emphasize the key elements that organizations must take into account when utilizing Power BI.

This includes the use of managed self-service BI, where data management is centralized and the main goal is to make centralized data reusable. This means that business users are responsible for creating reports and dashboards, while the dataset creation process is separate from the report creation process. To ensure that the shared datasets are reused, it is important to make them visible and easily accessible.

**Managed self-service BI**
Reuse of a centralized shared dataset by other report creators

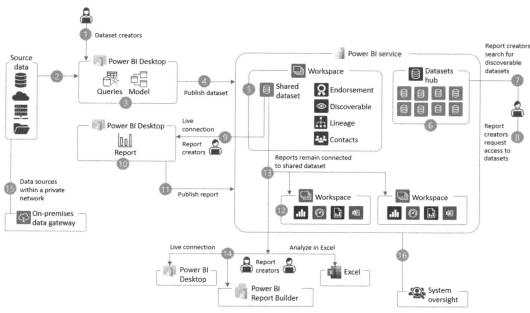

Figure 8.25 – Managed self-service BI with Power BI

The self-service data preparation scenario can be seen in the following figure. In this scenario, Power BI dataflows are a useful tool for consolidating data preparation activities and increasing uniformity. This will reduce the amount of effort required, as the same Power Query logic does not need to be replicated in multiple Power BI Desktop files. Furthermore, the dataflow can be used as a data source for multiple datasets, thus streamlining the data preparation process.

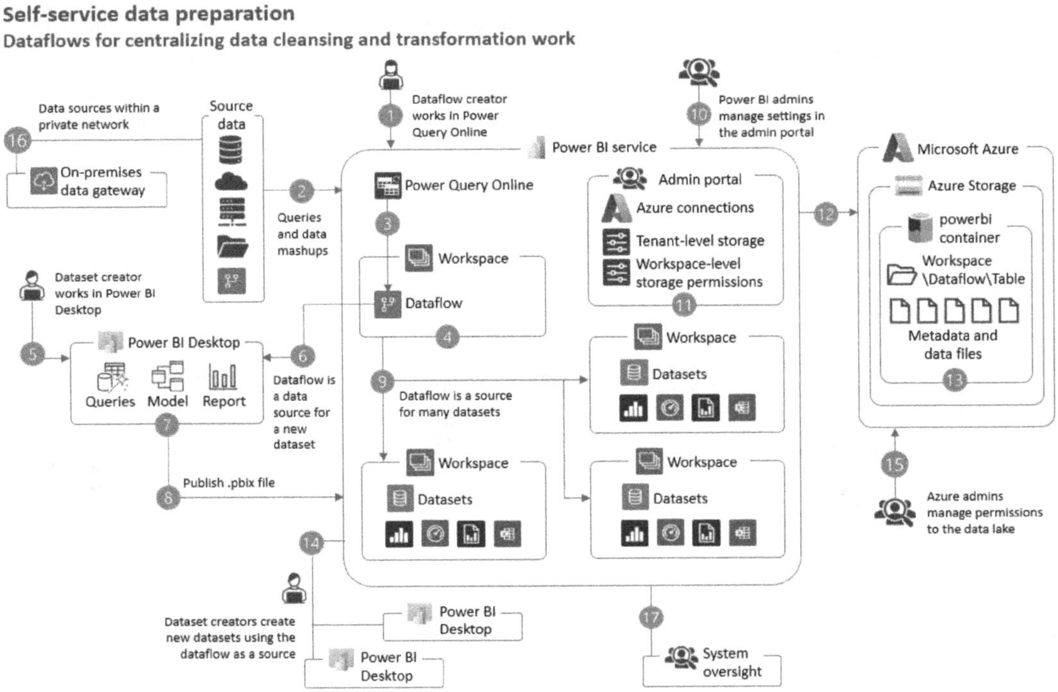

**Self-service data preparation**
Dataflows for centralizing data cleansing and transformation work

Figure 8.26 – Self-service data preparation with Power BI

Self-service BI has revolutionized the way organizations approach data analysis and decision-making. Empowering business users to independently access, prep, and visualize data has unlocked a new era of agility, data-driven insights, and collaborative decision-making, driving businesses toward greater efficiency and success in the dynamic and competitive landscape of today's data-driven world.

# Summary

This chapter provided a comprehensive overview of the essential elements involved in mastering Power BI and transitioning toward a self-service BI approach. We began by delving into the fundamental workings of Power BI, gaining valuable insights into its capabilities and understanding its significance in empowering data-driven decision-making.

The selection of the right license and pricing model was explored in detail, highlighting the importance of aligning the organization's needs with the appropriate licensing options. By making informed decisions, businesses can optimize their investment in Power BI and ensure they have access to the features that best support their unique BI requirements.

Furthermore, this chapter emphasized the significance of hands-on practice to effectively harness Power BI's potential. Through practical exercises and real-world scenarios, you had the opportunity to develop and refine your skills, becoming more adept at handling data, creating visualizations, and interpreting insights. Continuous practice is key to achieving mastery and enhancing your proficiency as a Power BI user.

Finally, we discussed the journey toward self-service BI, emphasizing the transformation from relying on IT departments for data and reports to enabling business users to access, analyze, and share data autonomously. By embracing self-service BI, organizations can foster a data-driven culture, where data insights are readily available to all stakeholders, promoting faster and more informed decision-making. Power BI reports often answer analytical questions such as *"What happened?"* (descriptive analytics) and *"Why did it happen?"* (diagnostic analytics).

In the next chapter, we'll explore advanced analytics using AI to answer questions such as *"What will happen in the future?"* (predictive analytics) and *"How should I act on it?"* (prescriptive analytics).

# Advanced Analytics Using AI

**Artificial Intelligence** (**AI**) is transforming businesses across various industries rapidly. Especially with the surge in popularity of large language models such as ChatGPT, AI adoption is increasing exponentially. Microsoft Azure provides a wide range of AI services to help organizations build powerful AI solutions. In this chapter, we will explore the different AI services available on Azure, as well as the roles involved in building AI solutions, and the steps required to design, develop, and deploy AI models on Azure.

Specifically, we will cover the following:

- The different roles involved in building AI solutions
- The questions a data architect should ask when designing an AI solution
- An overview of Azure's AI services, including Azure Cognitive Services, Azure Machine Learning, and Azure OpenAI Service
- An introduction to the concept of MLOps
- A reference architecture for batch and real-time scoring on Azure

By the end of this chapter, you will have a good understanding of the role of the data architect in the world of data science. Additionally, you will have a high-level overview of what the data scientist and machine learning engineers are responsible for.

## Knowing the roles in data science

The Azure cloud offers an extensive range of services for use in advanced analytics and data science. Before we dive into these, it is crucial to understand the different roles in the data science ecosystem. In previous chapters, while always looking through the lens of a data architect, we saw workloads that are typically operationalized by data engineers, database administrators, and data analysts.

Up until now, the chapters followed the journey of data through a data platform, from ingestion to raw storage to transformation, data warehousing, and eventually, visualization and dashboarding. The advanced analytics component is more separated from the entire solution, in the sense that most data architectures can perform perfectly without it. This does not take away from the fact that adding advanced analytics such as machine learning predictions can be a valuable enhancement to a solution.

The environment for advanced analytics introduces some new roles. The most prominent are the data scientist and the machine learning engineer, which we will look at in a bit more detail, starting with the following figure. Other profiles include roles such as data labelers and citizen data scientists.

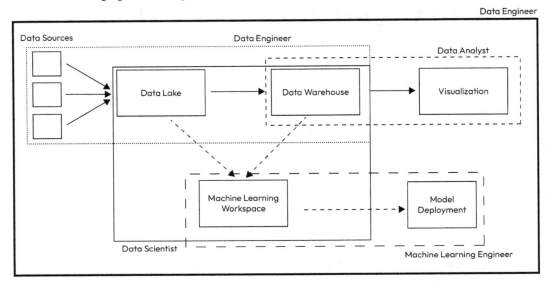

Figure 9.1 – An overview of the core components that each data role works with

*Figure 9.1* shows a very simplified data solution with a machine learning component attached to it. This consists of a workspace to build and train machine learning models and virtual machine clusters to deploy them in production.

The data scientist is responsible for building and training the machine learning model. This is done through experimenting with data, most of the time stemming from the data lake. The data scientist will often use data from the bronze or silver tier in the data lake (i.e., the raw or semi-processed data). Data in the gold tier or the data warehouse is often transformed and aggregated in ways that make it convenient for business users to build reports with. However, the data scientist might want to perform different kinds of transformations, which focus more on the statistical relevance of certain features within the data to optimize the training performance of a machine learning model. Regardless, in some cases, data scientists will still interact with the gold layer and the data warehouse to pull clean data for experimentation.

Using this data, data scientists will perform **exploratory data analysis** (EDA) to get initial insights into the dataset. This is followed by data cleaning and feature engineering, where features are transformed or new features are derived to serve as input for the machine learning model. Next up, a model is trained and evaluated, resulting in a first prototype. The experimentation does not stop here, however, as machine learning models have hyperparameters that can be adjusted, which might lead to increased performance, while still using the same dataset. This last process is called hyperparameter tuning. Once this is completed, we will arrive at the cutoff point between the responsibilities of a data scientist and a machine learning engineer.

The machine learning engineer is responsible for the machine learning operations, often referred to as MLOps. Depending on the exact definition, this usually encompasses the later stages of the machine learning model life cycle. The machine learning engineer receives the finished model from the data scientist and creates a deployment for it. This will make the model available through an API so that it can be consumed by applications and users. In later stages, the model will need to be monitored and periodically retrained, until the end of its life cycle. This is a brief summary, but the MLOps process will be explained in more detail further in this chapter.

Next, *Figure 9.2* provides an overview of the processes that take place in the MLOps cycle and who the primary contributor to each step is.

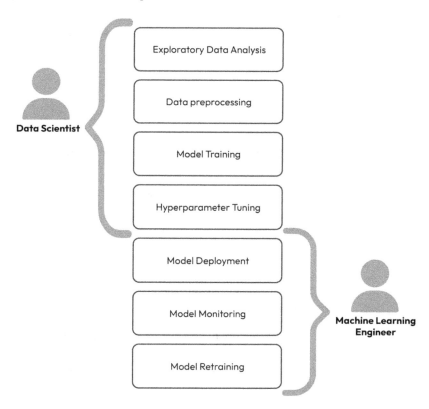

Figure 9.2 – The steps of the data science workflow and their executors

Finally, what we are most interested in is the role of the cloud data architect in this environment. First, the architect has to think about the overall AI approach, part of which is deciding whether to go for custom development or not. We will dive deeper into strategy soon.

If custom machine learning model development is involved, the architect will have to decide on a data science environment, or workspace, where the data scientists can experiment.

However, the architect will have more involvement in the work of a machine learning engineer. The optimal working of MLOps is considerably more dependent on good architectural design than the typical prototyping done by data scientists. Here, the architect is responsible for deciding on deployment infrastructure, choosing the right monitoring solutions, version control for models, datasets, code, retraining strategies, and so on.

A lot of the value that an architect brings to machine learning projects comes from design choices outside of the data science suite. The data architect can greatly facilitate the work of data scientists by envisioning efficient data storing structures at the data lake level, with a strong focus on silver (and bronze) tiers with good data quality. Often, extra pipelines are required to get *labeled* data ready to be picked up by the data scientists.

# Designing AI solutions

In this part, we will talk about the design of AI solutions, including qualification, strategy, and the responsible use of AI. Infusing AI into architecture has to be the result of some strategic consideration. The data architect should ask themself a series of questions, and find a substantiated answer, to end up with an optimal architecture.

The first set of questions is regarding the qualification of a use case.

## Is AI the right solution?

This can be further refined to the necessity of an inductive solution, compared to a deductive one. Business rulesets are deductive; machine learning is inductive. Business rules will provide you with a solid answer if the condition for that rule is met. Machine learning models will provide you with answers that have a high probability but not certain ones.

The big advantage of machine learning is its ability to cover cases in a much more granular manner, whereas business rules must group various cases within a single condition so as to not end up with an absurd or even impossible number of rules. Look at image recognition, for example. Trying to make a rule set for every possible combination of pixels that might represent a human is simply impossible. Knowing this, evaluate the proposed use case and confirm that the usage (and correlating costs) of AI is justified for this solution.

# Do we opt for pre-trained models or a custom model?

Although this question is more focused on implementation than qualification, it is crucial to answer it first, as this will directly impact the following two questions. As with most things in the broader field of IT, it comes down to not reinventing the wheel. Does your use case sound like something generic or industry-agnostic? Then there are probably existing machine learning models, often with far superior performance (general knowledge-wise) than your own data could train a model to have. Companies such as Microsoft and partners such as OpenAI invest heavily in getting these pre-trained models to cutting-edge standards.

It may be that the solution you want to create is fairly generic, but there are certain aspects that make it a bit more niche. An example could be a text analytics model in the medical industry. Text analytics models are great at the general skill of language understanding, but they might have some issues with grasping the essence of industry-specific language out of the box. In this case, an organization can provide some of its own data to fine-tune the model to increase its performance on niche tasks, while maintaining most of the general knowledge from its initial training dataset. Most of the pre-trained AI models on Azure, which reside in Azure Cognitive Services and Azure OpenAI Service, are fine-tuneable. When out-of-the-box models are not an option, then we need to look at custom development.

# Is data available?

If we opt for custom development, we will need to bring our own data. The same goes for wanting to fine-tune an existing model, yet to a lesser extent. Is the data that we need available? Does an organization have a significant volume of historical data stored already in a central location? If this data is still spread across multiple platforms or sources, then this might indicate it is not the right time to implement AI. It would be more valuable to focus on increased data engineering efforts in this situation. In the case of machine learning on Azure, data is ideally stored in tiers in Azure Data Lake Storage.

Keep in mind that machine learning model training does not stop after putting it into production. The performance of the production model will be constantly monitored, and if it starts to drift over time, retraining will take place. Do the sources of our current historic data still generate an adequate volume of data to carry out retraining?

In terms of data volume, there is still a common misunderstanding that large volumes of data are a necessity for any high-performant model. It's key to know here that even though the performance of a model still scales with the amount of training data, more and more new techniques have been developed to allow for valuable performance levels to be reached with a limited data volume.

## Is the data of acceptable quality?

Just like the last question, this only counts for custom development or fine-tuning. Data quality between sources can differ immensely. There are different ways in which data can be of bad quality. Some issues can be solved easily; others can be astonishingly hard. Some examples of poor data quality are as follows:

- **Inaccurate data:** This occurs when data is incorrect or contains errors, such as typos or missing values. This is not easy to solve and will often result in fixes required at the source.

- **Incomplete data:** This occurs when data is missing important information or lacks the necessary details to be useful. In some cases, data scientists can use statistics to impute missing data. In other cases, it might depend on the specific model that is being developed. Certain algorithms can perform well with sparse data, while others are heavily affected by it. Knowing which exact algorithms should not be in the scope of the architect but, rather, the data scientists.

- **Outdated data:** This occurs when data is no longer relevant or useful due to changes in circumstances or the passage of time. If this data is statistically dissimilar to data generated in the present, it is better to remove this data from the training dataset.

- **Duplicated data:** This occurs when the same data is entered multiple times in different places, leading to inconsistencies and confusion. Luckily, this is one of the easiest data quality issues to solve.

- **Biased data:** This occurs when data is influenced by personal biases or prejudices, leading to inaccurate or unfair conclusions. This can be notoriously hard to solve and is a well-known issue in the data science world. We will come back to this later when discussing responsible AI.

This concludes the qualifying questions on whether to implement AI or not. There is one more important topic, namely the **return on investment (ROI)** of the addition, but to calculate the investment, we need to have more knowledge on the exact implementation. This will be the focus of the next set of questions.

## Low code or code first?

The answer to which approach should be chosen depends on people, their skill sets, and the complexity of the use case. In the vast majority of cases, code-first solutions are preferred, as it comes with considerably more flexibility and versatility. Low-code simplifies development a lot, often by providing drag and drop interfaces to create workflows (or, in this case, machine learning pipelines). While low-code solutions often benefit from rapid development, this advantage in speed is slowly shrinking. Due to advancements in libraries and packages, generic code-first models are also being developed in a shorter amount of time than before.

While code-first solutions cover a much broader set of use cases, they are simply not possible for every organization. Data scientists tend to be an expensive resource and are often fought over, with competition due to a lack of them in the labor market. Luckily, low-code platforms are advancing fast to address this issue. This allows citizen data scientists (non-professionals) to create and train machine learning models easily, although it will still yield inferior performance compared to professional code-first development.

As a rule of thumb, if a professional data science team is present and it has already been decided that custom development is the way forward, choose a code-first solution.

## What are the requirements for the AI model?

Now, we will dive deeper into the technicalities of machine learning models. Note that not all answers here must come from the data architect. It is certainly a plus if the architect can think about things such as model selection with the data scientists, but it is not expected of the role. Leave it to the data science and machine learning team to have a clear understanding of the technical requirements for the AI model and allow them to leverage their expertise.

The minimum accepted performance is probably the most straightforward. This is a defined threshold on the primary metric of a model, based on what is justifiable for the use case to progress. For instance, a model might need to have a minimum accuracy of 95% to be economically viable and continue toward production.

Next, latency is an important requirement when the model will be used to make real-time predictions. The larger the model and the more calculations that need to happen (not counting parallelism), the longer it will take to make a prediction. Some use cases will require a prediction latency within milliseconds, which can be solved with lightweight model selection and specialized infrastructure.

Another requirement is the size of the model, which directly relates to the hosting costs when deployed into production, as the model will have to be loaded in RAM while the deployment runs. This is mostly a very binding requirement for IoT Edge use cases, where AI models are deployed on a small IoT device and make predictions locally before sending their results to the cloud. These devices often have very limited memory, and the data science team will have to figure out what the most efficient model is to fit on the device.

With the recently growing adoption of **large language models** (**LLMs**), such as the GPT-model family, power consumption has started to become an increasingly important topic as well. Years ago, this was a negligible topic in most use cases, but with the massive size of today's cutting-edge models, it is unavoidable. Whether these models are hosted privately or in the cloud, power consumption will be an incurred cost directly or indirectly. For natural language use cases specifically, consider whether the traditional (and significantly cheaper) text analytics models in Azure Cognitive Services can do the job at an acceptable level before heading straight for LLMs.

## Batch or real-time inferencing?

When a model is finished and ready for deployment, the architect will have to decide on the type of deployment. On a high level, we should decide whether the model will be used for either batch scoring or predicting in real time.

Typically, when machine learning predictions are used to enrich data, which is already being batch-processed in an OLAP scenario, the machine learning model can do periodical inferencing on large batches. The model will then be incorporated as an extra transformation step in the ETL pipeline. When using machine learning models in applications, for example, where users expect an instant prediction, real-time endpoints are required.

When deploying our model to an endpoint, the architecture might differ based on the type of inferencing, which we will look into in more depth later in this chapter.

## Is explainability required?

**Explainable AI**, often referred to as **XAI**, has been on the rise for quite a while now. For traditional machine learning models, it was straightforward to figure out why a model came to which conclusion, through statistical methods such as feature importance. With the rise of deep learning models, which are essentially black-box models, we come across more and more predictions that cannot be explained.

Techniques have been developed to make an approximation of the decision-making process of a black-box model. For instance, in the case of the mimic explainer, a traditional (and by nature interpretable) machine learning model is trained to mimic the black-box model and extract things, such as feature importance, from the mimic model. However, this is still an approximation and no guarantee.

Therefore, it is key to figure out how crucial explainability is for the use case. In cases that (heavily) affect humans, such as predicting credit scoring using AI, interpretability is a must. In cases with minimal or no impact on human lives, interpretability is more of a nice-to-have. In this instance, we can opt for a black-box model if this provides increased predictive performance.

## What is the expected ROI?

When the qualifying questions have been answered and decisions have been made to fulfill technical requirements, we should have sufficient information to calculate an estimated ROI. This will be the final exercise before giving the green light to start implementation, or at least the development of a proof of concept.

If we know what approach to use, what kind of models to train, and which type of deployment to leverage, we can start mapping it to the right Azure service and perform a cost calculation. This is compared to the expected added value of a machine learning model.

> Optimal performance of a machine learning model
>
> As a side note to calculating the ROI, we need to have an idea of what the optimal performance level of a machine learning model is. This is where the academic and corporate worlds tend to differ. Academics focus on reaching the highest performance levels possible, whereas business will focus on the most efficient ratio between costs and performance. It might not make sense for a business to invest largely in a few percent increase in performance if this marginal increase is not justified by bringing adequate value to compensate.

# Understanding AI on Azure

Microsoft has a globally leading role in terms of cloud-based AI. This is all thanks to performant infrastructure, strategic partnerships, and heavy investment in machine learning services.

The AI offering on Azure can be classified into two distinct categories:

- Pre-trained AI models
- Workspace for data scientists and machine learning engineers

The first contains a range of ready-to-use and pre-trained AI models that can be quickly implemented (and combined), allowing for an innovative way to process unstructured data or enhance applications with machine learning features. The latter provides the environment for a data science team to create their own custom models and maintain them throughout their life cycle.

The pre-trained models are, presently, available in two services:

- Azure Cognitive Services
- Azure OpenAI Service

Azure Cognitive Services is a collection of models meant to mimic most human functionalities, which can be used in various ways. The Azure OpenAI Service, a result of the close collaboration between Microsoft and its partner OpenAI, encompasses large-scale models to generate natural language, code, and images.

In terms of machine learning workspaces, the go-to option is Azure Machine Learning. Azure Machine Learning provides an Azure-native data science environment, with a complete MLOps framework and many built-in connectors to other Azure resources. Azure Databricks can be an alternative for data science teams that are fond of Spark, although Azure Machine Learning is increasingly getting Spark capabilities as well, due to integrations with Azure Synapse Spark. Whereas a full MLOps framework comes as a built-in feature of the Azure Machine Learning SDK, Databricks uses the open source MLflow framework to also provide MLOps functionalities. The MLOps functionalities refer to things such as model and dataset versioning, machine learning pipeline management, model life cycle management, and model deployment (monitoring).

Let's dive deeper into each of the key AI services on Azure.

## Azure Cognitive Services

Azure Cognitive Services holds many pre-trained models, covering numerous industry-agnostic use cases. It is divided into four categories:

- Speech
- Vision

- Language

- Decision making

All these models are readily available as API endpoints in a serverless solution. This means costs are only incurred for requests sent to the model. Hosting costs are not charged unless an organization chooses a private deployment, which is possible with a subset of the models.

## Speech models

Azure Cognitive Services for Speech has several models that can be used for speech-to-text, text-to-speech, speech translation, and speaker recognition.

The **Speech-to-Text** (**STT**) model is used to transcribe speech, providing the ability to easily transform audio data into text. It supports real-time and batch transcription, speaker diarization, and custom language models. Real-time transcribing is convenient to add instant subtitles to any video stream, while batch transcription is useful for call centers or interviewers, allowing them to turn all their recordings into text, which can then be further processed by text analytics models.

> **Speaker diarization**
>
> Speaker diarization is the ability to distinguish speech from multiple speakers (at the same time). This can be useful to segment parts of a transcription of a business meeting, for example. When combined with a speaker recognition model, which is also available in Azure, we can instantly transcribe who said what in a conversation.

The **Text-to-Speech** (**TTS**) model is used to produce natural-sounding text-to-speech voices. It supports standard and neural text-to-speech voices, custom voice creation, and **speech synthesis markup language** (**SSML**) for advanced customization. With SSML, we can adjust certain features of the synthetic voice if the default pronunciation is not satisfactory. It is possible to scale the pitch, adjust the speaking rate and volume, change the pronunciation and emphasis, and so on. TTS is often used at scale when creating audiobooks and the like. Nowadays, a lot of solutions are also popping up where TTS is used on the output of generative language models to quickly create a personal AI (home) assistant.

The **speech translation** model is built on the other models and is used to translate spoken audio in real time. This model can output either text or audio and is, like the STT and TTS models, able to be fine-tuned. Among other things, this technology allows the creation of solutions that can do real-time translation during voice or video calls.

With the **speaker recognition** model, we can identify and verify the speaker in a conversation, and it comes with fine-tuning capabilities as well. As previously mentioned, it is great to use in combination with the speaker diarization features of the STT model. This is perfect for use cases such as interview audio transcribing, where we want to automatically distinguish an interviewer and interviewee in the generated transcription.

## Vision

Azure Cognitive Services for Vision entails models such as Custom Vision, image analysis, spatial analysis, facial recognition, and optical character recognition.

**Custom Vision** is a core component of the Vision models in Azure Cognitive Services. It allows for convenient training of computer vision models, used for image classification or object detection. Organizations can simply upload their own data and train a computer vision model without a letter of code. The service also has an environment to label images, with a machine learning model in the background that will suggest labels after a while, which significantly speeds up the process as labeling efforts continue.

Next to Custom Vision, there is a range of models used for **image analysis**. Its most recent one, the Florence foundation model, understands over 10,000 concepts and objects, which it can detect in the images or classify into categories. With this knowledge, it is also capable of auto-generating alt-text for pictures (a brief description of what is shown). This can also be useful in cases where we want to have images as input for text-based foundation models (such as the GPT models). In this scenario, we can use the caption or description of an image as input for a language model.

Models for **spatial analysis** are used to detect people or vehicles and track their movements in 3D space. These models tend to go very well with CCTV footage, for either security purposes or for making estimates of queue lengths in a store or airport. Another example is (near)-collision detection for traffic cameras by detecting the speed and distance between two vehicles, in order to map highly dangerous road segments.

**Facial recognition** models are also included in Azure Cognitive Services and are capable of recognizing facial features and linking them to a person. However, this model is gated due to Microsoft's responsible AI guidelines, just like the models in the Azure OpenAI Service, as we will see later in the section on this service. As this model could be used for harmful actions at scale, access needs to be requested through a special application process before the model can be used.

Lastly, **Optical Character Recognition (OCR)** models allow you to automatically locate and extract text in images. It is a great way of turning images into text and can be valuable in cases of document digitalization. Since the latter has become a very popular use case, Microsoft has developed Form Recognizer, a service built on top of OCR to automatically extract key-value pairs from images of documents or PDF files. This way, the text in a document is extracted and instantly organized to conform to the document's structure.

## Language

The core language models include the following:

- Entity recognition
- Sentiment analysis

- Question answering
- Conversational language understanding
- Translation

The **entity recognition** models provide the ability to quickly extract concepts and objects from text data. A more specific version, **Named Entity Recognition** (**NER**) can extract the names of people and places from text. These models can be useful when looking for potential personally identifiable information in documents or extracting key stakeholders from lengthy contracts.

**Sentiment analysis** models can understand the sentiment of a given phrase. When passing large chunks of text data, a sentiment score is returned on a phrase-by-phrase basis. This can determine whether a text (especially reviews) is written in a positive or negative way. When used in combination with entity recognition, it is possible to extract sentiments on different concepts, such as different products in a single review. A restaurant can use something like this to determine which dishes are favored and which could use improvement.

**Question-answering** models are used to implement a conversational layer over knowledge bases such as FAQs or other documents. It is one of the components to create a custom chatbot. This is used in combination with a **conversational language understanding** model that focuses on interpreting the goal of a sentence or command, along with other types of information. Nowadays, however, many of these models are being outperformed by highly capable LLMs, but they still provide a relatively cheap alternative.

Finally, the **Translator** model is able to translate texts in over 100 languages and dialects, with the option to fine-tune very domain-specific data.

With the steep rise of LLMs such as the GPT family, which are available in the Azure OpenAI Service, it is unclear what the future holds for the language models in Azure Cognitive Services. Although the performance of LLMs is arguably better, they require a lot more memory and power to run. Therefore, the language models in Azure Cognitive Services still provide a cheaper and more energy-efficient method of processing natural language text data.

### Decision making

The fourth and last category of Azure Cognitive Services is defined as decision-making models, which is quite abstractly defined here. It is more of a collection of models that do not really fit the other (human sense-based) categories. The decision-making models include the following:

- Anomaly detector
- Content moderator
- Personalizer

The **anomaly detector** is a versatile model that can be used in various use cases, the only constraint being that time-series data is required. No matter the meaning of the data, the anomaly detector will find data points that are statistical outliers. In different situations, this can mean different things. For instance, when working with machine data, anomalies might hint toward defects in a machine or a sensor. In other cases, such as financial transactions, anomalies could be an indicator of fraudulent behavior. As with most Cognitive Service models, it is fine-tunable to optimize its performance for niche cases. Furthermore, it is integrated with other Azure services, such as Synapse and Azure Machine Learning, for out-of-the-box anomaly detection capabilities.

The **content moderator** model is made to track explicit content in text, images, and videos. Note that audio can also be analyzed by combining it with an STT model. This model is trained to find all sorts of profanity. It has a built-in tool for human review, which can be valuable to leverage for low-confidence predictions. When the model is not certain enough (and here, we define a certain threshold), it gets passed on to a human reviewer, which still saves tremendous time compared to a non-AI solution.

Finally, the **personalizer** model is designed for content recommendation. The model will carry out a series of A/B testing and evaluate the responding behavior on key performance indicators of our choosing. For something such as marketing content on a website, we would define things such as the click-through rate or average time on page, pass along all the available content, and let the model figure out the optimal recommendation strategy on its own.

Now that we have a good understanding of the available models in Azure Cognitive Services, let's look at the second set of pre-trained models, the powerful LLMs in Azure OpenAI Service.

## Azure OpenAI Service

OpenAI has risen immensely in popularity with the arrival of ChatGPT. The company, which started as a non-profit organization, has been the driving force behind the GPT and DALL-E model families, with intense research at a massive scale. The speed at which new models get released and become available on Azure has become impressive lately.

Microsoft has a close partnership with OpenAI, after heavy investments in the company from Microsoft. The models created by OpenAI use Azure infrastructure for development and deployment. Within this partnership, OpenAI carries the responsibility of research and innovation, coming up with new models and new versions of their existing models. Microsoft manages the enterprise-scale go-to-market. It provides infrastructure and technical guidance, along with reliable SLAs, to get large organizations started with the integrations of these models, fine-tuning them on their own data and hosting a private deployment of the models.

Like the face recognition model in Azure Cognitive Services, powerful LLMs such as the ones in Azure OpenAI Service could be used to cause harm at scale. Therefore, this service is also gated according to Microsoft's guidelines on responsible AI.

At the time of writing, Azure OpenAI Service offers access to the following models:

- GPT model family:

  - GPT-3.5

  - GPT-3.5-Turbo (the model behind ChatGPT)

  - GPT-4

- Codex

- DALL-E 2

Let's dive deeper into these models.

### The GPT model family

**GPT** models, which stands for **generative pre-trained transformer** models, made their first appearance in 2018, with GPT-1, trained on a dataset of roughly 7,000 books. This made good advancements in performance at the time, but the model was already vastly outdated a couple of years later. GPT-2 followed in 2019, trained on the WebText dataset (a collection of 8 million web pages). In 2020, GPT-3 was released, trained on the WebText dataset, two book corpora, and English Wikipedia.

In these years, there were no major breakthroughs in terms of efficient algorithms, but rather, in the scale of the architecture and datasets. This becomes easily visible when we look at the growing number of parameters used for every new generation of the model, as shown in the following figure.

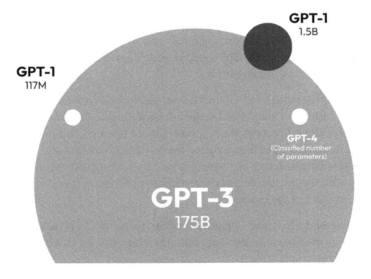

Figure 9.3 – A visual comparison between the sizes of the different generations of GPT models, based on their trainable parameters

The question is often raised of how to interpret this concept of parameters. An easy analogy is the number of neurons in a brain. Although parameters in a neural network are not equivalent to its artificial neurons, the number of parameters and neurons are heavily correlated – more parameters = more neurons. The more neurons there are in the brain, the more knowledge it can grasp.

Since the arrival of GPT-3, we have seen two major adaptations of the third-generation model being made. The first one is GPT-3.5. This model has a similar architecture as the GPT-3 model but is trained on text and code, whereas the original GPT-3 only saw text data during training. Therefore, GPT-3.5 is capable of generating and understanding code. GPT-3.5, in turn, became the basis for the next adaptation, the vastly popular ChatGPT model. This model has been fine-tuned for conversational usage while using additional reinforcement learning to get a sense of ethical behavior.

### GPT model sizes

The OpenAI models are available in different sizes, which are all named after remarkable scientists. The GPT-3.5 model specifically, is available in four versions:

- *Ada*
- *Babbage*
- *Curie*
- *Davinci*

The Ada model is the smallest, most lightweight model, while Davinci is the most complex and most performant model. The larger the model, the more expensive it is to use, host, and fine-tune, as shown in *Figure 9.4*. As a sidenote, when you hear about the absurd number of parameters of new GPT models, this usually refers to the Davinci model.

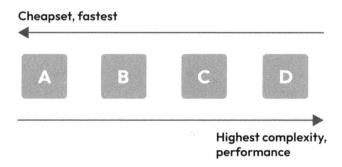

Figure 9.4 – A trade-off exists between lightweight, cheap models and highly performant, complex models

With a trade-off between costs and performance available, an architect can start thinking about which model size may best fit a solution. In reality, this often comes down to empirical testing. If the cheaper model can perform the job at an acceptable performance, then this is the more cost-efficient solution. Note that when talking about performance in this scenario, we mean predictive power, not the speed at which the model makes predictions. The larger models will be slower to output a prediction than the lightweight models.

**Understanding the difference between GPT-3.5 and GPT-3.5-Turbo (ChatGPT)**

GPT-3.5 and GPT-3.5-Turbo are both models used to generate natural language text, but they are used in different ways. GPT-3.5 is classified as a text completion model, whereas GPT-3.5-Turbo is referred to as conversational AI.

To better understand the contrast between the two models, we first need to introduce the concept of contextual learning. These models are trained to understand the structure of the input prompt to provide a meaningful answer. Contextual learning is often split up into few-shot learning, one-shot learning, and zero-shot learning. Shot, in this context, refers to an example given in the input prompt. With few-shot learning, we provide multiple examples in the input prompt, one-shot learning provides a single example, and zero-shot indicates that no examples are given. In the case of the latter, the model will have to figure out a different way to understand what is being asked of it (such as interpreting the goal of a question).

Consider the following example:

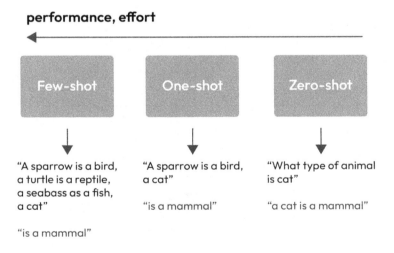

Figure 9.5 – Few-shot learning takes up the most amount of tokens and requires more effort but often results in model outputs of higher quality

While it takes more prompt engineering effort to apply few-shot learning, it will usually yield better results. A text completion model, such as GPT-3.5, will perform vastly better on few-shot learning than one-shot or zero-shot. As the name suggests, the model figures out the structure of the input prompt (i.e., the examples) and completes the text accordingly.

Conversational AI, such as ChatGPT, is more performant in zero-shot learning. In the case of the preceding example, both models able to output the correct answer, but as questions become more and more complex, there will be a noticeable difference in predictive performance. Additionally, GPT-3.5-Turbo will remember information from previous input prompts, whereas GPT-3.5 prompts are handled independently.

### Innovating with GPT-4

With the arrival of GPT-4, the focus has shifted toward **multimodality**. Multimodality in AI refers to the ability of an AI system to process and interpret information from multiple modalities, such as text, speech, images, and videos. Essentially, it is the capability of AI models to understand and combine data from different sources and formats.

GPT-4 is capable of additionally taking images as input and interpreting them. It has stronger reasoning and overall performance than its predecessors. There was a famous example where GPT-4 was able to deduce that balloons will fly upward when asked what will happen if someone cuts the balloons' strings, as shown in the following photo.

Figure 9.6 – The image in question that was used in the experiment. When asked what would happen if the strings were cut, GPT-4 replied that the balloons would start flying away

Some adaptations of GPT-4, such as the one used in Bing Chat, have the extra feature of citing sources in generated answers. This is a welcome addition, as hallucination was a significant flaw in earlier GPT models.

---

**Hallucination**

Hallucination in the context of AI refers to generating wrong predictions with high confidence. It is obvious that this can cause a lot more harm than the model indicating it is not sure how to respond or knowing the answer.

---

Next, we will look at the Codex model.

## Codex

Codex is a model that is architecturally similar to GPT-3, but it fully focuses on code generation and understanding. Furthermore, an adaptation of Codex forms the underlying model for GitHub Copilot, a tool that provides suggestions and auto-completion for code based on context and natural language inputs, available for various **integrated development environments** (**IDEs**) such as Visual Studio Code. Instead of a ready-to-use solution, Codex is (like the other models in Azure OpenAI) available as a model endpoint and should be used for integration in custom apps.

The Codex model is initially trained on a collection of 54 million code repositories, resulting in billions of lines of code, with the majority of training data written in Python.

Codex can generate code in different programming languages based on an input prompt in natural language (text-to-code), explain the function of blocks of code (code-to-text), add comments to code, and debug existing code.

Codex is available as a C (cushman) and D (Davinci) model. Lightweight Codex models (A series or B series) currently do not exist.

Models such as Codex or GitHub Copilot are a great way to boost the productivity of software engineers, data analysts, data engineers, and data scientists. They do not replace these roles, as their accuracy is not perfect; rather, they give engineers the opportunity to start editing from a fairly well-written block of code instead of coding from scratch.

## DALL-E 2

The DALL-E model family is used to generate visuals. By providing a description in natural language in the input prompt, it generates a series of matching images. While other models are often used at scale in large enterprises, DALL-E 2 tends to be more popular in smaller businesses. Organizations that lack an in-house graphic designer can make great use of DALL-E to generate visuals for banners, brochures, emails, web pages, and so on.

DALL-E 2 only has a single model size to choose from, although open source alternatives exist if a lightweight version is preferred.

## Fine-tuning and private deployments

As a data architect, it is important to understand the cost structure of these models. The first option is to use the base model in a serverless manner. Similar to how we work with Azure Cognitive Services, users will get a key for the model's endpoint and simply pay per prediction. For DALL-E 2, costs are incurred per 100 images, while the GPT and Codex models are priced per 1,000 tokens. For every request made to a GPT or Codex model, all tokens of the input prompt and the output are added up to determine the cost of the prediction.

Tokens

In natural language processing, a token refers to a sequence of characters that represents a distinct unit of meaning in a text. These units do not necessarily correspond to words, although for short words, this is mostly the case. Tokens are used as the basic building blocks to process and analyze text data. A good rule of thumb for the English language is that one token is, on average, four characters. Dividing your total character count by four will make a good estimate of the number of tokens.

Azure OpenAI Service also grants extensive fine-tuning functionalities. Up to 1 GB of data can be uploaded per Azure OpenAI instance for fine-tuning. This may not sound like a lot, but note that we are not training a new model from scratch. The goal of fine-tuning is to retrain the last few layers of the model to increase performance on specific tasks or company-specific knowledge. For this process, 1 GB of data is more than sufficient.

When adding a fine-tuned model to a solution, two additional costs will be incurred. On top of the token-based inference cost, we need to take into account the training and hosting costs. The hourly training cost can be quite high due to the amount of hardware needed, but compared to the inference and hosting costs during a model's life cycle, it remains a small percentage. Next, since we are not using the base model anymore and, instead, our own "version" of the model, we will need to host the model ourselves, resulting in an hourly hosting cost.

Now that we have covered both pre-trained model collections, Azure Cognitive Services, and Azure OpenAI Service, let's move on to custom development using Azure Machine Learning.

## Grounding LLMs

One of the most popular use cases for LLMs involves providing our own data as context to the model (often referred to as grounding). The reason for its popularity is partly due to the fact that many business cases can be solved using a consistent technological architecture. We can reuse the same solution, but by providing different knowledge bases, we can serve different end users.

For example, by placing an LLM on top of public data such as product manuals or product specifics, it is easy to develop a customer support chatbot. If we swap out this knowledge base of product information with something such as HR documents, we can reuse the same tech stack to create an internal HR virtual assistant.

A common misconception regarding grounding is that a model needs to be trained on our own data. This is not the case. Instead, after a user asks a question, the relevant document (or paragraphs) is injected into the prompt behind the scenes and lives in the memory of the model for the duration of the chat session (when working with conversational AI) or for a single prompt. The context, as we call it, is then wiped clean and all information is forgotten. If we wanted to cache this info, it is possible to make use of a framework such as LangChain or Semantic Kernel, but that is out of the scope of this book.

The fact that a model does not get retrained on our own data plays a crucial role in terms of data privacy and cost optimization. As shown before in the section on fine-tuning, as soon as a base model is altered, an hourly operating cost is added to run a private deployment of the model. Also, information from the documents cannot be leaked to other users working with the same model.

*Figure 9.7* visualizes the architectural concepts to ground an LLM.

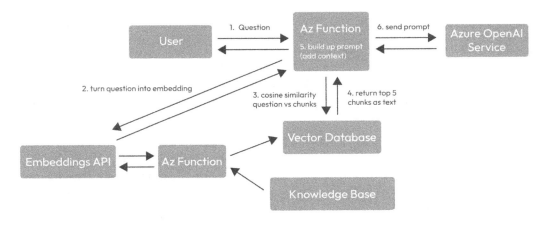

Figure 9.7 – Architecture to ground an LLM

The first thing to do is turn the documents that should be accessible to the model into embeddings. Simply put, embeddings are mathematical representations of natural language text. By turning text into embeddings, it is possible to accurately calculate the similarity (from a semantics perspective) between two pieces of text.

To do this, we can leverage Azure Functions, a service that allows pieces of code to run in a serverless function. It often forms the glue between different components by handling interactions. In this case, an Azure function (on the bottom left of *Figure 9.7*) will grab the relevant documents from the knowledge base, break them up into chunks (to accommodate for the maximum token limits of the model), and generate an embedding for each one. This embedding is then stored, alongside the natural language text, in a vector database. This function should be run for all historic data that will be accessible to the model, as well as triggered for every new, relevant document that is added to the knowledge base.

Once the vector database is in place, users can start asking questions. However, the user questions are not directly sent to the model endpoint. Instead, another Azure function (shown at the top of *Figure 9.7*) will turn the user question into an embedding and check the similarity of it with the embeddings of the documents or paragraphs in the vector database. Then, the top $X$ most relevant text chunks are injected into the prompt as context, and the prompt is sent over to the LLM. Finally, the response is returned to the user.

With Azure OpenAI and generative AI covered, there is one key Azure AI service left – Azure Machine Learning.

## Azure Machine Learning and MLOps

Azure Machine Learning is a workspace primarily focused on supporting custom development and maintenance of machine learning models throughout their whole life cycle.

To understand the full capabilities of Azure Machine Learning, we first need to introduce the concept of **Machine Learning Operations (MLOps)**.

MLOps is a core function of machine learning engineering that focuses on streamlining the process of taking machine learning models to production and then maintaining and monitoring them. MLOps is often the result of collaboration between data scientists and machine learning engineers.

In other words, MLOps is an engineering discipline that aims to unify machine learning system development and machine learning system deployment, in order to standardize and streamline the continuous delivery of high-performing models in production.

As shown in the following figure, MLOps can be divided into the following steps:

1. Enabling collaboration across data scientists.

2. Training the machine learning model.

3. Validating the machine learning model.

4. Deploying the machine learning model.

5. Monitoring the machine learning model.

6. Retraining the machine learning model.

This eventually forms a feedback loop, also shown in the following figure.

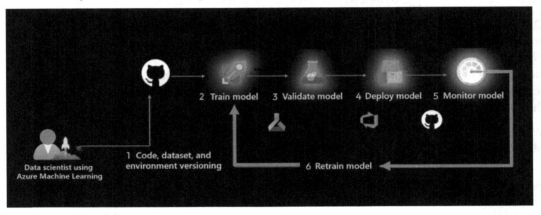

Figure 9.8 – A visual overview of the MLOps flow and model feedback loop

Let's cover the steps in detail now:

1. **Enabling collaboration across data scientists**: Data scientists working in the Azure Machine Learning workspace can make use of the built-in asset-sharing functionalities. As well as sharing, there is also the need to version artifacts. In terms of MLOps, the artifacts that we look to version are code (notebooks and scripts), datasets, and trained models.

   For code versioning, we can make use of remote repositories on GitHub or Azure DevOps. Dataset, environment, and model versioning are incorporated into the Azure Machine Learning workspace.

2. **Training the machine learning model**: In this overview, training the model includes all initial development by data scientists, including exploratory data analysis, data pre-processing, and model prototyping (training and hyperparameter tuning).

The Azure Machine Learning workspace provides many options to perform these tasks. As well as code-first options such as notebooks and scripts, automated machine learning (no-code) and designing (low-code/drag-and-drop) are performant alternatives aimed at citizen developers.

Automated machine learning will take in a dataset and train a variety of models on it. For citizen data scientists, this is a great way to easily acquire a trained model. However, professional data science teams can also use this, just in a different context. When starting a new project and dataset, a data scientist can run an automated machine learning job within minutes and get a good idea of which type of models perform significantly better on the dataset. This gives a strong indication of what algorithms can be further explored during custom development.

For large jobs, such as model (re)training or batch inference, we can leverage the machine learning pipelines provided by Azure Machine Learning. Machine learning pipelines form an essential component in AI development. It conveniently orchestrates entire end-to-end machine learning workflows, from data pre-processing to model training, validation, and deployment. These pipelines are often used when the code remains relatively unchanged over time, typically after the experimentation phase.

3. **Validating the machine learning model**: Although model validation is listed as a separate step in the MLOps process, in reality it is often performed during or immediately after training. For deep learning models, this happens during the training process; in between every pass throughout the entire training dataset (also called **epochs**), to find the ideal moment to stop training. Without going too deep into the mathematics of machine learning, model performance can deteriorate when training for too long, often referred to as overfitting, or when training is too short, known as underfitting.

4. **Deploying the machine learning model**: From this step onwards, the machine learning engineer comes into play. While the data scientist has a good understanding of mathematics and statistics, the machine learning engineer usually brings DevOps and containerization (Docker, Kubernetes, etc.) knowledge to the table.

When deploying a model and making it available through an API, we need three things:

- A compute target
- An environment
- An entry script

For compute targets, when deploying into production, we often make use of an **Azure Kubernetes Services (AKS)** cluster. With the newer version of the Azure Machine Learning SDK (V2), it is possible to have managed endpoints to outsource some of the cluster management. Another option is deploying a single container using **Azure Container Instances (ACI)**, although this is usually used for prototyping, as it does not provide a scalable solution. Models can also be deployed on IoT Edge devices or on-premises hardware (using Azure Arc, a service to simplify hybrid cloud architectures), as shown in the following figure.

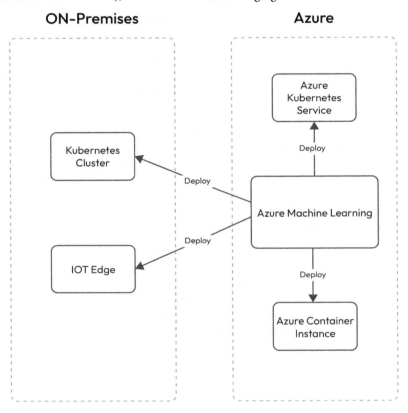

Figure 9.9 – Common deployment options for trained machine learning models in Azure Machine Learning

Next, an environment needs to be provided to the deployment container, holding all the necessary dependencies for the model. For this, we can either upload our own custom environment to Azure Machine Learning or use one of the curated (pre-built) environments available in the workspace.

The final required component is the entry script. This is a brief script that fetches the model from the model registry in Azure Machine Learning, loads it into memory, transforms the incoming data from POST requests in the right format for the model (note that this is model-specific, so most entry scripts are unique), makes a prediction, and returns it. The following code snippet is an example of a minimalistic entry script:

```python
import os
import pickle
import json
import numpy as np
# this function runs when the container starts
def init():
    global model
    # get the path in the model registry
    model_path = os.path.join(os.getenv('AZUREML_MODEL_DIR'),
'model.pkl')
    # load model in memory
    model = pickle.load(open(model_path, 'rb'))
# this function runs for every request made to the model
endpoint
def run(data):
    try:
        # unpack the incoming data
        body = json.loads(data)
        sample = body['data']
        # reshape the data
        sample = np.array(sample).reshape(1, -1)
        # predict and return the prediction
        pred = model.predict(sample)
        return str(pred)
    except Exception as e:
        return str(e)
```

5.  **Monitoring the machine learning model**: Good monitoring is the result of collaboration between the machine learning engineer and the data scientist. The machine learning engineer mainly monitors the health of the deployment (less so when using the managed online endpoints). For this, the engineer can make use of Azure Monitor.

The data scientist will monitor the performance of the model as time goes on. For this, the scientist can leverage the built-in data drift monitoring in the workspace. When monitoring data drift, two datasets are defined in the workspace, the baseline and target dataset. A dataset can be dynamic (for example, the last two weeks of data) or static (all data from a certain month).

The baseline dataset is a static dataset referring to the training data for the model currently in production. The target dataset is usually a dynamic dataset referring to the most recent weeks or months of data. Checks are continuously performed between the baseline and the target dataset to check whether they remain statistically similar.

Once the **statistical difference** (also called **drift magnitude**) exceeds a threshold, this means our model may have become outdated. The new, incoming data has significantly changed, and our model might require retraining. Before we move on to model retraining, we have to perform one more check – the health of the data sources. For instance, if a sensor breaks and faulty data is ingested, this will also be seen as data drift. Once we can rule out that this happened, we can start the retraining process.

6.   **Retraining the machine learning model**: By retraining the model, we restart the continuous MLOps loop of training, validating, deploying, and monitoring. For retraining, we use deployed machine learning pipelines. Machine learning pipelines can be deployed when the code does not change anymore, which is the case for retraining and batch inference. The pipeline can still be dynamic, using pipeline parameters. These pipelines can be triggered using an API call. Data drift monitoring can kick off a retraining pipeline, but the best practice is to have a human actor in between to check the case of faults at the data source.

The efficiency of data drift monitoring and retraining pipelines is heavily dependent on the work of the data architect and data engineer. A well-structured data lake and well-architected ETL pipelines go a long way and greatly improve the quality of MLOps processes.

## AI architectures on Azure

To understand the addition of AI components in a larger solution, we will take a look at some common architectures. Similar to the way data is ingested, machine learning predictions occur either in real time or in batches.

Let's explore a sample architecture of each approach.

# Scoring data in batches

The following figure is an example of a data architecture on Azure with batch scoring.

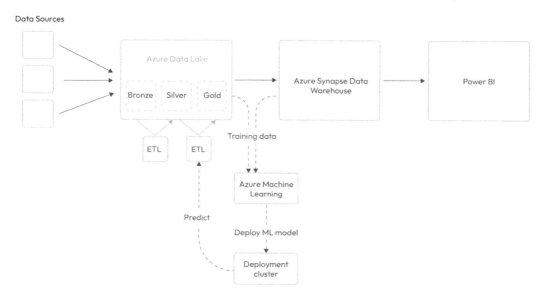

Figure 9.10 – An example data architecture involving batch scoring in the ETL process

Using data from the data lake and data warehouse, a custom model can be developed in the Azure Machine Learning workspace. The workspace does not copy data, so there are no additional storage costs. It will either mount data from the data lake or load tabular data straight into memory during training jobs in machine learning pipelines. When performing batch scoring, we do not want to deploy the model as an endpoint but, rather, have a deployed pipeline. This pipeline includes data cleaning, preprocessing, and inferencing.

The machine learning pipeline can be triggered using the data pipelines in Azure Data Factory or Azure Synapse pipelines. In the data pipelines, the machine learning pipeline can be integrated as part of the data transformation workflow. These predictions will mostly take place between the silver and gold layers, as the initial training dataset for the model usually originates from the silver layer.

When opting for a pre-trained model instead of custom development, the Azure Machine Learning component can be swapped out for any pre-trained model endpoint, which can then be integrated into an ETL pipeline in a similar way.

Next, we will look at an example of real-time scoring.

## Scoring streaming data with a custom model

The following figure is a Lambda architecture, with a hot and cold path, where a custom-developed machine learning model makes predictions on the real-time data stream.

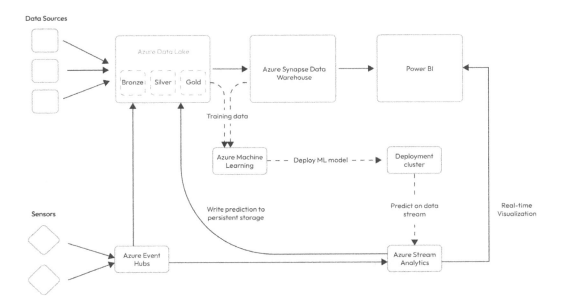

Figure 9.11 – An example data architecture involving scoring on streaming data

Everything regarding model training and validation happens in the same manner as in the example for batch inference. Once the model is finished, however, we will deploy the model to a Kubernetes cluster, instead of deploying a machine learning pipeline. With the model deployed on Kubernetes, we can have it predict on a stream of data in Azure Stream Analytics by integrating it in the Stream Analytics query as a **user-defined function (UDF)**.

The model predictions will enrich the data stream, yet aside from this, much of the architecture remains similar to a standard lambda architecture without machine learning. The same goes for batch inference. Therefore, machine learning and advanced analytics are components that can easily be added at more mature stages of the data platform, without having too great of an impact on its normal operations.

# Summary

This chapter focused on data science and AI on Azure. We started by outlining the different roles involved in a data science team, including the responsibilities of data architects, engineers, scientists, and machine learning engineers, and how the collaboration between these roles is key to building successful AI solutions.

We then focused on the role of the data architect when designing an AI solution, outlining the questions they should ask themselves for a well-architected design.

Next, we delved into the various AI services offered by Azure, including Azure Cognitive Services, Azure Machine Learning, and Azure OpenAI Service. For Azure Cognitive Services, we saw speech, vision, language, and decision-making models. For Azure OpenAI Service, we explored the GPT model family, Codex, and DALL-E 2.

We then introduced the concept of MLOps, along with mapping the different steps in the MLOps process to components with Azure Machine Learning, the workspace used for custom AI development.

Finally, we introduced a reference architecture for batch scoring and real-time scoring on Azure, which are applicable to a wide range of use cases.

In the next chapter, we will explore how to enforce data governance and compliance, essential components for scalable and highly performant data platforms.

# Part 4:
# Data Security, Governance, and Compliance

In this section, you will learn about scalable methods of applying data governance and compliance. You will also learn how to monitor data and enforce data policies, as well as learning about best practices for data security, both in transit and at rest.

This part has the following chapters:

# 10

# Enterprise-Level Data Governance and Compliance

As organizations continue to generate and consume vast amounts of data, it has become increasingly important to manage this data in a strategic and structured manner. This is where data governance comes in, providing a framework for managing data as a valuable organizational asset. With data governance practices in place, we can ensure that an organization's data is accurate, secure, and accessible, while also complying with relevant regional or industry-specific regulations. Without proper data governance practices, we run the risk of struggling with disparate data sources and inaccurate data and having difficulties in ensuring data privacy and security. As such, data governance and compliance have become essential components of any organization's data strategy.

In this chapter, you will learn about the importance of data governance, the roles involved in its implementation, and tools such as Microsoft Purview that can be used to facilitate data governance. Additionally, we will explore two assessment frameworks and two data governance models to help you establish and apply effective data governance practices in your organization.

By the end of this chapter, you will have a solid understanding of the concepts of data governance and compliance, the required profiles, Microsoft Purview as a governance service, and several proven frameworks to assist in the adoption of data governance in an organization.

We will be covering the following topics in the chapter:

- The importance of data governance and compliance
- Governing data with Microsoft Purview
- Applying enterprise-level data governance

# The importance of data governance and compliance

Businesses are becoming more and more data-driven as time goes on. They have good reason to do so, as revenue, time-to-market, profits, and customer satisfaction increase greatly for data-driven businesses. Given this trend, the need for data governance is higher than ever.

The goals of data governance can be summarized as follows:

- Managing an ever-growing data landscape
- Overcoming data silos
- Increasing data agility
- Complying with data regulations

More data-driven organizations mean a faster growth of the global data volume, but also a larger data landscape per organization. The latter will cause serious issues in the long run when managed incorrectly. With a strong data governance strategy alongside the right tools and services, a data landscape will remain clear and structured at scale. The data landscape tends to grow exponentially with the business. When the business grows, new subsidiaries or acquisitions bring new data, but existing departments also start to use more **Software-as-a-Service** (**SaaS**) applications (such as software for planning, HR management, decision-making, and so on), develop their own applications, or generate more data in another way.

Next, overcoming silos is nothing new in the data world. Data silos could refer to databases of different departments that are not integrated with each other. On a larger scale, subsidiaries or acquired organizations also tend to be seen as silos as their data often resides in different data centers, cloud tenants, or even cloud providers. Organizations have long been working on centralizing data in a (cloud-based) data lake and/or data warehouse. Data governance solutions such as Microsoft Purview provide insights into every silo without the immediate need for data migration. In mature scenarios with a central data warehouse, Purview grants insights into all the surrounding data transformation processes, source databases, and downstream data usage – for instance, in dashboards or reports. An example is shown in the following figure:

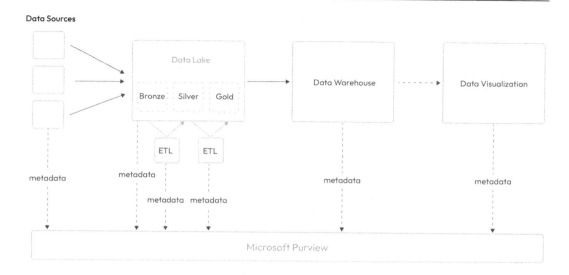

Figure 10.1 – Architecture representing Microsoft Purview
ingesting metadata from the entire data platform

Excellent data governance should also result in a vast increase in data agility. This comes as a consequence of having fast organization-wide insights into all data. Data strategists such as the **chief data officer (CDO)** can adapt rapidly to changes in the data. These changes can reflect new trends or influences from external factors, or quickly provide results from altered internal business processes.

Good data governance also forms the basis for data compliance. Without governance, it is not possible to efficiently verify whether data fully complies with all kinds of regulations, be they regional or industry-specific. With hefty fines for violations, this is something we should avoid at all costs. An example of regional regulation is the **General Data Protection Regulation (GDPR)** in the **European Union (EU)**, focusing on data protection and privacy. Simple examples of industry-specific regulations are the handling and storage of sensitive data regarding client-attorney privilege in the law sector or patient data in the medical sector.

Now that we have seen the results of strong data governance, let's dive deeper into the roles that are essential for designing, implementing, and enforcing such a strategy.

## The roles in data governance and compliance

The field of data governance and compliance is becoming increasingly interdisciplinary. Many different roles collaborate to design and execute the strategy at the enterprise level. In this domain, we introduce a few new roles:

- **C-level executives**:
  - **Chief data officer (CDO)**
  - **Chief information officer (CIO)**
  - **Chief technology officer (CTO)**
  - **Chief information security officer (CISO)**
- **Data administrator**
- **Data steward**
- **Data owner**
- **Subject-matter expert (SME)**

Executives, data administrators (in a data governance board), and stewards are typically situated in a hierarchical structure such as the following:

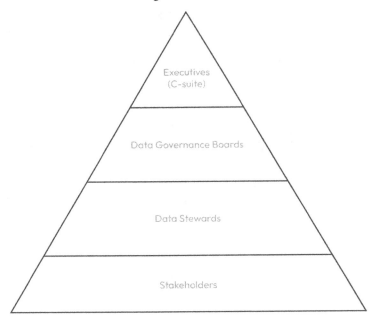

Figure 10.2 – Data governance organizational model

We will look at all data governance roles in more detail, starting with the C-suite executives.

## Executive roles in data governance

The roles of CDO and CISO are relatively new but are becoming increasingly important as companies continue to rely more heavily on data and technology.

A CDO is responsible for managing an organization's data assets and ensuring that data is properly stored, managed, and used to achieve the company's objectives. This includes developing data governance policies and procedures, managing data quality and integrity, and overseeing data analytics and reporting. The CDO works closely with other senior leaders to ensure that data is effectively used to support business decisions and drive innovation. More specifically, in data governance, the CDO will (indirectly) overlook the core governance and compliance team, consisting of data officers with elevated permissions to enforce governance.

A CISO, on the other hand, is responsible for managing an organization's information security program. This includes developing and implementing security policies and procedures, managing security risk assessments, and overseeing security monitoring and incident response. The CISO ensures that the organization's information is protected from cyber threats and designs strategies for responding to security incidents. This will be further covered in *Chapter 11, Introduction to Data Security*.

The CTO and CIO would usually cover the entire technical landscape of the organization: the CTO might focus more on the technological aspects of the company's products and services while the CIO focuses on the management and security of the company's IT systems. Although the scope of the CTO and CIO is broader than the data domain, in less mature or more traditional organizations without a CDO, they carry out the CDO responsibilities in data governance and compliance.

## Data governance boards

Next is the data governance board. It is a governing body that strategizes data governance programs in collaboration with the CDO, raises awareness of its importance, approves enterprise data policies and standards, prioritizes related projects, and enables ongoing support. The board typically includes delegates from the core function teams of marketing, sales, finance, and HR – all teams that depend on accurate data to perform their jobs effectively.

In its simplest form, a robust data governance team consists of data administrators and data stewards. Data administrators oversee the implementation of the entire data governance program.

## Data stewards

A data steward is a person who is responsible for managing the data assets at a departmental or business unit level. They ensure that data is properly managed, maintained, and used to meet the needs of their specific area of the organization. Although the role of a data steward may vary between organizations, in mature environments, it comes down to the following areas:

- **Data quality**: Ensuring that the data within their department is accurate, complete, and consistent

- **Data access**: Managing who has access to the data within their department and ensuring that access is appropriate and secure
- **Data security**: Ensuring that the data within their department is protected from unauthorized access or breach
- **Data governance**: Helping to develop and enforce data governance policies and procedures within their department or business unit
- **Data usage**: Ensuring that the data within their department is being used appropriately to meet the needs of the organization
- **Data training**: Providing guidance and training to their colleagues on the proper use of data within their department

Data stewards work closely with other stakeholders, including the governance board and end users, to ensure that the data at the operational level is properly integrated, maintained, and aligned with the overall data strategy of the organization.

### Data owner and SME

Contrary to the data steward, the data owner and SME are not full-time roles. These are dedicated individuals for a data asset, whose contact information will be visible to those who seek more information about the asset.

The data owner carries the final responsibility for the data asset. The data owner overlooks the data governance, data quality, security, and compliance for its data asset. To accomplish this, the data owner can leverage data stewards. By appointing a data owner, thereby having someone responsible for every single data asset in the organization, the risk of an ever-growing unmanageable spaghetti of data assets is mitigated.

The SME is, just like the data owner, an individual appointed to give insights into the data. The SME is typically someone with hands-on experience with the data and good theoretical knowledge of the field and use cases. They can provide clarity on data columns, values, aggregations, derivations, and so on.

Now that we have covered the importance of data governance and the roles that are applicable to this domain, let's move on to Microsoft Purview. This tool will allow us to manage organization-wide data assets conveniently.

## Governing data with Microsoft Purview

Microsoft Purview is a unified data governance service that allows organizations to manage and govern data that resides anywhere, from on-premises data stores to multi-cloud and even SaaS data.

Purview enables data discovery by providing data scanning and classification for assets across the entire data landscape. Metadata and descriptions of discovered data assets are integrated into a holistic map of the data estate, as shown in the following figure:

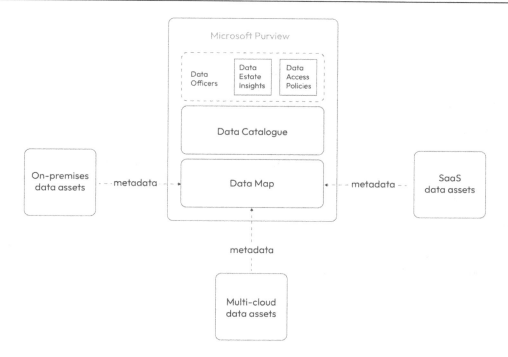

Figure 10.3 – Purview is built upon core components: Data Insights, Data Catalog, and Data Map. The Purview data map holds important metadata from multi-cloud, SaaS, and on-premises sources. Data officers can also set data access policies, which are straightforward.

The service consists of three core components:

- Data Map
- Data Catalog
- Data Estate Insights

Let's take a look at each of them.

## Data Map

Purview Data Map provides the foundation for discovery and governance. It is a unified map of all data assets and their relationships and enables more effective governance for the data estate. It is a knowledge graph that forms the basis for the Purview data catalog. It is crucial to get the data map right, as it has a large impact on the performance of all other governance and discovery efforts.

We will now cover the different concepts within the data map, starting with the connection to various data sources.

## Sources

The first step of building a data map is connecting to all data sources. Most of these, including third-party software, can make use of built-in connectors to rapidly create a link between the data source and Microsoft Purview. By registering an external data store as a source, the connection information for that data source is securely kept within Purview, allowing for easy manageability.

Using this method, Purview connects to all data storages spanning the entire data landscape of the organization, going from Azure services to on-premises data sources, Power BI, Amazon Web Services, Google Cloud Platform, SAP, Salesforce, Snowflake, and many more. This means that in a typical data platform (sources, data lake, data warehouse, and reporting), Purview has information on the whole data journey from start to finish.

## Scans

Purview does not copy the data from the source to its service. This would incur a significant amount of unnecessary costs. Instead, it periodically scans the registered data sources and stores metadata of all data assets. For example, Purview will ingest metadata such as the following:

- Data asset name
- File size
- Schema (columns, data types, and so on)

On top, Purview will apply classifications and labels during the scanning process, which will be further discussed later in this chapter.

The use of scans is the main cost driver for Microsoft Purview. Therefore, it is possible to apply scan rule sets to perform periodic scanning in the most cost-efficient way possible.

Scans can be scoped and individually scheduled, on different levels of granularity. We can decide what sources to scan, what file types, and which classifications should be applied. For example, all structured data in a data lake can be scanned daily, while unstructured file types are scanned twice per week.

Remember to make use of this to adjust the scan interval according to the importance of the data and the speed at which it changes, as this greatly affects the resulting costs incurred from the service.

---

**Data asset**

A data asset in the context of Microsoft Purview is an abstract concept and can point toward different layers in the data hierarchy. Data assets include data storage services, workspaces, tables, files, dashboards, and reports. For example, an SQL table is considered a data asset, as well as the schema, database, and SQL server it resides in. Data assets can be grouped logically using hierarchical collections.

---

Lastly, the scans that are performed by Purview on the data sources leverage Azure Data Factory pipelines under the hood. This means that in terms of compute or integration runtimes, the approach is very similar to that of Azure Data Factory.

### Pattern rules

Pattern rules in Purview are used to customize or override how Purview detects which assets are grouped as resource sets and how they are displayed within the catalog. Each set of rules is applied relative to a specified folder path scope.

### Classifications

As mentioned before, Purview applies classifications while scanning the data sources. Classifications categorize columns according to a specific pattern and are useful to automatically detect certain types of data. More specifically, **personally identifiable information** (**PII**) can be distinguished upon scanning, so that sensitivity labels can be applied where necessary. The organization is then able to leverage the result of this labeling process to enforce compliance.

Classification rules are set up using regular expressions in combination with a threshold of match percentage. These regular expressions can be applied to column names or data values. For instance, we could apply a rule set looking for the words *phone* or *mobile*, while also matching the cell values to a specific phone number pattern. Purview has a vast range of classifications readily available, such as passport numbers (for different countries), credit card numbers, and email addresses. The next pillar of Purview we will cover is the data catalog, which builds upon the metadata in the Data Map.

## Data Catalog

The Data Catalog provides a complete overview of the data landscape with automated data discovery, data lineage, and sensitive data classification, along with some other features. The data catalog is to be used by business end users to find any data asset (given that permissions allow it) and receive key information on it.

Within the data catalog, we will zoom in on the semantic search, data asset overview, and business glossary.

### Semantic search

Data assets residing anywhere in the organization's data landscape can be easily found using the semantic search in Purview. This makes a task that used to be extremely cumbersome, awfully simple. End users can simply browse the data catalog to retrieve any data asset within their scope of permissions.

### Data assets

When a data asset is retrieved, users are able to access various metadata, such as the following:

- Schema
- Data lineage
- Contacts
- Related data assets

We are able to view the schema (if applicable) of the data asset – the column names, column descriptions, data types, and the classifications and sensitivity labels applied by Purview. These columns can also be linked to certain terms in the business glossary to create more clarity on otherwise ambiguous column names.

Next to the schema, we get access to the data lineage, one of the most powerful and sought-after features within Purview. It provides a comprehensive, visual overview of the journey of data from its origin to its destination(s). End users can easily trace the flow of data through ETL pipelines, understand transformations happening along the way, and gain insights into how data is used within the organization. Furthermore, Purview allows us to drill down on specific columns in aggregated datasets to see where the data originated and in which dashboards and reports it is being used. The lineage is also useful for root cause analysis and data quality analysis. The following figure shows an example of data lineage in Microsoft Purview from start to finish:

Figure 10.4 – An example of a data lineage in Microsoft Purview. We get a view of the upstream sources and downstream usage of data in the chosen data asset (in this case, a SQL table)

When using Azure-native data pipelines, such as in Azure Data Factory or Synapse, this data lineage is automatically generated. For this reason, it is recommended to use Azure-native services for ETL pipelines, as this greatly increases the convenience of building up data lineages. However, it remains possible to add custom data lineages, yet this requires some custom coding and making use of the underlying Apache Atlas API.

Every data asset has a list of relevant contacts. These contacts are divided by role. Using this list, we can easily discover who is the designated data owner, the stewards governing the data asset, and the SMEs, along with their contact details. Additionally, it is possible to define custom roles and add them to the list.

Purview also provides the option to retrieve relevant data assets, such as parent and child assets. For instance, when looking up a SQL table, Purview also returns links to the schema, database, and server asset.

Lastly, access can be requested instantly from the data asset page and a `.pbix` file can be downloaded to quickly open up the data in a dashboard or report for analysis.

### Business glossary

The business glossary is our last component in the data catalog. It is a tool that allows the business to define and manage business terms, concepts, and relationships in a centralized and standardized manner. It helps organizations to establish a common understanding of the meaning and context of the data they use across various teams, systems, and processes. For larger corporations, this becomes absolutely essential, as the smallest ambiguity in term definitions can have a major impact on larger workflows.

An organization can benefit in many ways from leveraging a business glossary such as the one in Purview. The business glossary provides a single location to manage all business terms and definitions, centralizing the overhead management. Furthermore, it establishes a standardized naming convention in a clear manner. This helps to avoid confusion and ensure everyone is using the same terminology.

Next, the business glossary provides a search and discovery feature that allows users to quickly find the relevant business terms and definitions they need. Lastly, the glossary is integrated with other components of Purview, such as data assets. As mentioned before, we can link certain data columns to business terms in the glossary to provide more clarity.

In the end, the data catalog can be visualized as follows:

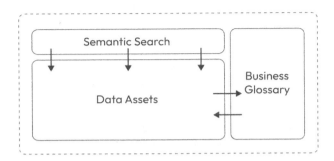

Figure 10.5 – The data catalog provides a powerful semantic search on
top of the data assets, accompanied by a business glossary

After exploring the data map and data catalog, there is one pillar left to cover: Data Estate Insights.

## Data Estate Insights

Data Estate Insights provides an overview of the assets that have been scanned into the data map and views key gaps that can be closed by governance stakeholders for better governance of the data estate. Access to Data Estate Insights should be more restricted than the data catalog. It is mainly to be used by executives and the governance boards.

Data Estate Insights comprises a collection of pre-built dashboards, showing aggregated information about the data landscape. More specifically, an executive or a member of the governance board can leverage these dashboards to get insights on the following topics:

- *The state of data stewardship*: Here we can see the level of data curation across all data assets. A data asset is seen as fully curated when it has an assigned data owner, description, and classification.

- *Data catalog adoption*: This shows the usage of the data catalog's semantic search, which data assets were the most retrieved, which keywords were the most popular, and so on.

- *Insights on data assets*: Aggregated information is available here on data assets that can be drilled down in many ways, such as Purview collection, source type, and file type.

- *Curation of the business glossary*: This shows both the curation of the business term in the glossary (does it have an owner, a definition, ...?) as well as their level of linkage with data assets.

- *Insights on classifications and sensitivity labels*: As the name suggests, this shows information on the usage and curation of both classifications and sensitivity labels.

In summary, Data Estate Insights is a restricted area within Microsoft Purview that provides leaders with a cross-tenant bird's-eye view of the current state of the organization's data landscape.

These were the three main pillars of Microsoft Purview: data map, data catalog, and data insights. Understanding the tool is one thing, but implementing data governance requires transformational steps to be taken on the business level as well. Let's find out how we can do this.

# Applying enterprise-level data governance

Not every cloud data architect will have to be as well-versed in the following part, as the implementation of data governance is something that happens organization-wide, rather than on the level of a single data solution. It would mainly involve a chief architect, CDO, or CIO.

Data governance forms an essential component for any data estate at scale, yet we cannot implement data governance blindly. As we will see later, data governance can be implemented too late or too early.

Neglecting the need for governance over a longer period of time, until the data platform reaches full-scale maturity, will cause many issues in the long run. The longer governance, compliance, and data management are neglected, the more technical debt is built up. The data landscape will turn into an unmanageable swamp, making it hard or near impossible to clean up and organize. Therefore, the key takeaway here is to think about data governance from the start.

On the other hand, data governance can be implemented too fast. First, the organization needs a good idea of the designated roles, such as the data owners and data stewards. Second, the business has to decide on a solid data governance and management strategy. To do this, we can leverage a couple of frameworks. It is recommended to follow one of the proven assessment frameworks (to assess the organization's maturity) and a governance framework (for the actual governance model to be used). Jumping straight into implementing data governance while disregarding these crucial steps runs the risk of having an unscalable governance model, resulting in a chaotic governance structure further down the road.

## Preparing the business for data governance and management

Before deciding on a governance framework, the main goal is to understand the organization's maturity level when it comes to data. This can be done in various ways, but two widely adopted assessment frameworks are as follows:

- **Data Management Capability Assessment Model (DCAM)** assessment
- **Data Management Association International (DAMA) Data Management Body of Knowledge (DMBOK)**

Let's take a closer look at these two approaches.

## DCAM assessment

The first step that an organization can take to prepare for implementing data governance and management is to perform a DCAM assessment. The DCAM is a framework designed to assess an organization's data management capabilities across various domains. This model helps organizations evaluate their current state of data management and identify areas for improvement in their data management practices.

The DCAM assessment typically involves a comprehensive evaluation of an organization's data management capabilities, including data governance, data architecture, data integration, data quality, and data security. The assessment model is based on a maturity model approach, where organizations are evaluated against a set of criteria that reflect best practices for each domain. The criteria are organized into maturity levels, which indicate the level of maturity an organization has reached in each domain.

DCAM defines maturity levels based on the following six dimensions:

- **Governance**: The ability to manage data as a strategic asset across the enterprise
- **People**: The skills and competencies needed to manage data effectively
- **Process**: The methods and procedures used to manage data across its life cycle
- **Technology**: The tools and infrastructure used to manage data
- **Data**: The quality, consistency, and completeness of data across the enterprise
- **Business**: The alignment of data management with business objectives

The DCAM assessment typically follows a structured approach involving a series of steps that include data gathering, analysis, and reporting. The assessment may be conducted by internal or external auditors, and the findings are typically presented in a report that outlines the areas of strengths and weaknesses in the organization's data management capabilities. The report may also include recommendations for improvement and remediation.

## DAMA DMBOK

DAMA DMBOK is a framework developed by DAMA that provides a comprehensive guide to data management practices and principles. It can be seen as a solid alternative to DCAM. Much like the DCAM framework, DMBOK is also used to evaluate the data maturity level of the organization.

The DMBOK framework consists of a set of guidelines, best practices, and standards that cover all aspects of data management, including data governance, data architecture, data quality, metadata management, data modeling, and many other topics. The framework is organized into 10 functional areas:

- **Data governance**
- **Data architecture management**
- **Data development**

- **Database operations management**

- **Data security management**

- **Data integration management**

- **Document and content management**

- **Reference and master data management**

- **Data warehousing and business intelligence management**

- **Metadata management**

Each functional area contains a set of activities, tasks, and deliverables that are essential for effective data management. The DAMA DMBOK framework is intended to be a flexible guide that organizations can adapt to their specific needs and requirements.

## Comparing the DCAM and DAMA DMBOK frameworks

Now that we have discussed both frameworks, we can start comparing them. The following table shows the differences between DCAM and DMBOK, or more specifically, DMBOK2 versus DCAM 2.2.

| Level | Level name | | Level description | |
|---|---|---|---|---|
| | DAMA-DMBOK2 | DCAM® 2.2 | DAMA-DMBOK2 | DCAM® 2.2 |
| Level 0 | No capability | Non initiated | No organized data management practices or formal enterprise processes for managing data | Ad-hoc data management (performed by heroes) |
| Level 1 | Initial/Ad Hoc | Conceptual | • Little or no governance<br>• Limited tool set<br>• Roles defined within silos<br>• Controls applied inconsistently<br>• Data quality issues not addresses | Initial planning activities (white board sessions) |
| Level 2 | Repeatable | Developmental | • Emerging governance<br>• Introduction of a consistent tool set<br>• Some roles and processes defined<br>• Growing awareness of impact of data quality issues | Engagement underway (stakeholders being recruited and initial discussions about roles, responsibilities, standards and processes) |
| Level 3 | Defined | Defined | • Data viewed as an organizational enabler<br>• Scalable processes and tools<br>• Reduction in manual processes<br>• Process outcomes are more predictable | Data management capabilities established and verified by stakeholders (roles and responsibilities structured, policy and standards implemented, glossaries and identifiers established, sustainable funding) |
| Level 4 | Managed | Achieved | • Centralized planning and governance<br>• Management of risks related to data<br>• Data Management performance metrics<br>• Measurable improvements in data quality | Data management capabilities adopted and compliance enforced (sanctioned by executive management, activity coordinated, adherence audited, strategic funding) |
| Level 5 | Optimization | Enhanced | • Highly predictable processes<br>• Reduced risk<br>• Well understood metrics to manage data quality and process quality | Data management capabilities fully integrated into operations (continuous improvement) |

Table 10.1 – A comparison between DMBOK and DCAM maturity levels

While both frameworks categorize organizations into six levels of maturity, these levels cannot be directly mapped against each other. As just described, DCAM defines maturity levels based on 6 dimensions that reflect an organization's overall data governance and management capability, while DMBOK defines maturity levels based on 10 knowledge areas.

## Data governance frameworks

Once an acceptable maturity level has been defined (around level 2 for DMBOK and level 2-3 for DCAM), the organization can think about actually implementing data governance. Much like the initial assessment, it would be strongly recommended to follow a proven framework. The difference now is that we are looking for a data governance model.

Two well-known data governance models are as follows:

- The centralized data governance model
- The federated data governance model

Each model has its own benefits and drawbacks. The optimal choice for the governance model depends on the size of the business, its structure, and management needs.

Centralized data governance is a model in which a single governing body or team within an organization is responsible for managing and maintaining all of the organization's data. This governing body creates and enforces policies and procedures for how data is collected, stored, and used across the organization. This model is typically more hierarchical and has a top-down approach to managing data. It is most convenient and ideal for smaller businesses. Large organizations can also incorporate the centralized model if their business units are well integrated and data management requirements are roughly similar across the organization.

On the other hand, the federated data governance model is a more decentralized approach to managing data. In this model, multiple governing bodies or teams within an organization are responsible for managing different sets of data. Each team creates and enforces policies and procedures for the data under their purview (pun intended). This model is typically more collaborative and allows for greater flexibility in how data is managed. However, without careful coordination between business units, it runs the risk of resulting in data governance silos – the exact thing we are trying to avoid.

The federated data governance model is often used in larger organizations that have multiple business units, where the data requirements and governance needs vary greatly between them. By decentralizing governance, each business unit can manage its data more efficiently and effectively, while still adhering to overall organizational standards.

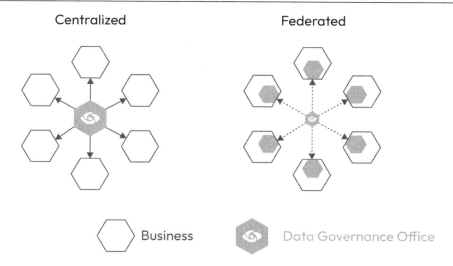

Figure 10.6 – The centralized and federated data governance model

To conclude, the main difference between the two models is that centralized data governance is managed by a single governing body, whereas federated data governance is managed by multiple governing bodies or teams.

## Summary

Data governance and compliance are critical components of any data strategy. In this chapter, we explored the importance of data governance, its goals, and the roles involved in its implementation, along with Microsoft Purview and data governance frameworks.

We highlighted four main goals of data governance, namely managing an ever-growing data landscape, overcoming data silos, increasing data agility, and complying with data regulations.

The chapter also discussed the different roles involved in data governance. Executives, governance boards, data stewards, data owners, and SMEs all have a part to play in ensuring that data is managed effectively and efficiently.

We explored Microsoft Purview as a core component for the implementation of data governance and compliance, which provides a Data Map, Data Catalog, and Data Estate Insights. This tool can help organizations understand their data landscape (even in its most decentralized form) and make better decisions about how to manage it.

Applying data governance in an organization requires a structured approach. We discussed two assessment frameworks, DCAM and DAMA DMBOK, which can help organizations evaluate their current level of data maturity and provide a clear path forward. We also explored two data governance models, centralized data governance and federated data governance, which organizations can use to determine the best approach for their needs.

Briefly, data governance and compliance are essential for organizations that want to manage their data effectively and comply with regulations. With the right tools, roles, and frameworks in place, organizations can achieve their data governance goals and realize the benefits of better data management.

In the next chapter, we will learn how to improve the security aspect of our data solutions. This is the last pillar of knowledge required to turn you into a well-versed data architect.

# Introduction to Data Security

Azure has an extensive range of data services, as we have seen throughout previous chapters, which can bring immense value to organizations of all sizes. However, the security of these services must be taken seriously as they are vulnerable to various threats, including hacking, data breaches, and cyber-attacks. Implementing robust security measures and regular monitoring can help prevent unauthorized access and ensure the confidentiality, integrity, and availability of the data. A business can easily justify the security investment, knowing it is protected from financial losses, reputation damage, and compliance violations, while also building trust with the end customers and other stakeholders.

There are many steps we can take in different security layers to increase the security of the organization's data estate. Microsoft's Azure Synapse security white paper distinguishes five layers:

- Data protection
- Access control
- Authentication
- Network security
- Threat protection

In this chapter, we will explain the relevant bits for the cloud data architect. As an extra at the end, we will also introduce Azure Policy and Azure Key Vault, as these are crucial to support efforts taken in the five layers.

## Data protection

The core component in data protection, apart from discovery and classification covered in the last chapter, is data encryption. This can be done depending on the state of the data, as seen in *Figure 11.1*.

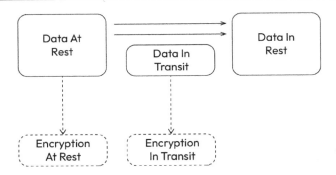

Figure 11.1 – Data is either at rest, in transit, or in use

Data is either at rest (inside the database or storage), in transit (when moving the data from one place to another), or in use. While the data is at rest or in transit, the data should be encrypted to maximize security.

## Encryption at rest

The first layer of protection is provided by Azure automatically, by encrypting data at rest using one of the strongest block ciphers in the world, 256-bit **Advanced Encryption Standard** (**AES**) encryption.

The key for this **server-side encryption** (**SSE**) can be managed either by the **platform** (*Microsoft-managed key*) or by the **organization** (*customer-managed key*).

A second layer of data encryption can be added for SQL databases: **transparent data encryption** (**TDE**). This will encrypt and decrypt database files, transaction logs, and backups automatically, using the same 256-bit AES.

For TDE, we have a similar choice of having the key database encryption key managed by Azure or providing our own key. If any of the keys for either the first or second layer of security were to be managed by the organization itself, it is strongly recommended to store these securely in **Azure Key Vault**. Azure Key Vault is explained further at the end of this chapter.

## Encryption in transit

Azure SQL databases and data warehouses use the **Tabular Data Stream** (**TDS**) protocol to encrypt data in transit. It requires the popular **Transport Layer Security** (**TLS**) protocol to ensure the channel in which the data moves is encrypted.

Luckily for the cloud architect, most of this is done automatically under the hood. The only significant choice to make here is which version of the TLS protocol to choose: TLS 1.0, TLS 1.1, or TLS 1.2. This choice depends on the supported TLS versions on the other side of the connection.

Now that we have concisely covered data protection, we will move on to the next layer of data security, which is access control.

# Access control

Without a doubt, controlling access to services and the data stored in them plays a major role in a successful data security strategy. We can control permissions of services using **role-based access control (RBAC)**, have fine-grained or temporal access to data lakes using shared access signatures, and put methods in place to control access for different user groups in the same database or data warehouse. Note that there are still other methods of controlling access on Azure that are not covered in this book. We are covering the most important ones, starting with RBAC.

## RBAC

**Identity and Access Management (IAM)** is a broad topic and is of most importance to the Azure administrator. However, a good cloud data architect knows at least the core principles as well. IAM forms the foundation for many concepts in access control. IAM is designed to allow the verification and management of (digital) entities, which could refer to a person, a group of people, an application, a service, and so on.

The **principle of least privilege (PoLP)** states that a user or identity should only have access to resources or data if this is required for the task they carry out. Access should be limited in both permissions and time.

Within the domain of IAM, the number one core component is RBAC. RBAC on Azure is based on role assignments. The concept of a role assignment is the combination of three components:

- An identity
- A role
- A scope

An identity is an abstract term for any user or entity in the (Azure) Active Directory. An identity could be any of the following:

- User
- User group
- Service principal
- Managed identity (system-assigned or user-assigned)

A user and user group (simply a group of users) should be fairly straightforward. A service principal is an identity that can be created within **Azure Active Directory (AAD)** for applications or services to connect to resources programmatically. *Figure 11.2* provides an overview of service principals in AAD. Service principals are typically made for an application and allow them to connect to different Azure resources, which may be provisioned in different subscriptions or even different tenants.

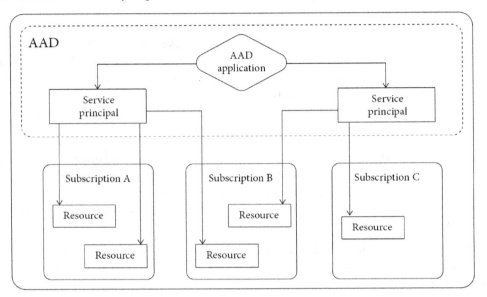

Figure 11.2 – Service principals allow applications to connect to
different resources in different subscriptions or tenants

Lastly, managed identities are identities where a lot of the management is outsourced, as the name suggests. For instance, the credentials of a managed identity are accessible to no one and are managed behind the scenes. Under the hood, a managed identity is a special type of service principal in AAD. Some Azure resources allow for quick enablement of managed identities, which are the system-assigned managed identities. User-assigned managed identities can cover one or more resources – ideal when a workload spans multiple resources.

The next component of role assignments is the role itself. A role is basically a set of permissions, allowing or denying access to certain services, features, or functionalities. Every resource in Azure has three standard roles:

- Owner
- Contributor
- Reader

To put this briefly, the owner has all permissions on the given scope. A contributor can make changes within the scope, but unlike the owner, cannot elevate permissions of other identities. Lastly, the reader can simply view without the ability to make changes.

On top of these three roles, most Azure services have their own unique roles as well. A Key Vault has roles for getting and setting secrets, a data lake has roles for editing blobs while denying edits to the file share, and so on.

The final component of a role assignment is the scope. This refers to the typical Azure hierarchy introduced in *Chapter 2, Preparing for Cloud Adoption*, using management groups, subscriptions, resource groups, and individual resources. A role assignment on a specific level of the hierarchy will be inherited automatically by lower levels. For example, the owner of a resource group is, by default, the owner of all resources in the resource group. The following figure sums it all up:

## Role Assignments

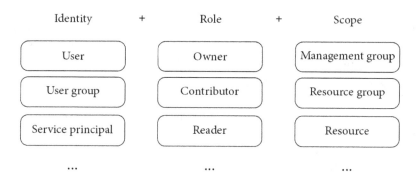

Figure 11.3 – A role assignment consists of the combination of an identity, a role, and a scope

Apart from the role assignments, there are a few other ways of receiving permissions. One of them that is relevant to the data architect is the **shared access signature** (**SAS**).

## Shared access signatures

Looking at the example of Blob Storage or Azure Data Lake Storage, remember that these are made up of blob containers (next to the lesser-used File, Queue, and Table storage).

The storage account has access keys, but it is strongly recommended to not distribute these. Access keys give permission to everything. The same goes for RBAC on the service level. RBAC can also be configured on the container level.

If we want to grant access to a blob storage or data lake, we should look at SAS tokens. SAS tokens provide granular data access and do not require an identity to be created in AAD. SAS tokens are split up into either account SAS tokens or service SAS tokens. While account SAS tokens have the entire storage account in scope, a service SAS token lives inside a blob container and applies to either a container or individual blobs.

This method of access is often used for temporary and granular access – ideal for external consultants and the like. When creating a SAS token, we specify a given start and end time, the permissions associated with the token, IP addresses that can connect, and whether we would only allow HTTPS connection (which is strongly recommended).

Now that we have discussed RBAC and SAS tokens, we will introduce methods of restricting access for users in the same database or, even more granular, querying the same table.

## Restricting internal data access

RBAC is a great method of providing access to a SQL server, database, or data warehouse, but what if we need more granular permissions for database users? In a large centralized data warehouse, for example, we want to have each department only to be able to access its relevant data. In another instance, we want to only have personnel with the right clearance to be able to access sensitive data. To solve these issues, we introduce the following concepts:

- **Row-level security (RLS)**: RLS can be implemented by database administrators to limit the rows certain users or groups of users can retrieve by querying the data. A typical example is users from Ireland will only see rows where the value of the Country column equals Ireland (as seen in *Table 11.1*). Likewise, end users in the sales department will only see records where the Department column equals Sales. These rules are set up in a similar fashion as a WHERE clause in SQL statements.

| OrderID | CustomerID | Country | Value |
|---------|------------|---------|-------|
| 42565435 | 11004 | Ireland | €245,000.00 |
| 41525462 | 11004 | Ireland | €13,650.00 |
| 52635676 | 15056 | Ireland | €42,950.00 |
| 54637642 | 16460 | Belgium | €24,630.00 |
| 14316753 | 10392 | Belgium | €65,099.00 |

Table 11.1 – We can use RLS so that salespeople in Ireland can only view the
top three rows, containing orders placed from Irish customers

- **Column-level security (CLS)**: CLS is similar to RLS, as it denies access to certain parts of a single table. Instead of rows, columns are made inaccessible to a subset of users. This is a convenient way to limit access to columns that might contain sensitive information.

- **Object-level security (OLS):** Where RLS and CLS are used to differentiate access for users querying the same table, OLS is meant for different user groups in the same database. Objects in this context refer to SQL tables, views, stored procedures, and functions. An administrator can give user groups `SELECT`, `READ`, `WRITE`, `EXECUTE` permissions, and so on. OLS can be combined with both RLS and CLS, as well as dynamic data masking.

- **Dynamic data masking:** With dynamic data masking, all rows and columns are returned to the user but individual cell values may be masked for certain user groups. This should be applied generously to sensitive data. The following figure shows a quick example of what data masking looks like:

Credit card

1234  5678  8765  4321  ⟶  XXXX XXXX XXXX 4321


Email address

johndoe@mail.com  ⟶  xxxx@xxxx.com

Figure 11.4 – An example of what sensitive data can look like for
end users after applying dynamic data masking

Regardless of the method of retrieval (table querying, view, or stored procedure), the data masking will apply according to the permissions of the user carrying out the operation.

Next, we will cover the authentication layer.

# Authentication

Having the correct permissions set up for every identity is a crucial step to take to secure the entire environment. However, if legitimate identities get compromised, all the efforts were in vain. Therefore, it is necessary that we verify that whoever logs in to a certain identity is who they claim to be. This is typically performed using well-protected credentials, such as a password or key.

With the number and scale of cyber-attacks increasing, we need to take extra steps to achieve an acceptable level of data security. Here are a few options:

- Strong password policies
- Encryption of user passwords
- Multi-factor authentication
- Firewall rules

The strength of a password can be increased by adding numbers or special characters, as they increase the complexity of the password and make it more resistant to certain types of attacks – mostly, dictionary attacks and brute force attacks. However, the exact impact of adding numbers or special characters to a password depends on various factors, including the length of the password. A strong password has a considerable length, uses capital letters, lowercase letters, numbers, and special characters, avoids using natural language words (to deter dictionary attacks), and is refreshed frequently.

Passwords should never be stored in plain text. To encrypt passwords, we can make use of techniques such as hashing, salting, and key strengthening. Hashing is a one-way process that converts a password into a fixed-size string of characters, typically a hexadecimal or Base64 encoded value, using a cryptographic hash function. The resulting hash is unique to the input password and is generally irreversible, meaning it cannot be reversed to obtain the original password.

Next, a salt is a random value that is generated for each user and combined with the password before hashing. The salt is then stored alongside the hash. The purpose of the salt is to add an additional layer of randomness and uniqueness to the hash, making it more difficult for attackers to use precomputed tables (rainbow tables) or other types of attacks, such as dictionary attacks or brute-force attacks.

Finally, key strengthening techniques, such as **key derivation functions (KDFs)** or **password-based key derivation functions (PBKDFs)**, can be used to make the hashing process slower and more resource-intensive. This can increase the time and computational effort required for attackers to crack the hashes using brute force or rainbow table attacks.

**Multi-factor authentication** (MFA) is crucial for enhancing the security of online accounts and systems by adding an additional layer of protection beyond traditional username and password credentials. MFA requires users to provide multiple forms of verification, such as a password and a temporary code sent to their phone, use the Microsoft Authenticator app on their phone, a fingerprint scan, or a smart card, to authenticate their identity. This adds an extra layer of security because even if one factor (such as the password) is compromised, the attacker would still need to bypass the additional factor(s) to gain unauthorized access. MFA helps prevent unauthorized access if the previous two steps fail.

Lastly, firewall rules for authentication are important for protecting the security and integrity of networks and services, such as an Azure SQL database. Firewalls act as a barrier between a trusted internal network and an untrusted external network, filtering incoming and outgoing network traffic based on predefined rules. Azure SQL Database and Azure Synapse Analytics have built-in firewall functionalities, allowing us to specify IP address ranges or specific IP addresses that are allowed to have access.

Now that we have covered authentication, let's move on to the network security layer.

# Network security

Much like IAM, networking and network security are huge domains. The exact network security configurations are often best kept for experts in the field, but it is still valuable for a cloud data architect to grasp the principles of securing networks.

The PoLP in access management stated that any identity should have the least amount of access to complete the job. Similar to this, in network security, endpoints should have the least possible exposure.

First, this comes down to not blindly opening up all endpoints to the public internet. This is, however, the default option in many Azure services. It is possible to deny public network access on the resource level, or we could enforce any resource of a given type to have disabled public network access by using Azure Policy. Azure Policy is further explained at the end of this chapter.

By disabling all access from the public network, the resources can only be accessed through private endpoints. This prevents data from being sent over the public internet when interacting with the endpoints. Private endpoints are **virtual network (VNet)** interfaces with their own private IP address and are created within a VNet subnet. Azure Data Lake Storage, Azure SQL Database, and Azure Synapse Analytics all support private endpoints.

Private endpoints greatly limit the exposure of endpoints. More specifically, there are only three options to get access to private endpoints:

- All resources within the same VNet as the private endpoint.

- All resources in peered VNets. Briefly put, peered networks are other networks linked to the VNet.

- On-premises network if they are connected to the VNet using either a VPN or Azure ExpressRoute.

The following figure shows the workings of private endpoints and VNets:

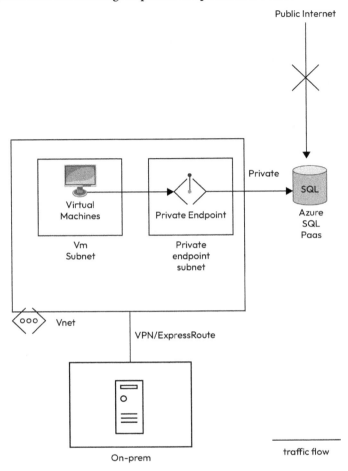

Figure 11.5 – An overview of Vnets and private endpoints. Subnets are simply a logical subset of a VNet. In this case, you can connect the Azure SQL DB over a private connection

Azure Synapse Analytics goes a bit deeper than the other data services in terms of network security. The Synapse workspace is an integration of many different components and they need to be connected with each other. This happens under the hood using a managed VNet, which, as the name suggests, is a completely managed version of a VNet. The managed VNet of the Synapse workspace can be further configured when setting up the workspace to manage network isolation for the Synapse Spark pools and pipeline orchestration runtimes between Synapse workspaces, as seen in *Figure 11.6*.

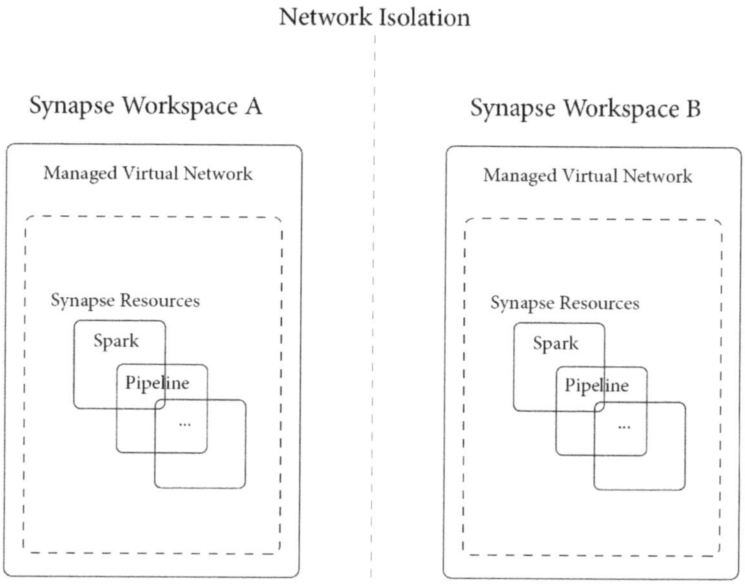

Network Isolation

Synapse Workspace A

Managed Virtual Network

Synapse Resources

Spark

Pipeline

...

Synapse Workspace B

Managed Virtual Network

Synapse Resources

Spark

Pipeline

...

Figure 11.6 – Network isolation between multiple Synapse workspaces

A Synapse workspace with a managed VNet can also leverage a built-in data exfiltration protection feature. It limits outbound connections to a whitelist of AAD tenants. This minimizes the risk of data in the lakehouse or data warehouse being stolen by malicious actors.

With network security covered, we move on to the final layer: threat protection.

# Threat protection

Threat protection will be a joint effort of multiple roles and tends to be mostly out-of-scope of the data architect. This is because services here are mostly used platform-wide, spanning more than just the data services. We will look at the relevant parts of Microsoft Defender for Cloud to assess vulnerabilities and perform advanced threat protection, and Microsoft Sentinel to monitor security incidents.

## Microsoft Defender for Cloud

Microsoft Defender for Cloud is a broad solution covering all kinds of services on Azure, external clouds, and on-premises. Defender for Cloud encompasses three main pillars:

- **Cloud security posture management (CSPM)**
- **Cloud workload protection platform (CWPP)**
- **Development security operations (DevSecOps)**

First, CSPM refers to the process of continuously monitoring and assessing the security configuration of cloud resources, and identifying and remediating misconfigurations, vulnerabilities, and compliance violations to maintain a secure posture in the cloud. CSPM solutions automate the monitoring and enforcement of security policies, provide visibility into cloud assets and configurations, and help organizations ensure that their cloud resources are configured securely and are compliant with industry regulations and best practices, reducing the risk of security breaches and data leaks in the cloud. Additionally, with the usage of Azure Arc, Defender for Cloud CSPM can be used for multi-cloud and on-premises environments as well.

> **Azure Arc**
>
> Azure Arc extends the capabilities of Azure to on-premises, multi-cloud, and edge environments. It allows management and governance of resources across diverse infrastructures from a single Azure portal. With Azure Arc, it is possible to bring existing resources such as servers, Kubernetes clusters, and data services into Azure to apply consistent management, security, and governance policies. It enables organizations to have a unified control plane for managing resources in a hybrid cloud setting.

An example of the hybrid cloud setting in which Azure Arc can operate is shown in *Figure 11.7*.

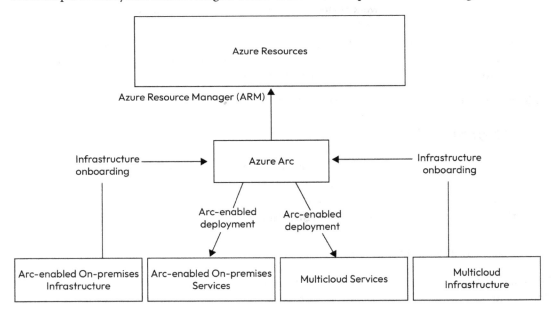

Figure 11.7 – Azure Arc easily connects on-premises, multi-cloud, and edge environments to the Azure cloud

Next, the CWPP refers to the fact that Defender for Cloud offers various workload-specific security options to protect components such as databases, servers, containers, and so on. Taking into account the scope of the cloud data architect, we are mainly interested in Defender for Databases, which we will explore further soon.

Lastly, DevSecOps might not be as relevant to the data architect as the previous two pillars. In the context of Defender for Cloud, this mostly refers to the workload-specific Defender for DevOps. It provides insights to security administrators into the DevOps inventory and pre-production code security posture, allowing for strengthened cloud resource configurations. Additionally, contextual insights from code to cloud enable prioritization of critical code fixes through customized workflows, expediting the remediation process. We will not go much deeper into this, given the scope of the data architect.

Let's dive deeper into CSPM and CWPP.

## CSPM

Defender for Cloud provides basic CSPM by default. When Defender for Cloud would be enabled for an Azure tenant, we would strongly recommend at least making use of the free tier if this has not been enabled already. Basic CSPM is a costless solution as the underlying technology (Azure Policy) is free as well. Azure Policy will be explained later in this chapter.

Defender for Cloud monitors the Azure estate and provides insights in a single, easy-to-use dashboard. The core metric in CSPM is the secure score, displayed as a percentage. The secure score in Defender for Cloud is a measure of an organization's overall security posture in the cloud environment. It provides a numerical score that reflects the effectiveness of the security controls and configurations in place, based on best practices recommended by Microsoft. The secure score is calculated by evaluating various security configurations, settings, and activities, based on Azure Policy. The score can be used as a benchmark to assess cloud security maturity and identify areas for improvement.

Along with the secure score, Defender for Cloud provides active recommendations on various topics. The more an organization complies with the active recommendations, the higher its secure score will become. As we are not talking about any specific workload yet, all these recommendations are purely related to Azure platform management. There are no configurations inside virtual machines or inside SQL databases being checked yet. These are addressed in the CWPP.

The following screenshot provides an example of a CSPM dashboard:

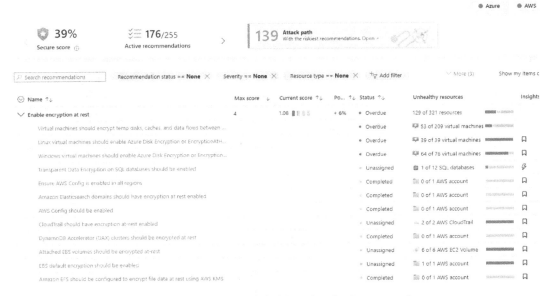

Figure 11.8 – The CSPM dashboard in the Azure portal

In this instance, the secure score is relatively low, sitting at a mere 39%. Active recommendations are listed along with their status and the number of unhealthy resources. Note that Defender for Cloud also tracks multi-cloud, such as AWS or GCP, resources.

## CWPP

CWPP offers Defenders for specific workloads – more specifically, servers, containers, databases, app service, storage, key vault, resource manager, DNS, and DevOps. Given the scope of the cloud data architect, we will mainly zoom in on database protection.

Database protection within Defender for Cloud contains four specialized defenders:

- Defender for Azure SQL Databases (PaaS SQL)
- Defender for Cloud for SQL servers on virtual machines (IaaS SQL)
- Defender for open-source relational databases
- Defender for Azure CosmosDB

The Defender for Azure SQL Databases protects both OLTP (Azure SQL DB and Azure SQL Managed Instance) and OLAP (Azure Synapse Dedicated SQL Pool) services. It carries out **vulnerability assessments (VAs)** and **advanced threat protection (ATP)**. The cost structure is a billing per server.

VAs in this context are scans that are performed on SQL databases to discover, track, and remediate vulnerabilities. For instance, it will check whether firewall rules are applied correctly, configurations are set correctly, and best practices are applied across the board. Then, it will return actionable steps to help solve security vulnerabilities. The VA covers both SQL servers and SQL databases.

Whereas VAs perform periodic scans on configurations, ATP is a continuous monitoring service. It monitors for all sorts of attacks and sends out alerts on suspicious activity. Later, we will discuss Azure Sentinel, where multiples of these alerts can be correlated to determine which activities are part of the same overarching security incident. The ATP for SQL databases focuses on SQL injection attacks, brute force attacks, and suspicious activity in general.

The Defender for Cloud for SQL servers on virtual machines (IaaS) has pretty similar outcomes, meaning it carries out the same VAs and applies ATP. This defender is meant for Azure Arc-enabled, on-premises virtual machines, SQL Server on Azure virtual machines, and multi-cloud (AWS accounts and GCP) projects. An agent is deployed on the virtual machines and performs the scanning and monitoring. Contrary to Defender for Azure SQL databases, costs are incurred on a per-vCore (virtual core of compute) basis.

Both Defender for open-source and Defender for CosmosDB only have ATP availability. No VAs are performed. Both have alert types that are very similar to those in Defender for Azure SQL databases. For open source databases, this Defender is available for PostgreSQL, MySQL, and MariaDB. On the other hand, the Defender for CosmosDB will only work for the NoSQL API. Defender for open-source databases is billed per server, and the costs of Defender for CosmosDB scale with the number of **request units per hour (RUs/h)** being used in the database.

## Microsoft Sentinel

Microsoft Sentinel is a **security information and event management** (SIEM) solution that helps detect, investigate, and respond to cybersecurity threats across the entire organization. It offers **security orchestration, automation, and response (SOAR)** capabilities. Microsoft Sentinel is built on top of Azure Log Analytics, which uses the same kind of technology for storage as Azure Data Explorer. This means high scalability and easy log querying using **Kusto Query Language (KQL)**. We are not going in-depth into KQL, but it is good to know that it is a query language that is optimized for time series analysis. The following code snippet will give you an idea of what the syntax looks like, as it is quite similar to SQL query writing. This simple KQL query fetches the last 7 days of attempted logins, up to a maximum of 100 records:

```
AttemptedLoginLogs
| where Timestamp >= ago(7d)
| sort by Timestamp, Identity desc
| take 100
```

Microsoft Sentinel offers a wide range of features to help organizations strengthen their security posture. It collects and analyzes data from various sources such as logs, events, and security alerts from across both cloud and on-premises environments. It can ingest logs from components such as firewalls, databases, AAD, and so on. It uses advanced machine learning algorithms to detect and respond to threats in real time, helping organizations identify potential security incidents before they can cause significant damage. Microsoft Sentinel also provides rich visualization and reporting capabilities to enable security teams to gain insights into their security posture and make informed decisions.

Microsoft Sentinel offers several benefits to organizations:

- Firstly, it provides a unified and centralized view of security events and alerts from across the organization, helping security teams get a holistic view of their security posture. This enables them to quickly detect and respond to security incidents, reducing the time to detect and respond to threats.

- Secondly, Sentinel can scale dynamically based on demand. This helps organizations to be agile and responsive to changing threat landscapes.

- Lastly, Microsoft Sentinel integrates with other Microsoft security products, such as the previously mentioned Defender for Cloud.

More specifically on this last topic, Sentinel ingests logs from Defender for Cloud, audit logs, and more and starts to link logs and alerts from different sources to find patterns and create incidents. An incident refers to a security event or occurrence that requires investigation and response by the security team. This can be useful to detect malware infections, suspicious user behavior, and data breaches. It can also be used for compliance monitoring, helping organizations meet their regulatory and compliance requirements by providing insights into security events and incidents that may impact compliance. Another interesting use case for Microsoft Sentinel is security analytics and threat hunting, allowing organizations to proactively search for potential threats and vulnerabilities in their IT environment.

## Azure services supporting data security

Azure Policy and Azure Key Vault were mentioned throughout this chapter. Both these services play a critical role in the security of the Azure environment and its data services.

### Azure Policy

We have seen before that Azure Policy forms the basis for Microsoft Defender for Cloud. Policies provide a way to define and enforce rules and standards that must be met by resources within your Azure environment.

Firstly, Azure policies are defined using JSON-based policy definitions. These policy definitions should be the result of business rules and cloud governance strategies, along with general best practices. They can specify a wide range of conditions, such as resource types, regions, tags, and metadata, to ensure that resources deployed in Azure comply with requirements set by the business. This should be leveraged to ensure that all services have secure configurations. For instance, a policy can be set to enforce that all PaaS databases (Azure SQL family) must make use of private endpoints for connectivity.

Secondly, Azure policies can be assigned to different scopes, such as management groups, subscriptions, resource groups, and individual resources. Policies can be set on either of these levels, where inheritance will trickle down the enforcement rules to all child objects. Policies can also be applied to multiple subscriptions or management groups using Azure Policy initiatives. Initiatives are basically a grouping of multiple policies. Azure Policy provides premade initiatives (for generic scenarios) as well as the option to introduce custom initiatives.

Thirdly, Azure policies can be used to audit and remediate non-compliant resources. When a policy is applied, it scans the resources for compliance and generates reports on non-compliant resources. Additionally, policies can be set to automatically remediate non-compliant resources by taking actions such as modifying or deleting resources or triggering custom scripts. This ensures that Azure resources are constantly monitored for compliance, and any violations are automatically corrected.

Lastly, Azure Policy integrates with other Azure services such as Azure Monitor, Azure DevOps, and Microsoft Defender for Cloud, providing a comprehensive governance framework for your Azure resources. Azure Monitor can be used to track and alert on policy compliance, Azure DevOps to incorporate policies into your CI/CD pipelines, and, as seen earlier in this chapter, Defender for Cloud to assess the security posture (CSPM) of resources against policy requirements.

### *Azure Key Vault*

Storing credentials such as passwords, keys, and tokens in plain text or, worse, having them hardcoded in application code or data transformation scripts is never a good idea. To conveniently solve this issue, we can make use of Azure Key Vault.

Azure Key Vault provides a secure and centralized location for storing and managing cryptographic keys, secrets, and certificates used for connecting services or authenticating APIs. It offers a robust solution for protecting sensitive data (mostly credentials) from unauthorized access. Key Vault uses industry-standard security controls, including **Hardware Security Modules** (**HSMs**), to ensure the highest level of data protection. HSMs are physical devices that provide a high level of security for storing and managing cryptographic keys and secrets. They are also remarkably resistant to tampering.

Azure Key Vault can seamlessly integrate with other Azure services, making it easy to securely access secrets and keys in data engineering scripts or service connection setups. It supports various key types, including symmetric keys, asymmetric keys, and certificates, making it versatile for different encryption scenarios. Key Vault also provides options for key rotation and versioning, allowing for effective management of the life cycle of cryptographic assets.

Additionally, Azure Key Vault is scalable and resilient out of the box, providing automatic replication of keys and secrets across Azure regions for high availability and disaster recovery scenarios. It also supports **Bring Your Own Key** (**BYOK**) scenarios, allowing for the import of own keys and use of them for encryption within Key Vault. It can be accessed and managed through various Azure management interfaces, such as the Azure portal, Azure **command line interface** (**CLI**), Azure PowerShell, Azure SDKs, and so on. To minimize any risk during transit, Key Vault also supports Azure Private Link (as seen in *Figure 11.8*), which allows secure access to Key Vault over a private connection, eliminating the need to expose it to the public internet.

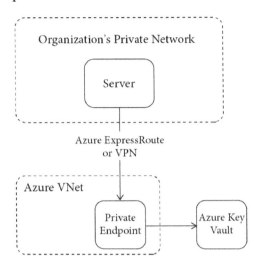

Figure 11.9 – Connection to Azure Key Vault with Azure Private Link

Finally, Key Vault provides backup and restore capabilities, along with a soft delete, which protects the keys and secrets from data loss or accidental deletion. With soft delete enabled, any data that is being deleted will be kept for a certain amount of time. It works similarly to the Recycle Bin on your computer, giving the option to restore any accidentally deleted data.

## Summary

In this chapter on data security, we discussed five layers of data security that are crucial for protecting sensitive data. These layers are data protection, access control, authentication, network security, and threat protection.

We covered data protection, which involved implementing data encryption at rest and data encryption in transit. We also discussed access control, which involved controlling who had permission to access data. We explained various access control mechanisms, such as RBAC, SASs, RLS, CLS, OLS, and dynamic data masking. These mechanisms ensure that only authorized users can access specific data based on their roles or permissions.

Authentication is another important layer of data security that we covered. We emphasized the use of strong passwords, MFA, and firewall rules to prevent unauthorized access. Strong passwords and MFA help enhance security by requiring users to provide additional proof of their identity beyond just a password. Firewall rules help regulate inbound and outbound network traffic to prevent unauthorized access to data.

We also discussed network security, including the use of VNets and private endpoints. VNets provide an isolated and secure environment for services, while private endpoints allow secure access to resources over a private network connection, mitigating the risk of data exposure over the public internet.

Threat protection is the final layer of data security. We discussed tools such as Microsoft Defender for Cloud, its Defender for Databases, and Microsoft Sentinel to aggregate correlated alerts and logs to create security incidents.

As an additional topic, we touched upon Azure Policy and Azure Key Vault. Azure Policy enables organizations to define and enforce policies for managing and securing resources in Azure, while Azure Key Vault provides a secure and centralized location for managing and storing cryptographic keys, secrets, and certificates.

Data security was the last, yet most important, topic to cover to grasp the essentials of Azure data and AI architectures. By now, you should have a solid understanding of cloud-based data engineering, data warehousing, data science, data governance, and data security concepts, all of which turn you into a well-versed cloud architect. If you wish to pursue a further career in this path, we wish you the best of luck on your journey!

# Index

www.packtpub.com

Subscribe to our online digital library for full access to over 7,000 books and videos, as well as industry leading tools to help you plan your personal development and advance your career. For more information, please visit our website.

## Why subscribe?

- Spend less time learning and more time coding with practical eBooks and Videos from over 4,000 industry professionals

- Improve your learning with Skill Plans built especially for you

- Get a free eBook or video every month

- Fully searchable for easy access to vital information

- Copy and paste, print, and bookmark content

Did you know that Packt offers eBook versions of every book published, with PDF and ePub files available? You can upgrade to the eBook version at packtpub.com and as a print book customer, you are entitled to a discount on the eBook copy. Get in touch with us at customercare@packtpub.com for more details.

At www.packtpub.com, you can also read a collection of free technical articles, sign up for a range of free newsletters, and receive exclusive discounts and offers on Packt books and eBooks.

# Other Books You May Enjoy

If you enjoyed this book, you may be interested in these other books by Packt:

**Practical Guide to Azure Cognitive Services**

Chris Seferlis, Christopher Nellis, Andy Roberts

ISBN: 978-1-80181-291-7

- Master cost-effective deployment of Azure Cognitive Services
- Develop proven solutions from an architecture and development standpoint
- Understand how Cognitive Services are deployed and customized
- Evaluate various uses of Cognitive Services with different mediums
- Disseminate Azure costs for Cognitive Services workloads smoothly
- Deploy next-generation Knowledge Mining solutions with Cognitive Search
- Explore the current and future journey of OpenAI
- Understand the value proposition of different AI projects

**Modern Generative AI with ChatGPT and OpenAI Models**

Valentina Alto

ISBN: 978-1-80512-333-0

- Understand generative AI concepts from basic to intermediate level
- Focus on the GPT architecture for generative AI models
- Maximize ChatGPT's value with an effective prompt design
- Explore applications and use cases of ChatGPT
- Use OpenAI models and features via API calls
- Build and deploy generative AI systems with Python
- Leverage Azure infrastructure for enterprise-level use cases
- Ensure responsible AI and ethics in generative AI systems

## Packt is searching for authors like you

If you're interested in becoming an author for Packt, please visit `authors.packtpub.com` and apply today. We have worked with thousands of developers and tech professionals, just like you, to help them share their insight with the global tech community. You can make a general application, apply for a specific hot topic that we are recruiting an author for, or submit your own idea.

## Share your thoughts

Now you've finished *Azure Data and AI Architect Handbook*, we'd love to hear your thoughts! Scan the QR code below to go straight to the Amazon review page for this book and share your feedback or leave a review on the site that you purchased it from.

`https://packt.link/r/1-803-23486-5`

Your review is important to us and the tech community and will help us make sure we're delivering excellent quality content.

# Download a free PDF copy of this book

Thanks for purchasing this book!

Do you like to read on the go but are unable to carry your print books everywhere?

Is your eBook purchase not compatible with the device of your choice?

Don't worry, now with every Packt book you get a DRM-free PDF version of that book at no cost.

Read anywhere, any place, on any device. Search, copy, and paste code from your favorite technical books directly into your application.

The perks don't stop there, you can get exclusive access to discounts, newsletters, and great free content in your inbox daily

Follow these simple steps to get the benefits:

1.  Scan the QR code or visit the link below

https://packt.link/free-ebook/9781803234861

2.  Submit your proof of purchase
3.  That's it! We'll send your free PDF and other benefits to your email directly

www.ingramcontent.com/pod-product-compliance
Lightning Source LLC
Chambersburg PA
CBHW060524060326
40690CB00017B/3379